Charles Alden John Farrar

Through the Wilds

A Record of Sport and Adventure in the Forests of New Hampshire and Maine

Charles Alden John Farrar

Through the Wilds
A Record of Sport and Adventure in the Forests of New Hampshire and Maine

ISBN/EAN: 9783744756266

Printed in Europe, USA, Canada, Australia, Japan

Cover: Foto ©Andreas Hilbeck / pixelio.de

More available books at **www.hansebooks.com**

CAPTAIN FARRAR AT HOME.

THROUGH THE WILDS

A Record of Sport and Adventure in the Forests of New Hampshire and Maine

BY

CAPT. CHARLES A. J. FARRAR

AUTHOR OF "THE ANDROSCOGGIN LAKES ILLUSTRATED," "CAMP LIFE IN THE WILDERNESS," "MOOSEHEAD LAKE AND THE NORTH MAINE WILDERNESS," "EASTWARD HO!" "WILD WOODS LIFE," "DOWN THE WEST BRANCH," "UP THE NORTH BRANCH," "FROM LAKE TO LAKE," ETC.

Profusely Illustrated

WITH OVER THREE HUNDRED ENGRAVINGS

BOSTON
ESTES & LAURIAT
PUBLISHERS

University Press:
JOHN WILSON AND SON, CAMBRIDGE.

TO

MY ESTEEMED FRIEND,

Dana J. Flanders,

OF MALDEN, MASS.,

TO COMMEMORATE CERTAIN TRIPS TO THE MAINE WOODS,

This Volume

IS RESPECTFULLY DEDICATED.

CONTENTS.

CHAPTER PAGE
I. Down Boston Harbor. — On the Briny Deep. — Along the Coast. — Places of Interest. — Cape Ann. — Man Overboard. — The Rescue. — Isles of Shoals. — Portland Head. — Cushing's Island. — Portland Harbor. — The Forest City 1
II. Sight-seeing in Portland. — A Trip in the Harbor. — A Tough Story. — An Angry Sheriff. — The Launch. — A Runaway Horse. — Beautiful Scenery. — Legends. — Gorham, N.H. — Ascent of Mount Hayes. — The Last Mouthful 36
III. A Country Show. — Side Trip to the White Mountains. — Sight-seeing. — Back to Gorham. — An Amateur Dramatic Performance. — The Mascot Mine. — Berlin Falls. — Pleasant Acquaintances. — The Mormon Elder. — The Picnic Dinner 71
IV. From Berlin to Colebrook. — Scenes En Route. — Fishing for Brook Trout. — Beaver Falls. — A Deer Story. — Ascent of Mount Monadnock. — An Amateur Show 107
V. Colebrook to the Dix House. — Catching Trout with a Silver Hook. — Dixville Notch. — A Day's Fishing. — Lost in the Woods. — Shooting a Deer. — Camping over Night. — The Rescuing Party. — Return to the Hotel 125
VI. Return to the Hotel. — Old Friends. — Climbing Table Rock. — A Peep at the Snow Cave. — Viewing the Profile. — A Rainy Day. — A Glance at Pulpit Rock. — Inspecting the Flume. — The Lower and Upper Cascade 168
VII. A Tour through the Lakes. — Umbagog. — Middle Dam. — Lake Welokennbacook. — Molechunkamunk. — The Upper Dam. — Mooselucmaguntic Lake. — Cupsuptic. — Indian Rock. — Oquossoc Lake. — Rangeley Village. — Haines' Landing. — Ascent of Bald Mountain. — Return to Upper Dam 187

CHAPTER		PAGE
VIII.	Upper Dam to South Arm. — Buckboard Ride. — Devil's Oven. — Black Brook Notch, Devil's Den. — Hermit Falls. — Silver Ripple Cascade. — A Night in Andover. — A Jolly Ride. — A Picnic Dinner. — Sights by the Way. — The Lakeside Hotel. — Cambridge. — Lake Umbagog. — Steamer Parmachenee	227
IX.	From Cambridge to Sunday Cove. — Errol Dam. — The Magalloway River. — Points of Interest	257
X.	The Berlin Mills House. — Gunning and Fishing. — Ascent of Aziscohos. — From Brown Farm to Errol. — Departure of the Girls	278
XI.	Return to Lowe's. — Camping Out. — Camp Cooking. — A Little Difficulty. — A Trip to Diamond Ponds	297
XII.	A Little Difficulty. — The Start Northward. — Boating on Magalloway. — Camping Out. — A Visit from a Moose	317
XIII.	An Unsuccessful Moose-hunt. — A Move up River. — Rainy Days. — A Night Alarm. — Difficult Navigation. — The Forks. — "Which Road shall we take?" — Parmachenee	338
XIV.	Up the Lake. — Danforth's Camp. — The Head of the Lake. — Up the River. — Little Boy's Falls. — A Permanent Camp. — Wood Rambles. — Rare Fishing. — A Moose Hunt. — Breaking Camp. — The Start for Home. — Almost an Accident	364
XV.	Baked Beans. — Campfire Music. — The Green Cook. — A Cook's Trick. — Arnold's Bog. — A Successful Moose Hunt. — "Through the Wilds." — Almost an Accident. — Return to Camp	384
XVI.	Through the Wilds. — Travelling by Compass. — Seven Ponds. — Head of Kennebago Lake. — Foot of Kennebago Lake. — John's Pond. — Down the Kennebago River. — Indian Rock again. — Down through the Lakes. — Cambridge. — Stage Ride through Grafton Notch. — Moose Cave. — The Jail. — Screw Auger Falls. — Bethel. — Homeward Bound by Rail. — Farewell	398

LIST OF ILLUSTRATIONS.

SUBJECT.	DRAWN BY	ENGRAVED BY	PAGE
Cover: designed and drawn by	J. J. Berry & Co.	J. J. Berry & Co.	
Captain Farrar at Home	Searles Gallagher	Lewis Engraving Co.	*Frontis.*
Initial Letter A : View in Boston Harbor	W. H. Garrett	Lewis Engraving Co.	1
The Camping Party	H. B. Colby	Lewis Engraving Co.	2
Steamer Cumberland	N. L. Stebbins, Photo.	John Andrew Co.	5
View in Boston Harbor	Photograph	Lewis Engraving Co.	6
Fort Independence, Boston Harbor	H. B. Colby	Lewis Engraving Co.	7
Fort Winthrop, Boston Harbor	H. B. Colby	Lewis Engraving Co.	8
Long Island Head Light, Boston Harbor	W. H. Garrett	John Andrew Co.	9
Deer Island Point Light, Boston Harbor	W. H. Garrett	John Andrew Co.	9
Nix's Mate, Boston Harbor	C. W. Reed	Lewis Engraving Co.	10
Fort Warren, Boston Harbor	C. W. Reed	Lewis Engraving Co.	11
Distant View of Boston Light	W. H. Garrett	John Andrew Co.	12
Bug Light, Boston Harbor	C. W. Reed	Lewis Engraving Co.	13
The Graves, Boston Harbor	W. H. Garrett	John Andrew Co.	14
"Breakers Ahead!" (Full page)	C. W. Reed	Geo. E. Johnson	17
Distant View of Egg Rock Light	W. H. Garrett	John Andrew Co.	21
Thatcher's Island Lights	W. H. Garrett	Adolf Borie	22
The Londoner	W. H. Garrett	John Andrew Co.	23
The Salvages	W. H. Garrett	John Andrew Co.	23
The Rescue. (Full page)	C. W. Reed	Geo. E. Johnson	25
The Chasm, Star Island	H. B. Colby	Lewis Engraving Co.	28
Smith's Monument, Star Island	W. H. Garrett	John Andrew Co.	29
Scene of the Wagner Murder, Smutty-Nose Island	Photograph	Ed. C. McClintock	30
Old Church, Star Island	W. H. Garrett	John Andrew Co.	31
"Dinner, Sar!"	H. B. Colby	Lewis Engraving Co.	31
Boon Island Light	H. B. Colby	Lewis Engraving Co.	32
White Island Light, Isles of Shoals	H. B. Colby	Lewis Engraving Co.	32
Distant View Double Lights, Cape Elizabeth	H. B. Colby	Lewis Engraving Co.	33

LIST OF ILLUSTRATIONS.

SUBJECT.	DRAWN BY	ENGRAVED BY	PAGE.
Portland Head Light	Special Photograph .	Ed. C. McClintock .	33
Cushing's Island, Portland Harbor . .	W. H. Garrett .	John Andrew Co. .	34
Breakwater Light	W. H. Garrett .	Lewis Engraving Co.	34
Tail-piece: Entrance to Portland Harbor .	H. B. Colby .	Lewis Engraving Co.	35
Initial Letter L: Observatory, Portland, Me. .	Bert Poole . .	Lewis Engraving Co.	36
Whitehead Cliff, Cushing's Island . .	H. B. Colby .	Lewis Engraving Co.	37
View from Western Promenade	W. H. Garrett .	Adolf Borie . .	38
Along the Wharves, Portland . . .	W. H. Garrett .	Lewis Engraving Co.	39
Trefetheren's Landing, Peak's Island .	W. H. Garrett .	Lewis Engraving Co.	40
The Willows, Cushing's Island . . .	Special Photograph .	Adolf Borie . .	41
Bathing House and Beach, Cushing's Island .	H. D. Murphy .	Lewis Engraving Co.	42
View on Cushing's Island . . .	Special Photograph .	Lewis Engraving Co.	43
Three Views on Cushing's Island . .	H. D. Murphy .	Lewis Engraving Co.	44
On the Beach, Cushing's Island	H. D. Murphy .	Lewis Engraving Co.	45
Cove, Diamond Island	Photograph . .	Lewis Engraving Co.	46
The Veracious Pilot .	E. L. Proctor .	Lewis Engraving Co.	47
Longfellow's Birthplace	A. E. Haynes .	Lewis Engraving Co.	48
The Longfellow House	A. E. Haynes .	Lewis Engraving Co.	48
Longfellow's Statue .	A. E. Haynes .	Lewis Engraving Co.	48
Dining-Room Office Preble House, Portland, Me. Reading-Room (Full page)	W. H. Garrett .	Lewis Engraving Co.	49
Dodging the Sheriff	C. W. Reed .	Johnson & Thompson	50
The Launch .	Bert Poole .	Lewis Engraving Co.	51
The Runaway .	E. L. Proctor .	Lewis Engraving Co.	55
Byrant's Pond, Maine . .	Special Photograph .	Chicago Engraving Co.	57
View from Bethel Station . . .	Special Photograph .	Adolf Borie . .	58
Wild River Bridge, Grand Trunk Railway	Myrick . . .	Geo. E. Johnson .	59
Treachery	E. L. Proctor . .	Lewis Engraving Co.	60
Meadows, Shelburne, N.H. . .	W. H. Garrett .	Adolf Borie .	61
Shelter from the Storm. (Full page)	E. L. Proctor . .	Lewis Engraving Co.	63
Gorham and Mount Hayes . .	Photograph . .	Chicago Engraving Co.	65
Suspension Bridge, Gorham, N.H. . .	W. H. Garrett .	John Andrew Co. .	66
"Now You see It, and Now You Don't." (Full page)	E. L. Proctor .	Lewis Engraving Co.	69
Initial Letter D: Imp Mountain .	Bert Poole .	Lewis Engraving Co.	71
The Prompter Does a Little Acting	C. W. Reed .	Johnson & Thompson	72
Lead-Mine Bridge . . .	Hassam . .	Geo. E. Johnson .	73
Lead-Mine Flume, Shelburne, N.H. .	W. H. Garrett .	Lewis Engraving Co.	74
Lead-Mine Brook, Shelburne, N.H. .	W. H. Garrett .	Lewis Engraving Co.	75

LIST OF ILLUSTRATIONS.

SUBJECT.	DRAWN BY	ENGRAVED BY	PAGE
Washington and Madison from Lead-mine Bridge	Myrick	Johnson & Thompson	77
Peabody River, Carter Notch	Bert Poole	Lewis Engraving Co.	78
Emerald Pool, near Glen House. (Full page)	Photograph	John Andrew Co.	79
On the Road to Glen House	Max Reder	Chicago Engraving Co.	80
Thompson's Falls, near Glen House, White Mountains. (Full page)	Photograph	John Andrew Co.	81
Glen House, White Mountains, N.H.	W. Bryant	John Andrew Co.	82
Crystal Cascade, near Glen House, White Mountains. (Full page)	Photograph	John Andrew Co.	83
Looking up the Notch	H. B. Colby	Lewis Engraving Co.	84
Glen Ellis Fall, Glen Road, White Mountains. (Full page)	Photograph	John Andrew Co.	85
View East from Crawford Notch	Photograph	Aldine Engraving Co.	86
The Gates of the Notch	Photograph	Aldine Engraving Co.	87
The Observatory, Summit of Mt. Washington	Bert Poole	Lewis Engraving Co.	88
Carriage Road and Railway, Mt. Washington	Bert Poole	Lewis Engraving Co.	88
Hard Travelling	H. D. Murphy	Lewis Engraving Co.	89
The Ledge, Mount Washington	Bert Poole	Lewis Engraving Co.	90
Half-way House, Mount Washington	Bert Poole	Lewis Engraving Co.	91
"Not Down on the Bills"	C. W. Reed	Johnson & Thompson	92
The Mascot Mine, Gorham, N.H.	Searles Gallagher	Lewis Engraving Co.	93
Two Views Alpine Cascades, Berlin Falls, N.H.	Photograph	Adolf Borie	94
Berlin Falls, Androscoggin River, N.H.	Myrick	Geo. E. Johnson	95
Androscoggin River, near Berlin, N.H.	Special Photograph	Chicago Engraving Co.	97
The Wrong Kind of Applause	C. W. Reed	Johnson & Thompson	100
"Chaffing!"	H. D. Murphy	Lewis Engraving Co.	102
On the Androscoggin, near Gorham, N.H.	Special Photograph	Chicago Engraving Co.	104
The Picnic Dinner. (Full page)	H. D. Murphy	Lewis Engraving Co.	105
Initial Letter T: The Young Fisherman	Max Reder	Lewis Engraving Co.	107
Devil's Slide and Stark Village. (Full page)	Special Photograph	Chicago Engraving Co.	109
Percy Peaks	Special Photograph	Chicago Engraving Co.	110
Pilot Range, from Groveton Junction. (Full page)	Searles Gallagher	Lewis Engraving Co.	111
On the Connecticut River, near North Stratford	Special Photograph	Chicago Engraving Co.	112
Where Boyton Took to the Water	Searles Gallagher		113
Mount Monadnock, and Colebrook, N.H.	Hassam	Geo. E. Johnson	114
Lunch in the Woods	W. H. Garrett	Lewis Engraving Co.	115
Beaver Falls, Colebrook, N.N.	Myrick	Johnson & Thompson	116
Fight with a Deer. (Full page)	W. H. Garrett	Lewis Engraving Co.	119

LIST OF ILLUSTRATIONS.

SUBJECT	DRAWN BY	ENGRAVED BY	PAGE
An Uncomfortable Seat	C. W. Reed	Johnson & Thompson	123
The Difference	C. W. Reed	Johnson & Thompson	124
Tail-Piece: Umbagog Lake	Max Reder	Lewis Engraving Co.	124
Initial Letter S: Log Camp	J. A. Kneeland	Lewis Engraving Co.	125
Fishing with a Silver Hook. (Full page)	W. H. Garrett	Lewis Engraving Co.	127
Frightened Deer	W. H. Garrett	Lewis Engraving Co.	129
Western Entrance to Dixville Notch	Special Photograph	Adolf Borie	132
Summit of Table Rock	Special Photograph	Adolf Borie	133
Pinnacles of Dixville Notch	M. M. Tidd	Nat Brown	135
Columnar Rock, Dixville Notch	W. H. Garrett	Lewis Engraving Co.	137
In the Forest	A. D. Nelson	Geo. E. Johnson	140
The First Bird	W. H. Garrett	Lewis Engraving Co.	142
A Deer Chase	W. H. Garrett	Lewis Engraving Co.	144
Run to Earth	H. D. Murphy	Lewis Engraving Co.	146
Camping Out. (Full page)	H. D. Murphy	Lewis Engraving Co.	151
The Wood Chopper	H. D. Murphy	Lewis Engraving Co.	153
Cooking Vension	H. D. Murphy	Lewis Engraving Co.	154
Scared by an Owl	Bert Poole	Lewis Engraving Co.	158
A Night Alarm	H. D. Murphy	Lewis Engraving Co.	161
Spying the Course	H. D. Murphy	Lewis Engraving Co.	165
To the Rescue	Bert Poole	Lewis Engraving Co.	166
Tail-piece: What Dick saw in His Dream	Herrick	Kilburn	167
Initial Letter C	H. O. Smith	Johnson & Thompson	168
A Reunion. (Full page)	W. H. Garrett	Lewis Engraving Co.	169
On the Cliffs, Dixville Notch	Photograph	Adolf Borie	171
Profile, Dixville Notch	M. M. Tidd	Nat Brown	172
The Flume, Dixville Notch	Photograph	Nat Brown	173
Dix House, Dixville Notch	Photograph	Crosscup & West	174
Lower Cascade, Dixville Notch	Special Photograph	Lewis Engraving Co.	175
Upper Cascade, Dixville Notch	Special Photograph	Adolf Borie	176
The Eagle's Nest			178
Along Clear Stream			179
The Bear Fight. (Full page)	W. H. Garrett	Lewis Engraving Co.	181
Errol Dam (1880)	Special Photograph	Nat Brown	182
The Steamer Diamond		Johnson & Thompson	184
Making a Landing	W. H. Garrett	Lewis Engraving Co.	186
Tail-piece: Aziscohos Mountain	H. B. Colby	Geo. E. Johnson	186
Initial Letter W	Bert Poole	Lewis Engraving Co.	187
The Old Union	M. M. Tidd	Johnson & Thompson	190
Quickwater Point	Bert Poole	Lewis Engraving Co.	191

LIST OF ILLUSTRATIONS.

SUBJECT.	DRAWN BY	ENGRAVED BY	PAGE
Eagle Point, Mouth of Sunday Cove	W. H. Garrett	Lewis Engraving Co.	193
Aziscohos Mountain from Lake Umbagog	H. B. Colby	Geo. E. Johnson	194
A Fisherman's Spoils, Middle Dam. (Full page)	Special Photograph	Lewis Engraving Co.	195
Camping Out on Middle Dam Carry	Special Photograph	Adolf Borie	198
Outlet of the Pond in the River. (Full page)	Special Photograph	Lewis Engraving Co.	199
Angler's Retreat, Middle Dam, Lake Welokennebacook	Photograph	Johnson & Thompson	201
A Middle Dam Trout. (Full page)	Special Photograph	Lewis Engraving Co.	202
The Old Middle Dam	Photograph	Johnson & Thompson	203
Old Middle Dam Camp	Photograph	Johnson & Thompson	204
Lake Welokennebacook from Angler's Retreat	W. H. Garrett	Lewis Engraving Co.	205
Lake Molechunkamunk from Metallak Point	Photograph	Johnson & Thompson	206
View down Lake Molechunkamunk from Birch Lodge	Photograph	Nat Brown	207
The Heron's Nest	Special Photograph	Adolf Borie	208
Brook Fishing, Lake Molechunkamunk	Special Photograph	Adolf Borie	209
Aziscohos Mountain from Upper Dam Landing	Photograph	Geo. E. Johnson	210
Upper Dam Camps	W. H. Garrett	Lewis Engraving Co.	211
Frye's Camp, Eagle Point, Lake Cupsuptic	W. H. Garrett	Lewis Engraving Co.	212
The Meeting of the Waters	Special Photograph	Adolf Borie	213
Camp Henry	Photograph	Johnson & Thompson	214
Rangeley Outlet	Photograph	Adolf Borie	215
Rangeley Dam, at foot of Oquossoc Lake	Photograph	Lewis Engraving Co.	216
Lake Point Cottage	W. H. Garrett	Lewis Engraving Co.	217
Rangeley Lake and Ram Island	Photograph	Johnson & Co.	218
Camp Kennebago, Indian Rock	Photograph	Lewis Engraving Co.	219
Mooselucmeguntic House, Haines' Landing	W. H. Garrett	Lewis Engraving Co.	220
Allerton Lodge, Bugle Cove	Photograph	Johnson & Co.	221
Lake Mooselucmeguntic	Photograph	Johnson & Co.	222
View at Bemis Stream	W. H. Garrett	Lewis Engraving Co.	223
Sport at Bemis Stream	Special Photograph	Lewis Engraving Co.	224
Camp Aziscohos, Molechunkamunk Lake	Photograph	Lewis Engraving Co.	225
Tail-piece: Cleft Rock, Bemis Stream	W. H. Garrett	Lewis Engraving Co.	226
Initial Letter D: The Lone Fisherman	Bert Poole	Lewis Engraving Co.	227
Camp Bellevue, Molechunkamunk Lake	Photograph	Geo. E. Johnson	228
Fishing at Mill Brook. (Full page)	Special Photograph	Lewis Engraving Co.	229
Metallak Brook	Special Photograph	Adolf Borie	230

LIST OF ILLUSTRATIONS.

SUBJECT.	DRAWN BY	ENGRAVED BY	PAGE
Wooding Up, Lake Welokennebacook	Photograph	Johnson & Co.	231
Lakeview Cottage, Lake Welokennebacook	C. W. Reed	Lewis Engraving Co.	233
I. Steamer and Buckboard at South Arm, Lake Welokennebacook			
II. Black Brook and Blue Mountain	Special Photograph	Adolf Borie	234
III. Devil's Oven, Black Brook Notch			
Natural Arch, Lake Road	Photograph	Johnson & Co.	235
The Devil's Den, Lake Road. (Full page)	Special Photograph	Lewis Engraving Co.	237
Andover House, Andover, Me.	Myrick	Johnson & Co.	239
Main Street, Andover, Me. (Full page)	Special Photograph	Lewis Engraving Co.	241
A Bit of Andover Corner	Photograph	Lewis Engraving Co.	242
Lower Fall, Cataract Brook	W. H. Garrett	Lewis Engraving Co.	243
Upper Fall, Cataract Brook	Special Photograph	Lewis Engraving Co.	245
The Flume, Cataract Brook	Photograph	Johnson & Co.	247
Dunn's Notch from Below and Above	Bert Poole	Lewis Engraving Co.	251
At Luncheon	Bert Poole	Lewis Engraving Co.	252
View from Lakeside Hotel, Looking Northwest	Special Photograph	Lewis Engraving Co.	253
View on Road, Lakeside Farm	Special Photograph	Lewis Engraving Co.	254
On the Piazza	Bert Poole	Lewis Engraving Co.	255
Initial Letter E: Old John and Buckboard	Bert Poole	Lewis Engraving Co.	257
Breakfast on Metallak Island	Bert Poole	Lewis Engraving Co.	259
The Lonely Camper		Lewis Engraving Co.	261
Pine Point, Umbagog Lake	Special Photograph	Adolf Borie	263
Steamer and Buckboard at Sunday Cove	Bert Poole	Lewis Engraving Co.	265
Canoes at Sunday Cove	M. M. Tidd	Geo. E. Johnson	267
A Deer Chase on Umbagog Lake	W. H. Garrett	Lewis Engraving Co.	268
Camping out on Moll's Rock	Special Photograph	Adolf Borie	270
A Shot at a Bald Eagle	W. H. Garrett	Lewis Engraving Co.	271
Camping at Foot of Big Meadow	Bert Poole	Lewis Engraving Co.	272
A Dry Crowd	Bert Poole	Lewis Engraving Co.	275
On the Magalloway	W. H. Garrett	Lewis Engraving Co.	276
Initial Letter A: Berlin Mills House	Bert Poole	Lewis Engraving Co.	278
A Camping-Party at Home	Special Photograph	Lewis Engraving Co.	279
Camping on the Magalloway River	Special Photograph	Lewis Engraving Co.	281
Shooting Partridges	W. H. Garrett	Lewis Engraving Co.	283
The Diamond Peaks	W. H. Garrett	Nat Brown	285
The Guide on the Summit	W. H. Garrett	Lewis Engraving Co.	288
Dinner on Aziscohos	W. H. Garrett	Lewis Engraving Co.	290
Bleak House, Mount Aziscohos	W. H. Garrett	Lewis Engraving Co.	293

LIST OF ILLUSTRATIONS.   xiii

SUBJECT.	DRAWN BY	ENGRAVED BY	PAGE
View on the Magalloway, just above the Bridge,	*W. H. Garrett*	Nat Brown	295
The Departure of the Girls	*Bert Poole* .	Lewis Engraving Co.	296
Initial Letter P: Our Treasurer . . .	*Bert Poole* .	Lewis Engraving Co.	297
The Way Country Boys fish. (Full page)	*Henry Linton* .	Lewis Engraving Co.	299
The Pickerel Party	*Bert Poole* . .	Lewis Engraving Co.	301
Pulpit Rock, Magalloway River. (Full page) .	*Special Photograph* .	Lewis Engraving Co.	302
Steamer Parmachenee, at Flint's Landing .	*Special Photograph* .	Lewis Engraving Co.	304
On the Tramp	*Bert Poole* .	Lewis Engraving Co.	306
Camp Furniture	*C. W. Reed* .	Johnson & Co.	307
The Kingfishers	*R. S. Ward*	Beckmann .	309
Dinner by the Roadside . .	*C. W. Reed*	Johnson & Co.	311
Building the Camp . . .	*C. W. Reed*	Johnson & Co.	314
Camp Complete . . .	*C. W. Reed*	Johnson & Co.	315
The First Night's Lodging .	*C. W. Reed*	Johnson & Co.	316
Initial Letter F: A Good Strike	*Bert Poole*	Lewis Engraving Co.	317
A Little Difficulty. (Full page)	*Bert Poole* . .	Lewis Engraving Co.	318
Across the Carry . . .	*Special Photograph* .	Lewis Engraving Co.	320
A Lucky Shot . .	*Bert Poole* .	Lewis Engraving Co.	323
A Fancy Sketch	*Guido Hammer* .	Lewis Engraving Co.	325
The Narrows, Looking down River . .	*Special Photograph* .	Lewis Engraving Co.	326
Camp at the Narrows, Magalloway River	*Special Photograph* .	Lewis Engraving Co.	328
Fishing on Magalloway River . . .	*Special Photograph* .	Lewis Engraving Co.	329
Camp near Lincoln Brook Rips (Full page) .	*Special Photograph* .	Lewis Engraving Co.	330
A Hunting Party on the Magalloway . .	*Special Photograph* .	Lewis Engraving Co.	332
A Queer Visitor	*Bert Poole* . .	Lewis Engraving Co.	334
Camp at Mouth of Lincoln Brook .	*Special Photograph* .	Lewis Engraving Co.	336
Initial Letter H: Moose Head .	*Searles Gallagher*	Lewis Engraving Co.	338
Trailing a Moose	*Searles Gallagher* .	Lewis Engraving Co.	339
Lower Metallak Pond, from Magalloway River	*Special Photograph* .	Lewis Engraving Co.	340
Lower Metallak Pond, Looking towards River,	*Special Photograph* .	Lewis Engraving Co.	341
Hunter's Camp, Magalloway River .	*Special Photograph* .	Lewis Engraving Co.	342
The Lucky Hunters	*Searles Gallagher* .	Lewis Engraving Co.	343
A Wet Time	*Searles Gallagher* .	Lewis Engraving Co.	344
A Logging-crew at Home. (Full page) .	*Special Photograph* .	Lewis Engraving Co.	346
Lumber Camp near Upper Metallak Pond .	*Special Photograph* .	Lewis Engraving Co.	347
A Gray Morning. (Full page) . .	*Searles Gallagher* .	Lewis Engraving Co.	348
"Very Thin Water"	*Searles Gallagher* .	Lewis Engraving Co.	349
Camp Landing, Little Magalloway . .	*Special Photograph* .	Lewis Engraving Co.	350
Camp on the Little Magalloway . .	*Special Photograph* .	Lewis Engraving Co.	351
Running the Rapids. (Full page) . .	*Special Photograph* .	Lewis Engraving Co.	352

LIST OF ILLUSTRATIONS.

SUBJECT.	DRAWN BY	ENGRAVED BY	PAGE
A Rest on Parmachenee Carry. (Full page)	Special Photograph	Lewis Engraving Co.	354
A Call to Supper	Searles Gallagher	Lewis Engraving Co.	357
In Camp on the Magalloway	Special Photograph	Lewis Engraving Co.	361
Flint's Camp, Sunday Pond	W. H. Garrett	Lewis Engraving Co.	362
A Party we saw on the Way	Special Photograph	Lewis Engraving Co.	363
Initial Letter O: The Camp Fire	Bert Poole	Lewis Engraving Co.	364
Sacking Canoes	Bert Poole	Lewis Engraving Co.	365
Stone Dam, Little Magalloway	Special Photograph	Lewis Engraving Co.	366
The Pool, Little Magalloway	Special Photograph	Lewis Engraving Co.	367
Parmachenee Lake, from Carry Landing	Special Photograph	Lewis Engraving Co.	368
Little Boy's Falls, Good Fishing. (Full page)	Special Photograph	Lewis Engraving Co.	370
Chasing a Caribou	Bert Poole	Lewis Engraving Co.	371
"Too Far Away"	Bert Poole	Lewis Engraving Co.	373
Little Boy's Falls. (Full page)	Special Photograph	Lewis Engraving Co.	376
"Death on Dumplings!"	Bert Poole	Lewis Engraving Co.	381
The Bear and the Berries	Bert Poole	Lewis Engraving Co.	382
Initial Letter F: The Brook	W. H. Garrett	Lewis Engraving Co.	384
"Baked Beans!"	W. H. Garrett	Lewis Engraving Co.	385
The Green Cook	W. H. Garrett	Lewis Engraving Co.	386
Beating Eggs	W. H. Garrett	Lewis Engraving Co.	387
Great Fishing	W. H. Garrett	Lewis Engraving Co.	389
Youthful Habit Strong in Age	Special Photograph	M. L. Brown	390
Shooting a Moose. (Full page)	W. H. Garrett	Lewis Engraving Co.	392
A Lunch by the River	Special Photograph	Lewis Engraving Co.	394
A Narrow Escape	W. H. Garrett	Lewis Engraving Co.	395
A Sympathetic Friend	W. H. Garrett	Lewis Engraving Co.	396
Letter S: Studying the Route	Searles Gallagher	Lewis Engraving Co.	398
The Forest Trail. (Full page)	Special Photograph	Lewis Engraving Co.	400
Looking for Game	Searles Gallagher	Lewis Engraving Co.	402
A Deer in Sight	Searles Gallagher	Lewis Engraving Co.	403
A Lucky Shot. (Full page)	Searles Gallagher	Lewis Engraving Co.	404
Saddle-Back Mt., Grafton Notch. (Full page)	Special Photograph	Lewis Engraving Co.	406
On Cambridge River, Grafton, Me. (Full page)	Special Photograph	Lewis Engraving Co.	408
The Landlady at South Arm	Special Photograph	Lewis Engraving Co.	409
Ready to Start	Special Photograph	Lewis Engraving Co.	409
Umbagog Lake from Rapid River. (Full page)	Special Photograph	Lewis Engraving Co.	410
Looking East from Lakeside Hotel	Special Photograph	Lewis Engraving Co.	411
Speckled Mountain, Grafton Notch, Me.	Special Photograph	Lewis Engraving Co.	412
Screw Auger Falls	Special Photograph	Lewis Engraving Co.	413
View on Bear River	Special Photograph	M. L. Brown	414
Tail-piece: The End of It All	Searles Gallagher	Lewis Engraving Co.	415

THROUGH THE WILDS.

CHAPTER I.

DOWN BOSTON HARBOR. — ON THE BRINY DEEP. — ALONG THE COAST. — PLACES OF INTEREST. — CAPE ANN. — MAN OVERBOARD. — THE RESCUE. — ISLES OF SHOALS. — PORTLAND HEAD. — CUSHING'S ISLAND. — PORTLAND HARBOR. — THE FOREST CITY.

VIEW IN BOSTON HARBOR.

ANY PERSON who had been on the forward deck of the steamer Fleetwing one fine July morning in the summer of '83, could scarcely have overlooked a group of four boys who were standing closely together, busily engaged in conversation both interesting and amusing, judging from their earnestness and the hearty peals of laughter that were occasionally wafted to the bystanders.

With an author's license, we will play eavesdropper for a few moments, while taking a mental survey of them. They are American boys, well dressed, with bright and intelligent faces, and their ages apparently from fifteen to eighteen.

"Quarter past eight," exclaimed the youngest, taking out a nice silver watch and referring to it; "in fifteen minutes more we shall be afloat on the briny deep."

"We are now, Dick," returned the eldest, laughing, "for the water under us is briny, and deep also. High tide, you know."

"Don't catch a fellow up so quick, George; if you begin that sort of thing now, and propose to continue it during the trip, we shall bury you somewhere in the wilds, and return without you," and Dick gave his elder friend a good-natured poke in the ribs.

The young gentlemen thus brought to our notice have long been friends, and are to take a summer vacation together in New England, and have already resolved to spend the most of it in the woods.

THE CAMPING PARTY.

The youngest of the party, Dick Burton, was the son of a wealthy speculator, whose parents, at the present time, were abroad, and being offered his choice between joining them for the summer in Europe or visiting the wilds of Maine with a party of his chums, had accepted the latter alternative as promising the most pleasure. Dick was a few months over fifteen, fond of shooting and fishing, and thought that a European tour would suit him a little better later in life. For the present, he preferred a visit to the bright lakes and sparkling streams where the speckled trout are easily lured to rise to an artificial fly, and in whose forest borders a quick eye, a steady hand, and a true aim, would furnish a fat buck for the camp larder.

His closest friend and steady companion, Fred Holmes, nearly a year older than Dick, was the son of a well-known clergyman of the Hub, whose family name, for various reasons, we have changed, and was known to his intimate friends only as the "Parson." Fred had studied a little too hard the past year, and his father had arranged the present excursion for his son, while the boy had made choice of companions, the three friends who accompanied him.

The third in the party, Edward Bailey, or "Ned" as his chums called him, was seventeen years of age, the son of a wealthy dry-goods merchant, who had intended him for the same business. But Ned declared he would never be a counter-jumper, his tastes running in an entirely different direction. He had a decided *penchant* for work requiring the use of tools, and he hoped to be a machinist or engineer.

The eldest of the group whom we are introducing, George Howe, was eighteen years old, tall, slim, and fine looking. His father was a newspaper publisher, and George, who aspired to either literature or the stage, had already begun reporting news items for the daily, and was a bright and shining light, perhaps we should say "star," in a South End Dramatic Club.

The friendship of the four boys was of several years' standing, and they had made other trips together before of two or three weeks in length. But this was to be a protracted one, it being their intention to remain away from the city three or four months. The excursion had been talked over for weeks and weeks, and their talk and plans had finally culminated in their presence on board the steamboat this pleasant Monday morning in July, *en route* for Portland.

George had favored making the run to Portland by rail, but

Dick, who was very fond of the water, represented the pleasures of a sea-voyage by daylight in such an enthusiastic manner, that he carried the point, and the party took passage on one of the St. John steamers.

"All ashore that's goin'," now sang out a darky, poking his head out of the saloon door for a moment, and ringing a large bell, to call attention to his words.

"Half-past eight," said Dick, consulting his watch again, "and now I suppose we are off."

"There goes the bow line," remarked Fred, who had stepped to the side of the steamer, and was looking down on the dock.

Just then the huge wheels began to revolve, one long whistle was heard,— a warning note for other craft,— and the beautiful boat moved slowly and majestically out from her dock.

It was a very hot morning on shore, with scarcely a breath of wind, and the current of air that the boat made as she gathered headway, was fully appreciated by our young friends, who had obtained stools, and were seated just in front of the pilot-house, where they could command an extensive view of the harbor.

A revenue cutter, several sailing and one steam yacht, and numerous vessels of all sizes and kinds peculiar to our merchant marine, were anchored near the wharves, and through these the steamer made her way, turning and twisting, as occasion demanded, until she had passed East Boston, and had a comparatively clear course, when her route was less circuitous, she only following the turns of the channel.

The boat passed a dredging-machine, and the boys were much interested in its workings. And for some time they watched the large iron buckets, that went down with a rattle and splurge, and then reappeared loaded with mud, the water pouring from it

STEAMER CUMBERLAND.

in a stream, as it was dumped into scows that were anchored near.

"That is a clumsy-looking machine," said Ned, as the dredger disappeared from sight; "I believe I could improve on that."

"Oh, let it alone," bantered the Parson; "you are always improving something."

"Yes, he's improving the shining hours now," put in Dick with a smile.

VIEW IN BOSTON HARBOR.

"Belay your puns, Dick!" exclaimed George with a make-believe frown.

"There comes the Nantasket, boys," cried Ned; "what a crowd there is on her."

"Yes; the business men who live at Hull and Hingham are just coming up to their stores," added the Parson.

"I am glad we are heading from Boston instead of towards it; ain't you, my boy?" and Dick gave the Parson a slap on his thigh that made him wince.

"You need not break a fellow's leg if you are," replied his friend, at the same time moving out of reach.

As the steamer reached Fort Independence, the attention of the boys was drawn towards it, and Ned asked his companions if either of them could tell him how old the fort was. All confessed ignorance to its age or history; but for the benefit of our readers, some of whom, like Ned, may have curiosity about it, we quote a few facts: —

"The first fort built upon Castle Island was constructed in 1634, and since that time the island has always been fortified. The works have been rebuilt a great many times. Castle William stood on this island when the Revolutionary War broke out, and when the British troops were obliged to evacuate Boston, they destroyed the fort and burned it to ashes. The Provincial forces then took possession of the island, and restored the fort. In 1798 its name was formally changed to Fort Independence, the President, John Adams, being present on the occasion. In 1798 the island was ceded to the United States. From 1785 until 1805 this fort was the place appointed for the confinement of prisoners sentenced to hard labor, provision having been made in the act of cession to the United States that this privilege should be retained. The present fort is of comparatively recent construction."

FORT INDEPENDENCE.

Directly opposite Fort Independence, across the main ship channel, is Fort Winthrop, still uncompleted, on Governor's Island.

"I should like to know if Uncle Sam intends to finish that fort?" queried Dick.

"He don't seem to be in much of a hurry about it," answered

George; "it has been in its present condition, as near as I can judge, since I was a child."

A writer says of it:—

"The island was granted to Governor Winthrop 1632, and was subsequently confirmed to his heirs. In 1640, the conditions of his ownership having already been once previously changed, he was granted the island on condition of paying one bushel of apples to the Governor and one to the General Court in winter annually. It continued in the sole possession of the Winthrop family until 1808, when a part of it was sold to the Government for the purpose of erecting a fort, which was named Fort Warren. The name given to the work now in process of erection is Fort Winthrop, in honor of the Governor of Massachusetts Bay and first owner of the island; while the name of the former fort has been transferred to the fortification further down the harbor. When fully completed, Fort Winthrop is intended to be a most important defence to the harbor."

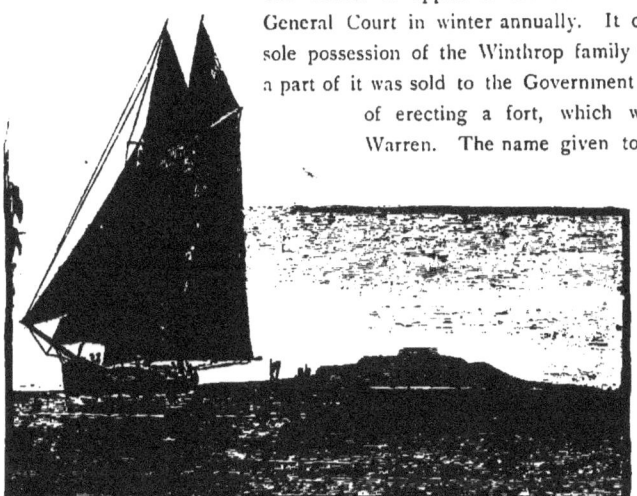

FORT WINTHROP.

The day, for a sea trip, was all that could be desired: warm and pleasant, with a perfectly clear atmosphere, enabling the boys to sight vessels a long distance off, and even George acknowledged that they were much more comfortable on the boat than they would have been on the cars.

"There's the Government boat that runs between the city and

Fort Warren," exclaimed Dick, as a very fast and handsome tug flashed by them, heading up the harbor. "Isn't she a daisy?"

"Ploughs the water as if she meant business," acknowledged the Parson. "I should not object to owning her."

"I wish you did," added Ned, "and then you could take us off for a three months' cruise."

The steamer now swung more to the eastward, heading for Broad Sound Channel, and the boys soon noticed Long Island on the starboard side, and Deer Island on the port, and questioned each other in regard to them, without gaining a great deal of information.

LONG ISLAND HEAD LIGHT.

On the bluff, or head, of Long Island, are a lighthouse and an uncompleted battery. The lighthouse was built in 1819. The tower is twenty-two feet in height, but the light is eighty feet above the sea. The tower is of iron, painted white; the lantern has nine burners; the light is fixed, and can be seen in a clear night about fifteen miles. The battery, intended to be a very strong one when completed, is still in course of construction, and will, no doubt, be finished some time, if Uncle Sam's purse is long enough.

Deer Island belongs to the city of Boston, and contains a number of fine buildings. It is noted as the place where common and uncommon drunks, after being run through the mill of the Police Court, and bounced out of the hopper, find rest for periods ranging from one to six months.

"There is Nix's Mate," said George, pointing to a peculiar-looking object, rising out of the water to the right.

"Does it mark a reef there?" asked Dick.

"I believe so. Either a reef or shoal, and it runs in towards the shore a long way, as seen at low water. I have an idea that I have read something interesting connected with it, but don't remember now what it was."

"You should cultivate your memory," declared the Parson. "Who knows but we have lost a first-rate yarn through your forgetfulness?"

As George could give no account of this well-known beacon, we quote the following for the benefit of those of our readers who may feel interested, many of whom have, no doubt, noticed it when down the harbor: —

"East of Long Island Head there is a low, rocky island on which stands a singularly-shaped monument. It consists of a solid structure of stone, twelve feet in height, and forty feet square. All the stones in this piece of masonry are securely fastened together with copper. Upon it stands an octagonal pyramid of wood, twenty feet high, and painted black. It is supposed that this monument was erected in the earliest years of the present century, though the date is not known. Its purpose was to warn vessels of one of the most dangerous shoals in the harbor. This island is called Nix's Mate, though for what reason is not known. There is a tradition, unsupported by facts, that the mate of a vessel of which one Captain Nix was master, was executed upon the island, for killing the latter. But it was known as 'Nix's Island,' as long ago as 1636, and this would seem to dispose of the story. It is, however, true that several murderers and pirates have been hanged upon the island, and one William Fly was hanged there in chains in 1726 for the crime of piracy, on which occasion, the *Boston News Letter* informs us, Fly 'behaved himself very unbecomingly, even to the last.' It is a part of the tradition above referred to that Nix's mate declared his innocence, and asserted as a proof of it that the island would be washed away. If any such prophecy was ever made, it has certainly been

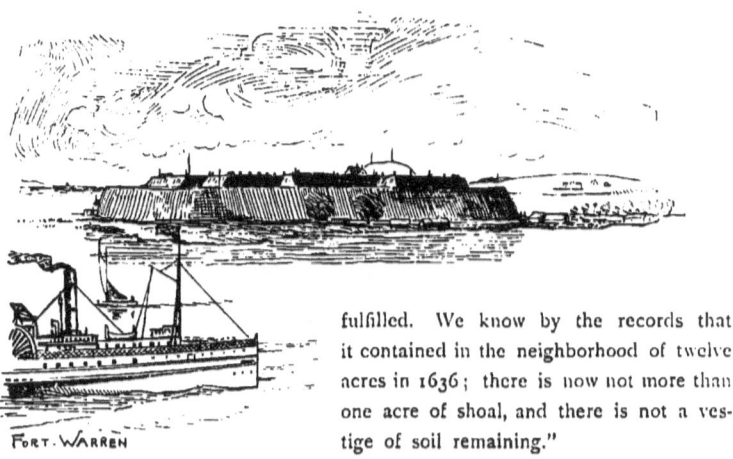

Fort Warren

fulfilled. We know by the records that it contained in the neighborhood of twelve acres in 1636; there is now not more than one acre of shoal, and there is not a vestige of soil remaining."

"There is Fort Warren," cried Ned, pointing off to starboard, "but we are not going very near it."

"Yes," said Dick, "and I can see Boston Light farther out, and way beyond it the tall shaft of Minot's."

"I mean to visit the islands in the harbor some time," said the Parson. "Wouldn't you like to, Dick?"

"First-rate. I should like to go up into one of the lighthouses also."

"We will take a day some time next summer, hire a steam-yacht, and do them all," added George. "I should like to know their history, — it must be interesting."

As some of my readers may be of George's opinion, I quote the following in regard to these well-known places : —

"Fort Warren is situated on George's Island, near the entrance to the harbor, and is the most famous of all the defences of the city. George's Island was claimed as the property of James Pemberton of Hull, as early as 1622. His possession of it having been confirmed, it was bought, sold, and inherited by numerous owners, until 1825, when it became the property of the city of Boston. It is now, of course, under the jurisdiction of the United States Government.

BOSTON LIGHT.

The construction of the present fort was begun in April, 1833, and was completed in 1850. The material is finely-hammered Quincy granite, and the stone faces, as well as those parts that have been protected with earth and sodded over, are as neat and trim as art can make them. The fort is one of great strength, but it has never yet been needed to defend the harbor of Boston. During the Rebellion, it was used as a place of confinement for noted Confederate prisoners, the most famous of all being the rebel commissioners to Europe, Mason and Slidell, who were sent here for confinement, after their capture on board the Trent by Commodore Wilkes.

"About two miles from Fort Warren, nearly due east, and at the entrance of the harbor, is the Boston Light. The island on which it stands has been used as a lighthouse station since 1715, when the General Court of the Colony passed the necessary acts. The land was generously given to the Colony by the owners of it, though as there is soil on only about three-quarters of an acre, the rest of the two or three acres being bare jagged rock, the gift entailed no great loss upon them. In the time of the Revolution, the lighthouse was the object of much small warfare, and was several times destroyed and rebuilt. In 1783 it was once more restored by the State, being built this time of stone ; and it is this light-house which still stands at the mouth of the harbor, though it has since been enlarged and refitted several times. The top of the lighthouse now stands ninety-eight feet above the level of the sea, and is fitted with a revolving light which can be seen from a distance of sixteen nautical miles in fair weather.

"Still nearer to Fort Warren, and on the direct line to Boston Light, is the Spit, or Bug Light. It is a curious structure. The lower part is a system of iron pillars fixed in the rock, affording no surface for the waves to beat against and destroy. The fixed red light is about thirty-five feet above the level of the sea, and can be seen at a distance of about seven miles in clear weather. This light was built in 1856. Its object is to warn navigators of the dangerous obstacle known as Harding's Ledge, about two miles out at sea, east of Point Allerton, at the head of Nantasket Beach."

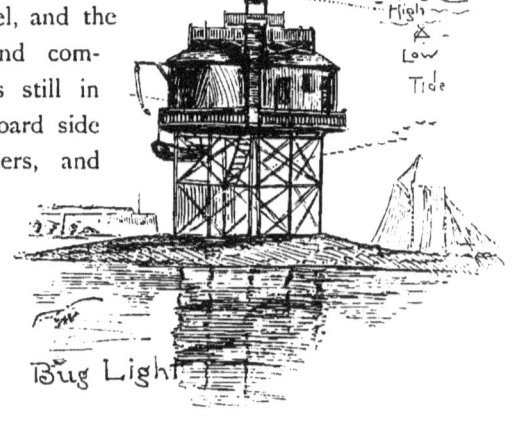

The boat was now well along in Broad Sound Channel, and the boys were watching and commenting on the islands still in sight. Off on the starboard side lay the three Brewsters, and beyond, westerly, the Graves. The ocean was comparatively quiet, and there was but little sea on. It looked as if one could land on the Graves from a row-boat with comparative ease, but to see these cruel rocks in a northeast gale, with the breakers dashing in immense volumes of white angry water, and with thunderous roar submerging these ledges, you would say these islands were rightly named.

An excursion steamer from Nahant now passed them, and the boys waved their hats and handkerchiefs at the passengers, some of whom returned the compliment.

"Were you ever at Nahant, Dick?" asked George.

"No; but I mean to go some time, and visit Maolis Garden."

"That don't amount to much; I have been in it. But I can never pass Nahant headland without a shudder. I had a narrow escape from death there one night."

"How was that?" eagerly inquired the Parson.

"A party of six of us left City Point, South Boston, one evening, about seven o'clock, to go down to Swampscott to a muster. Ned Bray was to be one of the party, but business called him to Lynn that afternoon, and he agreed to meet us at Nahant, if we would run in there and pick him up. We promised to do so, and I told him we should probably get there about eight or nine o'clock.

The Graves.

"We started from the Point in a large sloop yacht, all of us in first-rate spirits. There was a light southerly breeze, and I laid a straight course for Broad Sound. Only one of my companions was at all familiar with the art of sailing a boat, so he and I took turns in the management of our craft.

"The evening was beautiful when we left the wharf, and we naturally anticipated a very pleasant sail. But the poet says

'The best-laid schemes of mice and men gang aft aglee,'

and it was so in our case."

"Did the poet say that all alone by himself?" broke in Ned, with a roguish smile.

"Now, Ned, if you interrupt me in that way again, I'll call the captain and have you put down in the bilge hole," and George shook his finger warningly at the joker.

"Reel off your yarn, and I'll keep him quiet, George," added Fred.

"All right. Lay him on the deck and sit down on him if he speaks again," laughed George, and resumed his story. "We had passed Deer Island and were about half-way between that and Nahant, with all the harbor lights visible, when in five minutes, before I noticed it, talking and laughing as we were, there rolled in a fog as thick as mud, and hid everything from view.

"When the lights disappeared we were heading in a bee line for the steamboat landing at Nahant. But as the fog increased, the wind changed and came out from the eastward, and began to blow a little fresher than I cared to have it. I had neglected to take a compass, and, as you may suppose, that did not help matters any.

"We began to tear through the water at a rate that frightened two of the timid ones, and every few minutes we were plentifully spattered from the spray of some large roller breaking on the weather bow.

"It was not exactly dark, for the moon was shining above and making an ineffectual attempt to pierce the fog, but still we could only see for the length of a fathom or two around us, and I began to feel uneasy as to our exact position.

"For the last half-hour I had laid our course as near as I could by the wind, and I called Tom Smith up to me, on whom I depended for help in working the boat, and asked him in a whisper if he had any idea where we were. He thought we must be about opposite West Lynn, and said I had better change the course and run for the shore.

"As I could think of nothing better to do, I followed his advice. During the last half-hour the wind had increased very much, and the boat rushed through the water with 'a bone in her teeth,' and we were fast getting wet through.

"For fifteen minutes, I should judge, we dashed on in this manner, when suddenly I was startled by the noise of breakers. I cast an inquiring glance towards Tom, and saw that his face was turned in the direction of the sound, and that he was listening attentively.

"The next moment the fog lifted, or cleared, a little, so that a few rays of moonlight illumined the angry waters before us, and right ahead I saw"—

"What?" broke in Dick, excitedly.

"The ragged walls of Nahant, with the breakers dashing up on the scarred and honeycombed rocks some twenty or thirty feet.

"Tom took in the situation at the same moment, and being better acquainted with Nahant than I was,—he had lived there one summer,—knew exactly where we were.

"With an expression on his face that I shall never forget, he cried,—

"'The Swallow's Cave! Hard-a-port your helm—hard-a-port! If she misses stays our lives are not worth a farthing,' and seizing an oar he put it out on the port side and pulled for dear life.

"The boat came up to the wind lively, but moved slower as the sails shivered in the wind's eye, and I actually believe that if it had not been for Tom's oar she would have missed stays, for she had a trick of doing it sometimes in rough water, and there was a very heavy sea on by that time.

"I hauled the windward jib sheet as tight as I could draw it, and only slacked it off when the boat had swung around so far

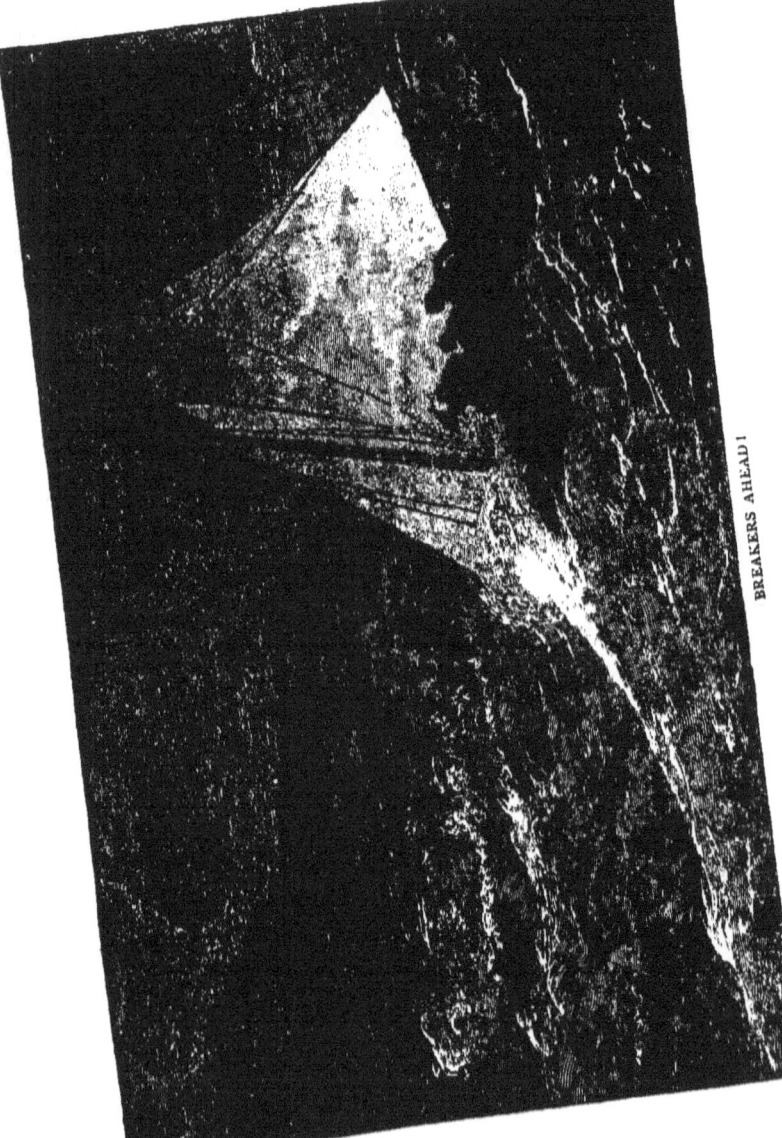

BREAKERS AHEAD!

that her lee rail was under water, and I knew there was no danger of her going back on us; then trimming the mainsail we hove away from our dangerous position.

"The fog thickened again; and after running on our present tack fifteen minutes by my watch, I slacked off the sheets, squared away, and run awhile before the wind until I felt satisfied that we had cleared Nahant, when I put my helm to port, hauled in our sheets, and stood for the shore.

"After running on that course as long as I dared, I brought the boat into the wind, had the boys haul down the jib, and we dropped anchor. Then Tom jumped into the tender and pulled away to see if he could discover where we were. It was then about ten o'clock.

"He was gone nearly an hour, and when he returned he brought Ned Bray with him, who told us he had been waiting on the wharf for two hours, and was half frozen.

"Tom informed me that we were not more than half a mile from the steamboat wharf. We hauled up the anchor, hoisted the jib, and Tom took the helm, as he had the best idea of where the wharf lay.

"The fog was as thick as ever; so I went forward, and, lying down on deck, peered into the mist, ready to announce the first sight of land.

"The boat sped toward the shore like an arrow, occasionally shipping a barrel or two of water, that wet us all to the skin, for none of the boys would go into the cabin, although they might have kept dry there; and in a few moments I saw off on the starboard bow a large white object, looking dim and ghostly, as it appeared suddenly through the fog. It was the steamboat lying at the wharf, and we were but a short distance from it, and were running parallel with it.

"I was just rising to my feet to slack away the jib halyards, when I made out a cat-boat at anchor directly ahead of us, and not twenty feet distant.

"'Starboard your helm!' I shouted. 'Quick! hard-a-starboard!' and, excited with the impending collision, my voice rose far above the roar of the wind and water. Tom heard me, and obeyed the order promptly. But he was not quick enough for the speed at which we tore through the waves, and the next moment we struck the boat amidships with a tremendous crash, cutting her almost in two, our boat swinging clear of her as she sank.

"The shock of the collision brought me to the deck all in a heap; but the moment I had scrambled up, I let go the jib and mainsail halyards, and yelled to Tom to haul in the main sheet; and the next moment we had landed on the beach, with our bow nearly out of water, bringing up so suddenly as to throw everybody down, while I went heels over head out on the shore. Luckily it was sand and gravel where I struck, and I was not hurt much; but my temper was terribly ruffled, and I inwardly consigned the fog to Davy Jones's locker.

"Rising to my feet, I called to Tom to light the lantern and bring it forward; and when he came we examined the boat carefully, but found our craft had escaped serious injury, having had only a few splinters knocked off, and her paint badly rubbed in two or three places. We had a nice job then in getting her afloat, for she had struck solid, and had only been so slightly damaged from the fact that there was not a rock on the spot where she had piled up on the beach. After half an hour's hard labor we succeeded in floating our yacht, and pulled her over to the wharf, which was but a short distance away, and made her fast.

"Then Tom and I took the tender, and rowed out to where

we had struck the other boat, to see if she had come to the surface. But we could see nothing of her. By the aid of our lantern, however, we found a rudder and pair of oars floating about: these we picked up, and carried back to the yacht.

"It was then nearly twelve o'clock, and we were all wet to the skin, and shivering with the cold; while Joe Chick said he was hungry enough to eat Limburger cheese, and he exactly voiced the sentiments of the entire party.

"As there was no stove in our boat, we climbed up on the wharf and skirmished around for fuel. An old dry-goods case and a fence in the vicinity supplied us, and we soon had a good fire under way, whose bright blaze both cheered and warmed us. Then we cooked our supper and made some coffee, and, while quieting our appetites, talked over the accident, for such it was, pure and simple; and as none in the party appeared anxious to pay for the boat we had unfortunately ruined, it was the unanimous opinion of the whole party, that the earlier we made sail in the morning, the better it would be. So with that understanding, we extinguished the fire, put our things on board, and turned in for a few hours' sleep.

"About four o'clock I awoke, called my companions, and after depositing the rudder and oars belonging to the sunken boat on the wharf, we cast off and made sail. There was just a light ripple on the water, barely enough to give us steerage-way, but by the aid of an ash breeze we lost no time running away from the scene of the accident.

"As we passed the steamboat, one of the deck-hands hailed us, inquiring if we did not run into a boat when we came in last night. Tom told him that was a great moral question, and we could not spare time to answer it; and we continued on our course without further talk. We had a good run to the city, reaching the Point about nine o'clock. After paying for the boat, we put for our homes; but, no matter how long I live, I never shall forget that night."

"Did you ever learn who owned the boat you sank?" asked Dick.

"No, I did not. As you may imagine, there were none of us particularly anxious to look the matter up; but it must have been a mystery to him unless he was enlightened by some of the steamer's crew."

By this time the Fleetwing was opposite Egg Rock Light, and the boys had a good view of that, also Lynn Beach. Occasionally some small coaster, three-masted schooner, or square-rigged vessels, passed them, drawing their attention for a few moments from the panoramic view of the coast they were enjoying so much. At a distance they saw the islands and hills, the summer hotels and villages, of

the North Shore, and passed successively the pleasant boroughs of Swampscott, Marblehead, Salem, Beverly, Gloucester, and Cape Ann. The steamer passed within a stone's-throw of Thatcher's Island, giving them a fine view of the Double Lights, so well known to our hardy mariners. After passing these, and when abeam of the Londoner, — a small rock marked with an upright pole, around whose foot the angry waters continually foam, — the steamer's course was changed more to the north; and shortly after they sighted Mount Agamenticus, which grew larger with each mile they advanced.

A mile beyond, the steamer reached the Salvages, a group of two or three low islands off to the left; and while passing these, an exciting event took place.

For some time past the boys had looked with disgust upon a rough specimen of humanity who had been staggering about the deck, and occasionally accosting one of the party in that foolish and unmeaning manner so natural to a drunken man.

THATCHER'S ISLAND LIGHTS.

Not receiving any encouragement from the boys to converse, he had "beat over," as Dick expressed it, to the starboard side of the steamer, and was leaning over the rail, when suddenly, in some unaccountable manner, he pitched head foremost over the bulwark. The Parson saw him, and promptly gave the alarm, crying out, "Man overboard!"

Instantly all was excitement. One of the pilots rang for the engineer to stop, yelled through the speaking-tube, "Man overboard!"

and ordered the man at the wheel to "keep her steady." The first mate happened to be in the wheel-house. Out he rushed, threw over two or three life-preservers, and, calling to some of the deck-hands, hurried aft to one of the starboard quarter boats.

The boys followed the mate, eager to see all of interest, and watched the process of launching the boat. This was accomplished more readily than sometimes happens in such cases, and showed the crew was well drilled for emergency; and in three minutes from the time the alarm was given, the boat was afloat, and under way on her humane mission.

As the boat struck the water, George jumped lightly up on the bulwark, and, holding on by a stanchion, took a look for the struggling man. He soon saw him, and pointed him out to the mate,

who was in command of the boat; while the crew bent to their oars with a will that sent their craft rushing through the water. Standing erect in the stern sheets, with the tiller lines in his hands, the mate kept his eye on the inebriate, and occasionally gave a command to his crew.

"It's lucky for that rum-sucker it is such a still day," said Dick.

"That's so," replied George; "and it is lucky for him that the mate was equal to the emergency, and backed by a willing crew. I tell you, boys, this boat is well manned. All the officers I have seen look and act like gentlemen, and the crew are proving their metal now. Don't they walk that boat along?"

"They pull handsomely," replied Ned; "but if that loafer hasn't caught a life-preserver, or can't swim, he'll drown before the boat reaches him."

"I guess the bath he's taken will sober him a little," added the Parson.

"It looks to me as if he had hold of something — hurrah! he has — either one or two of the life-preservers," cried George. "Now he's all right, for the boat is most up to him. My stars! how those fellows are pulling! They every one, mate included, deserve a medal from the Humane Society."

The boys, with many of the other passengers, watched the attempt at rescue, with anxious suspense, and were finally gratified by seeing the boat reach the unfortunate victim of his own indiscretion, and the crew haul him in.

The steamer meanwhile had been slowly backing, and had materially lessened the distance between the two boats.

As the rescuing party turned their boat to retrace their way to the steamer, a cheer went up from the passengers, and they watched its return with eager eyes, meantime speculating on the condition of the half-drowned man. It was amusing to hear the various opinions expressed, — some thinking he was hurt, and others not; but all seemed to be of the opinion that if he was alive he was pretty thoroughly sobered.

The wheels of the steamer yet revolved slowly, and she was backed to within a few fathoms of the boat, giving the passengers

THE RESCUE.

a chance to see inside of it plainly. The man who had fallen overboard was lying in the stern sheets with his head pillowed on the mate's breast, and the blood was seen running down his face, from a cut over his right eye.

A few moments later, and the party reached the steamer. The rescued man was passed up on board and carried down to the gentlemen's cabin, he being too weak to walk. The davit blocks were hooked into the rings, and the boat hoisted on board, and the steamer resumed her trip after an hour's delay.

There happened to be a physician among the passengers, and he attended the miserable victim of intemperance, and did what was necessary for the man's comfort.

When the doctor appeared in the saloon again he was besieged by the older passengers, who wished to satisfy their curiosity.

The doctor, who was rather a taciturn individual, told them the man would be all right the next day. That he must throw up the salt water he had swallowed, and get rested. That the cut on his forehead did not amount to much, and had been caused, the man thought, by one of the floats of the wheel striking him; and then refused to say anything more, and devoted himself to his book.

The boys now returned to their place of observation on the saloon deck, in front of the pilot-house, and took their former seats. Off to the left, or port side, they could see in the distance Ipswich and Newburyport, Plum Island, the mouth of the Merrimac, Hampton and its beaches, Rye and Rye Beach, and a number of lighthouses scattered along shore. The Isles of Shoals next attracted their attention, and from the steamer's deck, with their glass, they could easily discern the large hotels of that celebrated summer resort.

"Who has ever been to the Isles of Shoals?" asked Dick, after they had talked for some time about them.

"I have," replied George. "I was down there two years ago."

"Much of a place?" inquired Ned.

"So-so. Nice boating and fishing, bathing, too, if you like it. Fine, roomy hotels, with splendid piazzas. Just the thing for evening promenades, with a pretty girl hanging on your arm, and gazing up into your face with her soulful eyes."

"Yum, yum," broke in Ned. "Don't go on in that kind of a strain, or you will make me nervous."

"Any drives?" asked Dick, who was fond of horses.

"Well; no. The islands are all nearly barren rock. But around the hotels there are small patches of lawn, and some flower-beds on foreign soil. That is to say, all the dirt of which they are composed was brought from the main land, there not being any on the island."

"An expensive garden that, I should think," suggested the Parson.

"Yes. It must have cost a great deal of money to get the place into its present shape."

"How many islands are there in the group?" queried Ned.

"I don't know the exact number, but the principal ones are Duck, Hog, Smutty-nose, — which you may remember as the scene of a frightful tragedy a few years ago, — Star, and White. That is White Island, the one where you see the lighthouse."

A little information about this romantic group of islands may not come amiss at this time, and we quote what follows in regard to them : —

"The history of the Isles dates back to July 15, 1605, when the pinnace of the French navigators, DeMonts and Champlain, piloted by the ill-fated Panounias and his faithful bride Onagimon, sailed by them. The security which they offered from the Indians made them very early the resort of fishermen; and by the middle of the seventeenth century they were the home of a large and busy community of fishermen and traders. The first settlers appear to have been a wild and lawless set, among whom women were prohibited from living. With prosperity came better manners apparently, and the law became obsolete, as the following enactment of the General Court, held at Gorgeana in 1650, shows:—

THE CHASM, STAR ISLAND.

"'It was ordered, upon the petition of William Wormwood, that as the fishermen of the Isles of Shoals will entertain womanhood, they have liberty to sit down there, provided they shall not sell neither wine, beare, or liquor.'

"One cause of the degeneracy of the islanders a century later, it may be noted here, was attributed to their having substituted ardent liquors for the use of a wholesome drink called bounce, 'composed of two-thirds spruce beer and one-third wine,'—whether under the influence of 'womanhood' or not, our informant, Charles Chauncey, does not say. The principal settlement was at first upon Appledore, or Hog; but about 1679, for some unexplained cause, this island was entirely deserted, and a settlement was made on Star Island, which afterwards was incorporated as the town of Gosport. This soon became a town of some four hundred inhabitants, doing a very considerable fishing business. The town records contain many very curious and interesting entries, among which the following is perhaps unique:—

"'On March ye 25 1771, then their was a meating called and it was gurned until the 23d day of Apirel. Mr. Deeken William Muchmore Moderator.'

"At the outbreak of the Revolution the people were ordered off the islands, as it was feared that they would give aid to the British. A few only returned at the close of the war; and from that time the population has gradually diminished, until now the islands are simply the temporary abode of the valetudinarian and the summer idler.

"It were vain to attempt to describe the varied charms which these barren rocks have for those who love the ocean, to tell of the countless rifts and chasms into which the sea has rent the shore, or to point out the solitary cliffs on which, to one looking over the broad expanse of the deep, there comes such a strange exhilaration and fulness of enjoyment. But it is an experience of a lifetime to stand on such a spot during an easterly gale, and watch

"'The mad Atlantic,
When surge on surge would heap enorme
    Cliffs of emerald topped with snow,
    That lifted and lifted, and then let go.
A great white avalanche of thunder.

. . . . . .

And whenever the weight of ocean is thrown
Full and fair on White Island Head,
    A great mist-jotum you will see,
    Lifting himself up silently,
High and huge o'er the lighthouse top,
With hands of wavering spray outspread,
    Groping after the little tower.'

SMITH'S MONUMENT, STAR ISLAND.

"Each island has its peculiar attractions, as each has its own rote, or sound made by the surf upon the shore. On Star is the monument erected to Capt. John Smith, on which were originally three turk's-heads. He gave the islands his own name, and was for a long time supposed to have been their discoverer. On the same island is also Betty Moody's Hole, where a woman is said to have hidden herself during an Indian raid, with her two children, whom she killed, lest their cries should reveal her hiding-place. There is also here a fine chasm, with walls rising to a height of some fifty feet. A shelf of the bluff, facing the ocean, is called Miss Underhill's Chair, after a school-teacher who was swept from it by a great wave some years ago. Other accidents, it is said, have taken place here; and he is foolhardy who will risk his life for a seat in the fatal chair.

"On Smutty-Nose are the house of Samuel Haley (who in the last century did so much for the material prosperity of the islands), and the cottage where Wagner so foully murdered two women in 1873, as well as the graves of the fourteen Spanish sailors, the crew of some unknown ship wrecked here in 1813. Standing by these mounds, Mrs. Thaxter's lines have a tender significance:—

"'O sailors! did sweet eyes look after you
The day you sailed away from sunny Spain?'

"On Appledore there is a rude monument, or cairn of stones, which a doubtful tradition says was built by Captain Smith in 1613, or thereabouts. Hawthorne says of the valley which divides the island, that in old times 'the sea

SCENE OF THE WAGNER MURDER, SMUTTY-NOSE ISLAND.

flowed quite through, . . . and that boats used to pass.' During the storm which overthrew the Minot's Ledge Lighthouse he adds, 'a great wave passed entirely through this valley, and Laighton describes it, where it came in from the sea, as toppling over to the height of the cupola of his hotel.'

"White Island will always have a peculiar interest as the place where Mrs. Celia Thaxter spent six years of her childhood. Her father, the Hon. Henry B. Laighton, accepted the position of lighthouse keeper out of disgust for political life, and from the time he entered upon his duties till the day of his death, twenty-five years later, it is said he never again set foot on the main land. There are not many things in literature more touching than the account which Mrs. Thaxter gives in her book, 'Among the Isles of Shoals,' of life on the lonely rock. It is a beautiful picture which she paints of the child tending her solitary fern, watching the flowers, the insects, the birds, the sea, climbing the lighthouse stairs at dusk to light the lamps, or sitting in the outer darkness, lantern in hand, at the landing-place, to guide home her father's boat, — a picture whose fair beauty is but heightened by the shades which storm and shipwreck occasionally throw over it. Possibly there is no similar instance of so much of true poetry springing from such unpromising soil as a lighthouse keeper's home."

OLD CHURCH, STAR ISLAND.

"Thank fortune, that means dinner," said Dick, as a darky appeared, ringing a bell and announcing "Dinner, sar!"

The boys, who were all hungry, did not wait for a second invitation, but started for the forward part of the saloon, where dinner was served, and were shown seats at a table by the attentive waiters. They found the bill of fare very inviting, and kept four of the waiters trotting all the time, until they had blunted the edge of their hunger. Then they began to take breath, and talk a little, and the dinner came in for a large amount of praise.

"They set a splendid table on these boats, don't you think so, fellows?" inquired Ned, who was just about to attack his second plate of cream.

"DINNER, SAR!"

"They give a fine dinner," replied George, "and everything else about the boat seems to be first-class also."

"I told you this was the way to make the trip to Portland," said Dick.

"So you did, Parson, and I am glad you persuaded me to try the steamer."

After dinner the young fellows went out on deck, and made their way to the stern of the steamer, where they sat down on the port side, from which they had an interrupted view of the coast. The boat had just passed a lighthouse, to the left of them, which they learned on inquiry was Boon Island Light, when Dick caught sight of another further inshore.

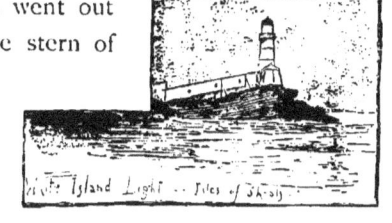

Boon Island was the scene of one of the most terrible shipwrecks ever happening on the New England coast. The Nottingham, an English vessel, was wrecked on this barren rock in October, 1811, and before being rescued her crew were compelled to resort to cannibalism to sustain life.

"I wonder what light that is inshore," remarked Dick, with an inquiring look at his friends.

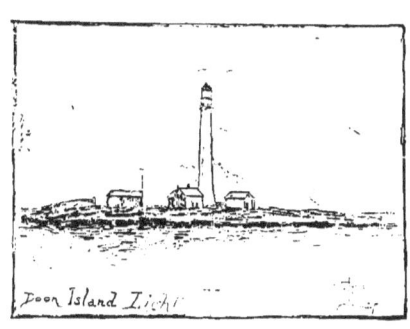

A gentleman who sat near, seeing that none of the party answered, informed Dick that it was Cape Neddick Light.

The boys remained at the stern of the boat for about two hours, watching the various vessels in sight, as, with white wings spread, they headed for near or distant ports, and the different lighthouses as the steamer passed them, obtaining a great deal of information from the gentleman who had answered Dick's query. He appeared to be perfectly familiar with all objects along the coast line, and

DISTANT VIEW DOUBLE LIGHTS, CAPE ELIZABETH.

pointed out to them successively, Wells Beach, Goat Island Light, Cape Porpoise, Wood Island Light, Old Orchard Beach, the White Mountains, which loomed grandly up in the northwest, sharply

PORTLAND HEAD LIGHT.

outlined against the turquoise blue of the sky, Scarborough Beach, and the Whistling Buoy off Richmond Island, and related many interesting incidents in connection with some of the places, which would almost fill a volume by themselves. As the boat drew near

CUSHING'S ISLAND.

the two lights on Cape Elizabeth, the boys thanked the gentleman for his timely information, and then went forward again. After passing the lighthouses, the steamer followed the shore on the port side, never at any very great distance from it, until she reached her dock in Portland.

The boys were delighted with what they saw of Portland Harbor, dotted with its numerous islands, and small steamers and sailing craft. None of them had ever seen it before, and Portland Head Light, Cushing's Island, with its sightly and handsome hotel and picturesque cottages, Forts Preble and Scammel, the breakwater and its modest lighthouse, were all objects of interest to them.

The steamer's landing was at Railroad Wharf; and from there the boys took a hack to the Preble House, the best-kept hotel in the city, where they arrived at five o'clock. As they felt rather tired from their steamboat ride and its attendant excitement, they concluded to spend the evening quietly at the house, go to bed early, and leave sight-seeing until the next day, as they would have the whole forenoon in the city, the train on which they were to depart for the north not leaving until one o'clock; and this programme was carried out to the letter.

CHAPTER II.

SIGHT-SEEING IN PORTLAND. — A TRIP IN THE HARBOR. — A TOUGH STORY. — AN ANGRY SHERIFF. — THE LAUNCH. — A RUNAWAY HORSE. — BEAUTIFUL SCENERY. — LEGENDS. — GORHAM, N. H. — ASCENT OF MOUNT HAYES. — THE LAST MOUTHFUL.

"LET US SEE all of the city possible while here," said George the next morning, as they descended to the dining-room.

"Right you are," replied the Parson, "we'll take it all in if we can."

After breakfast they adjourned to the office, and had a talk with one of the clerks, from whom they obtained a few points about the objects of interest, and then sallied out to do the city.

As it was nearly high water, they first took a horsecar, and rode out to Munjoy Hill, and visited the Observatory, the view from here being much finer at high tide, for then the unsightly flats that nearly surround the city are covered up. There is no better place from which to see the city and its environs than from the top of this Observatory; and much to the surprise of the boys, who were delighted with the views obtained through the telescope, an hour passed away before they realized it. An enthusiastic writer says, —

"It is impossible to describe in language adequate to its beauty the view which bursts upon one as he enters the lantern of the tower. The city, the bay with its hundred green isles, the illimitable ocean, long stretches of fertile land dotted with villages, innumerable hills culminating in Mount Washington, lie before one in almost bewildering beauty. Which ever way you turn, there meets the eye something which seems to surpass all other points in loveliness. To the east one can distinguish the lighthouse on Seguin Island at the mouth of the Kennebec. To the west one can look down upon Scarborough and Old Orchard beaches. In front are Peak's and Cushing's Islands, with the grand Whitehead Cliff guarding the harbor entrance, and beyond is the ocean. Cape Elizabeth, with its lighthouses and hotels, seems to lie at our feet, and we can almost fancy that we can hear the surf which beats upon its rocky shore. Inland the view is no less fine. There is no water, save that of the Back Cove just underneath us; but the smiling country, with the distant mountain range, combine to make a picture of such fascination, that it is difficult to tear one's self away from it. A short distance from the Observatory is the Eastern Promenade,— a broad esplanade bordered by noble trees, from beneath which one looks over the Bay towards Harpswell. The

WHITEHEAD CLIFF, CUSHING'S ISLAND.

large building beyond, in the opposite village of Deering, is the United States Marine Hospital. To the right, nearer the Portland shore, is a pretty island, owned and occupied by the Hon. J. H. Baxter, one of Portland's richest and most enterprising citizens, as a summer residence. The beautiful public library building on Congress Street was a gift from Mr. Baxter to the city. At the other end of the city, on Bramhall's Hill, is the Western Promenade, situated on the very edge of a steep pine-clad declivity. This spot, which is best visited towards sunset, is to the White Mountains what the terrace at Berne is to the Alps. The whole range from Washington to Chocorua stretches along the horizon, and one should wait and see how the different peaks glow in the last rays of the sinking sun, while the evening shades creep over the lowlands beneath. The building which crowns the hill on the right is the Maine General Hospital, and the noble structure beyond it, at the base of the hill, is the new and magnificent Union Railroad Station, of which the citizens of Portland are justly proud. The streets in the unburnt western part of the city are so densely shaded, that the title of 'Forest City,' by which Portland is known, seems most appropriate."

VIEW FROM WESTERN PROMENADE.

"Come, fellows, it is ten o'clock; time we were getting out of this, if we wish to see anything more," said the Parson, as he looked at his watch.

From the Observatory the boys rode as far as City Hall, and then made their way to Commercial Street, and started on a tour of observation along the wharves. They passed the Post-office *en route*, but it did not impress them sufficiently to cause them to look it over inside. They strolled for some distance along

Commercial Street, and at one of the wharves saw several small steamers, and walking down to them found a boat just starting for some of the islands.

"Suppose we take a cruise in the harbor," suggested Ned.

"I don't believe we have time," replied Dick.

"I will find out, for I should like very much to go, if we can get back in season for dinner and our train;" and George stepped on board the steamer, and asked the captain at what hour he was due at the city on his return.

"We reach here at noon," was the answer.

"That will just suit us," returned George; "come on, fellows."

The boys jumped on board,

ALONG THE WHARVES, PORTLAND.

and the next moment the lines were cast off, and the boat backed out from the wharf. The trip proved a very pleasant one, the steamer touching at several of the islands, and the boys saw a great deal that amused and interested them. At one landing they noticed a number of large buoys, such as are used to mark the channels and dangerous places in the harbor. On inquiry the party learned that part of the island was used as a government buoy and torpedo station. Peak's and Cushing's Islands were lively with summer cottagers and boarders, it being the time of harvest for the hotels. The boat stopped an hour at Cushing's, and the boys were enabled to visit the handsome Ottawa House, and take a short ramble about the island.

Cushing's Island is by all means the most attractive bit of land in Casco Bay, and its manifold beauties are rapidly becoming known to the vast concourse of summer ramblers, who each year

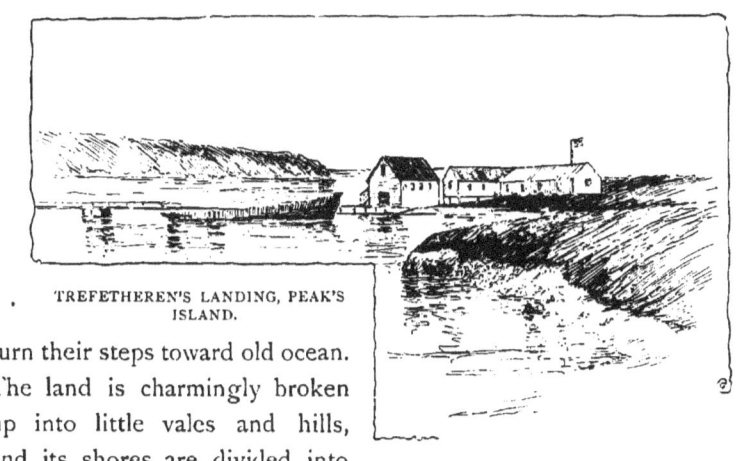

TREFETHEREN'S LANDING, PEAK'S ISLAND.

turn their steps toward old ocean. The land is charmingly broken up into little vales and hills, and its shores are divided into gently sloping beaches, and precipitous walls. Its hotel is a fine specimen of architecture, happily located on the highest swell of the land at the southern end of the island, and commanding the most entrancing views both inland and seaward. Its summer cottages are not the common seaside gimcracks one sees at the beaches, but beautiful and expensive residences, picturesque, and unique in many features, the homes of people of wealth and refinement, who find on Cushing's, with its careful and well-enforced restrictions, what they cannot find elsewhere. The natural beauties of the island have been improved under the direction of Frederick Law Olmstead, the famous landscape gardener, until now this brightest gem of Casco Bay has become a beautiful park, its entire arrangement being in complete harmony with its wildest features, and grand surroundings. One may travel far before

THE WILLOWS, CUSHING'S ISLAND.

finding its equal, and its accessibility to Portland, with its numerous rail and steamship lines, make it a most desirable resort for the summer tourist. The scenery of the island itself is pleasing and fascinating, and in many cases grand, while the views from the hotel piazza, Whitehead Cliff, and other points, awake the enthusiasm of the beholder, who stands spellbound with admiration and delight. A day — a week — a month — we might with simple truth say a summer, can be passed here, without exhausting the charms of this lovely dwelling-place by the sea. When Old Orchard Beach shall have lapsed into obscurity, and Mount Desert become but a pile of costly ruins, Cushing's Island will still shine forth resplendent, as the fairest haven of rest and pleasure whereon the summer tourist has ever set his foot.

BATHING HOUSE AND BEACH, CUSHING'S ISLAND.

Whittier says in one of his poems that nowhere is there fairer or sweeter sunshine—

> "Than where hillside oaks and beeches
> Overlook the long blue reaches,
> Silver coves, and pebbled beaches,
> And green isles, of Casco Bay."

Another writer says,—

"One is not inclined to doubt the truth of this assertion, when on some bright summer's day, he sails amid the islands of the bay,—those islands which were the Hesperides of Longfellow's boyish dreams,— and explores the green depths of the myriad coves which open before him at every turn in the intricate passages which his boat is threading. It is not difficult during the summer to visit nearly every part of the bay by means of the excursion steamers plying upon its waters. The most attractive of the islands, in some respects, is Cushing's, which lies just at the mouth of the harbor, between the two main entrances.

VIEW ON CUSHING'S ISLAND.

The land rises abruptly from the ocean side to a ridge crowned with trees, but descends more gradually to the beaches on the northern shore. There are many pleasant walks on the island; but the finest is that which leads through the pines to Whitehead,— the cliff which forms its eastern extremity. Here the rock falls precipitously one hundred and fifty feet to the water, which foams and surges amid the huge fragments of the cliff scattered along its base. To the east of Cushing's lies Peak's Island. Upon it there is a considerable village, the number of whose inhabitants is swelled many fold in the summer by visitors from the mainland. The island, in its main features, does not differ much from Cushing's, except that its shores are not so bold. Among the other of the one hundred and twenty-two islands with which the bay is studded, Long, Little Chebeague, and Diamond Islands, are worth visiting. The cove which makes into Great Diamond Island is remarkable for its rare beauty."

As the boys stepped on board the boat for the run to the city, the name of the steamer caught Ned's eye, and he repeated it over two or three times, as if trying to remember where he had seen or heard it before. "Tourist, Tourist," he muttered slowly. "Ah, now I have it! I read in the paper a few years ago about a boat by this name being run into, one morning in the fog, by the St. John's steamer, and sank."

"Do you suppose this is the one?" queried Dick.

"I don't know; this don't look as if it had ever been to the bottom, but we can ask the fellow at the wheel."

The boys went to the pilot-house, and George, stepping to the door, inquired of the pilot if this was the boat that figured in a collision a few years ago.

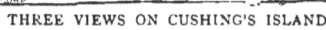
THREE VIEWS ON CUSHING'S ISLAND.

"The identical boat," replied the man.

"Was you on her at the time?"

"Yes, I was. But I got off mighty sudden."

"How did it happen?" asked the Parson.

"It was on our first trip down in the morning, and the fog was so thick you could walk to the shore on it."

"Not quite so thick as that, I guess," remarked the Parson with a laugh.

"Pos'tive fact," reiterated the old barnacle at the wheel. "Why, you never saw a down-east fog, and they are nothing here to what they are down along the Provinces. I run on a steamer

ON THE BEACH, CUSHING'S ISLAND.

one year down in the Bay of Fundy, and one morning the captain said we might as well lay at the wharf, for the fog was so thick the steamer couldn't force her way through it. He had a barn that had a leaky roof, and, as he hated to see us loafing, the old man thought that would be a good time to shingle it. So he put all the boat's crew to work on the barn. It was a large barn, and about seventy-five feet long. I worked just behind the old man, and we slapped the shingles on lively, I tell you. After working about an hour, without getting to the end of our course, I told the old man I thought something must be wrong: that we ought to have reached the end of the barn before; so we stopped to investigate. And upon examination we found, as true as I'm a living sinner, that we had shingled right off the end of the barn on to the fog for over thirty feet."

The boys looked at each other, and then burst into a gale of laughter.

"Oh, that's gospel truth," asserted the veracious pilot, as he gave the wheel a turn to starboard, to clear a small fisherman, and expectorated a mouthful of tobacco juice to leeward.

COVE, DIAMOND ISLAND.

"But how about your steamer getting sunk?" queried Dick.

"Oh, yes, I forgot about that. As I said before, the fog was very thick. We were running about half-speed, keeping a good lookout, when I heard a whistle so near that it made my hair stand on end. I rang to stop, and then to back, but before we had lost headway the big steamer struck us, and I out of this wheel-house and went overboard lively. I could swim, and I didn't stop for any life-preserver, you bet. The engineer followed me, and what few passengers there were on board. The steamer lowered two boats, and picked us all up, and the Tourist went to the bottom."

"I suppose it was a hard job to raise her," ventured Ned.

"Oh, no, not much of a one. It took us about half a day."

Just then the engineer rang to slow down, and the boys found on looking up that the steamer had nearly reached the wharf. As they were moving away from the pilot-house, the old salt said, —

"Perhaps you don't believe that fog story I told you; but it was so thick down there that season, that in the fall, instead of using boughs, as he usually did, the old man had us go down to the shore and cut the fog up into blocks, and used it to bank up his house," and squirting another cascade of tobacco juice over the rail, the pilot rang to stop. After the boys had stepped out on the wharf, George turned and called to the pilot.

"What's the rumpus?" asked that worthy.

"I wish to tell you one thing before we leave."

"If it's too good for you to keep, tell it."

THE VERACIOUS PILOT.

"I believe," replied George, waving his hand in token of farewell, "that in you we have found the champion liar of the State of Maine."

"I thought you was going to tell me something new," returned this modern Ananias, with a grin; "come and see us again."

"We will before the season is over," and the boys, hailing a hack, jumped in, and rode to the hotel.

After the excursion of the morning, our young friends had a good appetite, and they thoroughly enjoyed the fine dinner served at the Preble. They lingered at the table, loath to leave, but George hurried them away, and, settling their bill, they took a hack to the Grand Trunk Depot, stopping on the way at the corner of Hancock and Fore Streets, which is but a short distance from the station, to obtain a look at the "old, square, wooden house, upon the edge of the sea," where the poet Longfellow was born in 1807.

The dwelling next to the Preble House, on Congress Street, which the boys had also looked upon with veneration, known as the "Longfellow House," was not occupied by Stephen Longfellow until after his son Henry's birth.

The baggage of the party had been sent from the steamboat wharf directly to the railroad station, and the boys' first move, after paying the hackman, was to find and check

I. DINING ROOM
II. OFFICE &c.
III. READING ROOM

it for Gorham, N. H., at which place they were to make their first stop.

After seeing to their baggage, they stood idly by, watching the people who were taking seats in the cars of the Lewiston train. Just as the conductor shouted, "All aboard for Lewiston!" the boys noticed a man running from the back end of the depot. He reached the train just as it started, and jumped on the rear platform of the hind car. Two men who were following, a short distance behind, were not so lucky, and lost their passage. Much to the surprise of the boys, and their amusement also, the man who had gained the car, faced the two who had lost the train, and raising his hand to his face, placed the end of his thumb on his nose, and twirled his fingers at his pursuers in a manner highly exasperating.

DODGING THE SHERIFF.

"Stop him! stop that man! stop the train!" shouted the tallest of the two men in the depot, excitedly, stretching forth his hand in a vain attempt to reach the person guying him.

"The train will not stop," said the depot-master, who stood near. "What is the trouble?"

"I've a warrant for that man's arrest," replied the tall man, puffing and blowing, and looking with longing eyes at the fast disappearing train.

"Who are you?" inquired the depot-master, who noticed that the belligerent parties were dressed in plain clothes.

"I'm a sheriff, and I wanted that man."

"What for? Who is he?"

"That's my business," replied the sheriff, crossly, and speaking a few words in a low tone to his companion, they left the depot.

"'It's a cold day' for those fellows," remarked the depot-master, as he turned away laughing.

Another train now appeared, slowly backing into the depot, which the boys learned was the one for Gorham, and, finding a Pullman car at the rear of it, they secured seats in that.

"They don't trouble themselves about leaving on time," said Dick, who had just consulted his watch, and found it to be half-past one.

"No matter," replied George; "we are not in a hurry."

THE LAUNCH.

"But we might have had half an hour longer at that dinner," suggested the Parson, regretfully.

"Oh, nonsense," added Ned, "you had dinner enough. You should leave a little room for your supper."

"Here we go," cried Fred, as the engine gave two short whistles, and the train pulled out from the depot.

The boys had taken seats on the right-hand side of the car, and obtained a good look at the harbor and shipping and the islands in the bay. A mile out from the depot the train stopped at the Portland and Worcester Transfer Station, and took on some passengers. Then, after its customary two toots, the engine gave a warning snort, and the train dashed across a long wooden bridge, and pulled up in East Deering.

While the cars were crossing the bridge, the boys were treated to a very pretty sight. A large vessel that had been lying on the stocks in a shipyard close to the railroad was just gliding into the water, amid the shouts and hurrahs of an admiring throng of spectators. She presented a fine appearance, being freshly painted and handsomely decorated with flags.

A large towboat, also covered with bunting, lay off at a short distance, waiting to take charge of the new ocean ranger after she had taken a plunge into her natural element. The scene brought to George's mind Longfellow's poem, "The Building of the Ship," and, almost involuntarily, he recited a few lines, that were very apropos to the occasion, —

> "And see! she stirs!
> She starts, — she moves, — she seems to feel
> The thrill of life along her keel,
> And spurning with her foot the ground,
> With one exultant joyous bound,
> She leaps into the ocean's arms!
> And lo! from the assembled crowd
> There rose a shout prolonged and loud,
> That to the ocean seemed to say, —
> 'Take her, O bridegroom, old and gray.
> Take her to thy protecting arms,
> With all her youth and all her charms!'"

The boys stepped to the rear of the car, and, standing out on the platform, had just time to see the vessel glide gracefully into the water, when the train started. They watched the scene until the car swung around a curve, hiding the view from them, and then returned to their seats.

"No loss, without some gain," remarked the Parson. "If the train had not been late, we should have missed seeing that launch, and a very pretty sight it was."

"Right you are, my boy," answered Ned. "Why didn't you sketch it?"

"That reminds me, that I have not had my sketch-book out since we started, and I will get it now, and see if I can't catch some little bits from the window when the train stops at the stations."

The train being late, the stops were shorter than usual, and the cars sped rapidly along through Falmouth, Cumberland, and Yarmouth, until it reached Yarmouth Junction. The country was all new to the boys, but, through persistent questioning, they obtained a good deal of information about it.

"That is the Maine Central Railroad," replied the porter, to an inquiry of Dick's about a railroad they were crossing; "it runs to Brunswick and Augusta and on east to Bangor. And I want you to understand," added the darkey, "that it is one of the best-managed railroads in this country."

A few people of eccentric dress and appearance came on board the train here, and the porter told the boys they were French Canadians, who had probably been working in mills somewhere in Maine, and who were now on their way home.

From the Junction the train sped rapidly on its way, stopping for a moment at North Yarmouth, Pownal, and New Gloucester.

Just after leaving the latter station, Dick noticed another railroad to their left, and the porter told him that it was another branch of the Maine Central, running to Lewiston and Waterville. There was a train on the other road, going in the same direction they were, and, just as Dick caught sight of it, the car they were in gave a jerk, and seemed to spin along faster.

"They are racing to see who will get to the Junction first," remarked the porter.

"What junction?" asked Fred.

"Danville Junction — it is the next station, and the Maine Central crosses us there."

The boys watched the other train with interest, and noticed that its speed also was increasing. But their train kept the lead, and stopped first at the crossing. This gave it the right of way, and it reached the depot ahead. Quite a number of passengers took the train here, and the boys found amusement in watching them. Just as they left the station, the Maine Central train pulled up on the other side of the depot, and that was the last the boys saw of it, as beyond the tracks of the two roads widely diverged. From Danville the landscape improved rapidly, the country being more broken and more thickly wooded than nearer Portland. Hills and mountains began to appear in the distance, growing in size with each onward mile they travelled. At Lewiston Junction, the next stopping-place, there was a four-horse Concord coach in waiting, and this, the boys learned, was to convey passengers to Poland Springs, about three miles distant. The connection for Poland Springs is now made at Danville Junction, where the Maine Central Railroad Company, with its accustomed foresight and liberality toward the public, have built one of the finest depots in the State, outside of Portland. The porter pointed the hotel out to them, standing on a high hill off to the left of the railroad.

At Empire Road, the next station, a little incident caused

them some excitement. A horse, attached to an old-fashioned chaise, took fright as the cars pulled up at the station, and started off toward the village as if Old Nick was after him. A short distance from the depot, the runaway team collided with a hayrack, and the old chaise went into the air about ten feet, and, turning over, threw the horse down. Before any one could get hold of him, however, he struggled to his feet, and with only the shafts and one wheel, continued his mad race, and that ended the excitement, as far as the boys were concerned.

The next stop was at Mechanics Falls, a flourishing village situated on both banks of the Little Androscoggin River, where are located several paper mills, and other manufactories.

THE RUNAWAY.

The Rumford Falls and Buckfield Railroad connects here with the Grand Trunk, and runs to Canton. Beyond this station the train crossed the river over a handsome iron bridge, and continued northward. Along the river bank the boys espied several fishermen, who were trying to lure the trout from their cool retreat, and watched them while in sight.

At the next station, Oxford, the Parson made a pretty sketch while the train waited, and George improved the brief moments in carrying on a handkerchief flirtation with a young lady on the platform, who was evidently a summer boarder from the city.

As they approached South Paris, the mountains increased in height, and the view on all sides was lovely. The boys had been fortunate in selecting the shady side of the car, and could have the window-shades up without being annoyed by the sun, and were able to see all within their vision. The train pulled up opposite a neat brick depot, the platform of which was filled with a crowd of young and old of both sexes, half of whom, at least, had come to see and be seen, instead of to travel. The boys inspected the restless crowd outside, and were much amused by the appearance of several of the natives, who looked as if they had characters peculiarly their own.

On inquiry, the party learned that this was the shire town of Oxford County, and contained the court-house and jail. The village, one of the most flourishing in the county, lies to the northward of the station, and Paris Hill, so called, is about two miles beyond, and is thickly settled. A branch track leaves the main line at South Paris, extending a mile and a half to Norway, another smart and enterprising town. After a stop of nearly ten minutes here, the train moved onward again, and made a run of about seven miles to West Paris. From this village to the next station the grade of the road is very heavy, and the boys thought several times that the train would stop, so slowly did it move. But the engine, puffing and panting with all its strength, held steadily to its work, and finally the steepest part of the grade was passed, and, with increased speed, the train rushed along until it reached the Bryant's Pond Station.

Here is a pretty little hamlet, nestled among the mountains. The party were very much taken with the pond, some two miles in length, on the left of the railroad, overshadowed by a perpendicular bluff, Mount Christopher, several hundred feet in height, and were almost tempted to stop here and try their luck at fishing. But, after a short argument, concluded to keep on to Gorham.

With two short whistles the train bade farewell to Bryant's Pond, and skirting two or three other small sheets of water, each

BRYANT'S POND, MAINE.

attractive in itself, shortly reached Locke's Mills, where only a momentary halt was made. Then hurrying onward again for a few miles, slowed down at Bethel, where the boys caught their first glimpse of the Androscoggin River, one of the most charming and picturesque streams in New England. This station is the principal point of departure for the Androscoggin Lakes, over the most direct route. A daily stage runs from this point to the

Lakeside Hotel, Cambridge, at the foot of Lake Umbagog, connecting with a daily line of steamers on the lake. The road passes through Grafton Notch, and is deservedly popular from its wild and romantic mountain scenery, appealing to the artistic sense of all lovers of the beautiful.

"This is a very pretty country," remarked George, as the train left the Bethel station. "Could anything be more lovely than

VIEW FROM BETHEL STATION.

that charming meadow sweeping away on our right, with the silvery river meandering through it?"

"Hold on, George," cried the Parson, smiling; "you are becoming poetical."

"Who wouldn't, with such a view as that before them? and look at the mountains in the distance. There is plenty of material for your sketch-book."

"Yes, altogether too much; I can't do it justice, and I had rather gaze and admire, than make a caricature copy of it on paper."

From "Farrar's Androscoggin Lakes Illustrated," we quote the following about this locality: —

"Again we are speeding up the Androscoggin Valley, scenes of wild grandeur and romantic beauty meeting the eye on every side, a short ride bringing us to West Bethel, a station of but little importance as yet, seventy-four miles from Portland. A short distance beyond here the train passes over Pleasant River Bridge, and about a mile farther on you obtain a fine view far up the valley of Mounts Jefferson and Adams, lifting their conical summits over the shadowy ridges of Mount Moriah. Five miles from West Bethel we cross Wild River, over a fine bridge two hundred and fifty feet in length.

"This river is a child of the mountains, at times fierce, impetuous, and shadowy as the storms that howl around the bald heads of its parents, and bearing down everything that comes in its path; then again, when subdued by long summer calms, murmuring gently in consonance with the breezy rustle of the trees, whose branches droop over it. An hour's time may swell it into a headlong torrent; an hour may reduce it to a brook that a child might ford without fear.

WILD RIVER BRIDGE, GRAND TRUNK RAILWAY.

"This vicinity is rife with legends of the Indian wars. One of the last acts of the aborigines, ere their strength was forever broken, was an onset on the defenceless village of Bethel, made by a party of the St. Francis tribe, who had followed down the State line from Canada. They carried away a man named Pettingill, another named Sager, and two by the name of Clarke.

"Pettingill and one of the Clarkes, after proceeding a few miles, were unable, through lameness, to go on, and the savages finally consented to their return, advising them to keep to the same trail they had followed up, pretending that there were hostile scouts on all others. Clarke, who was well acquainted with the Indian character, suspected treachery in this apparent solicitude for their safety, and as soon as he was out of sight, struck into the woods, and, swimming the Androscoggin, passed down the opposite side with safety. During his

TREACHERY.

lonely tramp he heard the report of the gun which proved the death-note of his friend, who, taking the path designated, was followed back by the savages and shot dead. The mutilated body of poor Pettingill was subsequently found and buried on the bank of Wild River, just by the bridge.

"Beyond the bridge the railroad is almost closed in on either hand by rude cliffs towering many feet heavenwards. The Androscoggin River is still to be seen on our right, turning and twisting through the narrow strip of intervale between the railroad and base of the mountains. This land, although subject to overflow by the spring freshets, is all cultivated, and yields abundant crops. We now reach Gilead, eighty miles from Portland, and with but a moment's halt dash on. A mile or more above this station the track crosses the boundary between Maine and New Hampshire. Here, bidding farewell to the Pine Tree State, we soon find ourselves at Shelburne, a delightful summer resort, well patronized each year. At this point the mountains grow higher and still more rugged, and a short ride brings us within view of the lofty summits of. Mounts Washington, Jefferson, and Adams, that burst upon our sight from behind a

MEADOWS, SHELBURNE, N.H.

wooded ridge of Mount Moriah. For the next few miles, till we arrive within a short distance of the depot at Gorham, these mighty peaks remain constantly in view. Just after leaving the Shelburne station, the cars pass near a high bluff, called 'Moses' Ledge,' named for an early resident of the town, one Moses Ingalls, who is said to have once run up to the top of it. As it is almost perpendicular and nearly as smooth as glass, this was a feat that calls a smile to the face of the observer of to-day, although the story is apparently well authenticated. Near it formerly stood an immense granite bowlder, many thousand tons in weight, a great portion of which has been blown to pieces and used .in the construction· of the railroad, an act of vandalism entirely unnecessary. A fragment of this rock was secured by Judge Burbank, of Boston, who owns the White Mountain Stock Farm in

Shelburne, who had it manufactured into a settee, which is yet kept upon his place and is of interest to all visiting the farm. Under this rock, it is said, an aged matron named Starbird, who supplied the place of physician to the section, a long time ago, found refuge, during one of the wildest storms that ever smote the mountains. She was on her way, on horseback, alone, to visit a patient, where her presence was thought to be indispensable (so the story goes), when night and storm overtook her; bewildered by the pelting rain, she was glad to avail herself of such shelter as the rock could afford. House there was none for miles, and here she remained cowering all the long night, with a fearful chorus confusing her ear, — the rushing of the great rain through the darkness, the voice of the countless streams that flooded every cliff and ravine, the wail of the great trees on the ridges as they writhed and struggled and swayed in the merciless grasp of the gale, and the oft-repeated howl of the shivering wolf, driven from his lair by the incursions of the storm, commingled with the hoarse boom of the swollen river that made the very earth tremble. The laggard morning broke at last above the hills, but it brought no cheer to that 'weary auld matron.' Many a noble forest-giant lay shattered on the acclivities about her; the torrents still poured their turbid floods, and, filling the whole valley like a sea, the river swept onward, grinding and crashing, noisy and tumultuous, with its *débris* of trees and timber, gravel and rocks; nor was it till noon, when the clouds retired to the higher peaks, the sun shone out, and the streams began to fall as suddenly as they had risen, that she was able to resume her journey. To commemorate her unpleasant experience, the bowlder was named Granny Starbird's, or Starbird's Rock."

While passing through Shelburne, the boys obtained a fine view of Mount Winthrop, just back of the village. From the top of this sightly elevation, a beautiful view of the Androscoggin Valley may be obtained.

On the high plateau front of Mount Winthrop is the picturesque summer cottage of W. K. Aston, a New-York gentleman of wealth and refinement, who, tempted by the many beauties of the locality, has made it his summer home here for several years, and has handsomely and tastily combined art with nature in beautifying his

SHELTER FROM THE STORM.

charming estate. The view from the piazza of his palatial cottage is second to none in New Hampshire.

Skirting the base of Mount Moriah, with the silvery river on our right, washing the foot of Old Bald Cap, our attention is called to another elegant cottage, built of cobble-stones picked from the land on which it stands. This house also is charmingly located, and belongs to a wealthy gentleman by the name of Endicott. Beyond here a curve in the road suddenly brings one in sight of the station, and the train stops at Gorham, ninety miles from Portland. At this point passengers *en route* for the White Mountains leave the train, and proceed by Milliken's world-renowned Concord coaches to the Glen House, eight miles distant, at the foot of Mount Washington. A fine and commodious hotel, the Alpine House, built by the Grand Trunk Railway Company, stands directly opposite the depot. It occupies the same site as the old hotel of that name, destroyed by fire. The new house is a great improvement over the old building. Gorham is pleasantly situated on the Androscoggin River, at the entrance of Carter Notch, commanding fine views of the Carter Range and the monarchs of the White Hills. There are many attractive places of interest, and fine drives in its vicinity. Mount Hayes, on the right of the railroad, is noted for furnishing the best views of the higher White Mountain Peaks, of any height, on the easterly side of the range, and its ascent from the village is comparatively easy.

"This is Gorham, young gentlemen," said the porter, as the train stopped at the station, and the boys were quickly on their feet. As the porter had taken some trouble to answer their questions, and furnish them with desired information, George gave him half a dollar when they left the car, and the darky smiled all over his face.

As they stepped from the train a porter from the hotel met them, and they turned over their hand baggage to him, then went forward to the baggage-car. After seeing their trunks landed on the platform, they walked over to the hotel, booked their names, and secured rooms. They obtained two on the front side of the house, with connecting door, and Dick and George took possession of one, while Fred and Ned occupied the other.

GORHAM AND MOUNT HAYES.

After attending to their toilet, they descended to the piazza, where they sat down to enjoy the view.

"This is not a bad-looking place," remarked Dick, as they gazed about them.

"I like the appearance of it first rate," replied George; "and if they set a good table at this hotel we will stop here three or four days. We ought to find something to amuse us."

"How did you say we were going to the mountains, George?" inquired Ned.

"My idea was to go over to the Glen House on the stage, leaving our trunks, rods, and guns here, and only carry our valises. We would stop there over night, then go to Glen Station the next day, where we would take the Maine Central train, and ride through the Crawford Notch to Fabyan's, stopping there a night or two. Then to the top of Mount Washington by railroad; from the Summit walk down to the Glen over the carriage road, then by stage back to this house. That was my plan; if either of you can improve on it, I shall be glad to have you."

"I think I can suggest an improvement," ventured Ned. "If we go by stage to Glen Station, we shall have no time to visit the places of interest along the way; and I think we had better hire a team for this part of the trip: then we can travel at our pleasure, and see all there is worth looking at along the road."

SUSPENSION BRIDGE, GORHAM, N.H.

"Your suggestion is a good one, and we will act upon it, and now let's go in to supper."

The party retired early that night, and the next morning, after breakfast, learned from the hotel clerk the easiest route to the summit of Mount Hayes; then, procuring some lunch to carry with them, started off, intending to spend the greater part of the day on the excursion.

They passed through the village, and crossed the lovely Androscoggin, over a wire suspension bridge, built only for pedestrians. This is a private enterprise, and the toll is five cents for each person. From the opposite side of the river they followed the carriage road a short distance, then turned to the right, and began the ascent of the mountain path, the road behind them continuing on to the Mascot Silver Mine.

In former years, when Hitchcock kept the Alpine House, there was a small hotel on the top of Mount Hayes. Then many persons made the ascent of the mountain, some on foot, but more on horseback. But now the number who visit the summit is comparatively few, and it is the more to be wondered at from the fact that Mount Hayes furnishes more satisfactory views than many other peaks of the White Mountain range.

Upward, with joke and laughter, the boys made their way, and when they had accomplished a third of the distance, stopped to rest and look about them. From this point they had a fine view of the village of Gorham, and the river valley for many miles, environed by its mountain walls.

As they neared the summit the path grew rougher and steeper, and they were not sorry when they stood on top. They had been two hours from the hotel, but had walked leisurely all the way. Although hot, it was clear, and there were but few clouds in the sky: they could not have had a better day than the one selected for the trip. They visited the ruins of the hotel first, and speculated somewhat over them, and then sat down to rest, and enjoy the sight they had toiled for.

"That's a pretty hard climb," remarked the Parson, wiping his face with his handkerchief.

"I agree with you," said Dick. "I am tired."

"So is a wheel," put in George, dryly.

"Oh, none of that!" exclaimed Ned. "Save your puns until we get back to the hotel."

There can be no doubt in the mind of any sensible person, who has ever made the ascent of Mount Hayes, that in comparison with many of the other mountains, it stands head and shoulders above them, as affording the grandest landscape view of Madison, Adams, and Washington, to be obtained in the Granite State. That valuable handbook, "Eastman's White Mountain Guide," says : —

"The picture from the summit cannot be sufficiently praised. The view of Adams and Madison, sweeping from the uplands of Randolph, will never be forgotten. And Mount Washington shows no such height, or grandeur, when seen from any other point. Mount Washington does not show its superior height, or look grander in form than the associated peaks, from any position in the valleys near Gorham and the Glen. But from Mount Hayes its supereminence and majesty are caught and appreciated. That summit seems to be the chair set by Providence at the right distance and angle to observe and enjoy its majesty, its symmetry, and the proud grace with which its 'airy citadel' is sustained against the sky. And by way of desert to this substantial feast of mountain grandeur, a most charming view of the curves of the Androscoggin for twenty miles, of its exquisite islands, and of the meadows which it threads, is given from Mount Hayes."

At one o'clock the boys ate their lunch, the bracing mountain air giving them a keen appetite, and they looked regretfully at the empty paper bags when they threw them away.

"I declare, I haven't had half dinner enough," murmured Dick, looking wistfully at a fragment of doughnut that the Parson held between his thumb and forefinger.

"Haven't you?" said Fred; "then take this piece of doughnut. I should hate to see you starve."

Dick reached for the doughnut, but just as his fingers were about to grasp it, Fred threw it into his mouth, exclaiming as he tucked it away under his left cheek, —

"Now you see it, and now you don't," and he gave Dick a comical wink, as he swallowed the last morsel.

"NOW YOU SEE IT, AND NOW YOU DON'T."

"That was a mean trick, Parson," declared Dick, "and I owe you one."

"Well, I am safe, then, for you was never known to pay anything you owe."

The others laughed at this sally, and then the boys strolled all over the top of the mountain, stopping here and there to obtain views in different directions, and in a couple of hours found themselves once more at the ruins of the hotel. They sat down on one of the fallen timbers to rest before commencing the descent.

"What a pretty place this is!" said George. "I wonder that some one does not erect another hotel. I should think a carriage road might be built up here with less trouble and expense than up Mount Washington, and one could obtain a nice view from here a great many days when they could see nothing from the summits of the higher mountains."

"That is so," assented Ned; "and perhaps the next time we come up this way, there will be one. But suppose we start down now: I begin to feel hungry again."

"Hungry!" cried Dick, as they arose to their feet, and moved toward the path, "I feel wolfish!"

They stopped several times on their way down, to admire the lights and shadows on the towering peaks beyond them, thrown by the declining sun, and reached the hotel about six o'clock. Here they established themselves on the piazza until teatime, glad to rest a few moments. As they went in to supper, they noticed a bill hanging on the clerk's desk, which proved to be the programme of a dramatic show. They were too hungry to give it more than a casual glance, but, when they came out from the dining-room, they examined it with greater care.

CHAPTER III.

A COUNTRY SHOW. — SIDE TRIP TO THE WHITE MOUNTAINS. — SIGHT SEEING. — BACK TO GORHAM. — AN AMATEUR DRAMATIC PERFORMANCE. — THE MASCOT MINE. — BERLIN FALLS. — PLEASANT ACQUAINTANCES. — THE MORMON ELDER. — THE PICNIC DINNER.

"DO you suppose it will be much of a show?" queried the Parson, as they gathered in front of the playbill after supper and attentively scanned it.

"Give it up. Give me an easier one," answered George.

"Let's go," said Ned. "I approve of taking in all the shows we come across, for after we get into the woods we shall not see any."

"I'm with you," assented Dick. "Where is it? Oh, I see, Gorham House Hall. That must be over to the other hotel. What are the tickets? Reserved seats, thirty-five cents. That's what we want, fellows."

"Yes, we'll all have 'preserved seats,'" remarked George with a smile, "so let us fix up a little, and go over."

"I don't need any fixing," said Dick, looking himself over.

"You don't!" returned George. "Your hair needs combing, you young monkey; it looks like a hurrah's nest. If I had noticed your head when we went in to supper, I would not have occupied the same table with you."

"How particular the 'Star' is getting, fellows!" said Dick with a laugh, as they went to their rooms.

They had no trouble in finding the hall and obtaining good seats, but the show was not very satisfactory. To boys who had seen the best productions of the Boston theatres, the performance appeared thin. They obtained their money's worth of fun, however. For, just before the last piece was finished, the scenery accidentally caught fire, and fell over on the performers, burying some of them in the wreck, and the prompter, seeing a chance to do a little acting, rushed on the stage with a pail of water, and gave the unfortunate actors who were struggling under the curtain a good washing down. The fire was speedily extinguished, doing but slight damage; but that ended the show, and the boys returned to their hotel and went to bed.

THE PROMPTER DOES A LITTLE ACTING.

The next morning when they came down to breakfast, they were surprised to find it raining. It continued with but slight intermission all that day and the next, a most unusual occurrence for that time of the year. When they arose Saturday morning, however, the sun was shining brightly, and the storm was over.

While eating breakfast they discussed the best way to pass the day, and finally concluded to make an excursion to an abandoned lead mine in Shelburne, some two miles from the covered bridge. They learned that the entire distance was six miles, and that they could obtain some fine views of the mountains from the vicinity of the bridge, and concluded to take the day for it, and carry their dinner. After obtaining the lunch, neatly packed in two small baskets, they started off, crossing the river by the public bridge, at the lower end of the town, for the road they were to travel was on the eastern side of the river. They walked slowly, frequently stopping to admire the beauties of the landscape, and it was half-past ten when

LEAD-MINE BRIDGE.

they reached the bridge. They enjoyed the mountains from this point for a few moments, and then continued their way. A mile below, they reached a small graveyard, and turning to the left, crossed a pasture, went through a gate, and then followed a pleasant woodland road for a mile or so. On their way they passed a rocky flume in the mountains, that they were highly pleased with, and the Parson, who had brought along his sketch-book, made several sketches in the locality. It was half-past twelve when they reached the lead mine, and they were all tired and hungry.

"I guess this place will keep until after we eat," remarked Ned, seating himself amid the ruins of the boiler house; "I never was so hungry in my life."

"Or I either," added the Parson, "and it is six confounded long miles here."

"They are country miles," laughed George.

"Stop talking, fellows," cried Dick, "and open up the grub. That interests me more than distances and scenery just now."

When their hunger was appeased, they strolled about and examined the ruins of the buildings, threw large stones into the perpendicular shaft, which was three hundred feet deep, and full of water, and listened to the rocks as they struck first one side and then the other in their descent.

They examined and went to the end of a horizontal shaft, higher up the ravine, and after coming out obtained several specimens of the ore that contained both lead and silver.

"If they ever try to work this mine again, it will be a job to pump the water out," said Dick.

"Yes, it would," replied George. "But I doubt if this mine is ever worked again. I don't believe there is five dollars' worth of lead or silver in a ton of this rock."

"Come, fellows, let's be going. It's two o'clock now," urged the Parson, "and I wish to make a sketch of Washington and Madison from the bridge, and the bridge itself if I have time."

"I'm ready," said Ned, "but I'm glad we came here, for it is a very pretty place. That flume was well worth looking at also."

It was a very hot day; none of the party felt disposed to hurry, and it was half-past three when they arrived at the bridge. While the Parson was making his sketch of the mountains, his friends crossed the bridge to look at a row-boat on the opposite bank of the Androscoggin. As they did not come back, Fred also crossed the river, and made a sketch of the bridge from that side. Just as he finished, his companions joined him, and George told him they had been talking the matter over during his absence, and had concluded to return on the west side of the river, as it would give them some different views. This suited the Parson exactly. They enjoyed the walk back very much, and when they reached the hotel were all of the opinion that they had never passed a pleasanter day.

Of the excursion to the Lead-Mine Bridge, Eastman's "White Mountain Guide" says: —

"The name is derived from an abandoned lead mine about six miles below Gorham, on the eastern bank of the Androscoggin, in Shelburne. The bridge is about four miles from the hotels, and can be easily reached by team in three-quarters of an hour. The proper time to visit it is in the latter part of a summer afternoon, when the golden light is on the meadows, and the long shadows are falling athwart the mountains. There is no spot in the whole mountain region where the beauty of the river is joined so charmingly to the majesty of the hills. No river view can be more fascinating than that of the noble Androscoggin breaking around emerald islands with clean sandy shores, sweeping around the base of a lofty cliff, and joining its parted currents again into one strong tide just above the bridge where one stands. And then a few miles distant, enthroned over the narrow valley, as though the stream flowed directly from their base, rises the heavy dome of Mount Washington, in company with the clear-cut, exquisite pyramid of Madison, with the crest of Adams rising directly behind it.

"The height of the noblest mountains is never appreciated by going close to their base, if they are foreshortened by ridges intervening between the eye and the supreme summits. The Lead-Mine Bridge is just far enough away from the White Hills to allow their height to make its true impression. And whoever sees Mount Madison thus, in a clear afternoon, will recall the impression it makes, as perhaps the loveliest picture which the White Mountain journey leaves in the memory."

The next day being Sunday, the boys went to church in the forenoon, and passed the afternoon and evening quietly at the hotel. Monday, after the arrival of the morning train from Portland, they left Gorham for the Glen House. Having obtained outside seats, they enjoyed the beautiful ride up the Peabody Valley, with better appreciation for its beauties than many older people might have had. The stage-driver called their attention to the "Imp," and other objects of interest along the way, stopped while they viewed Garnet Pool, and regaled them with stories of incidents that had happened in the mountains, in which nine grains of lie and one of truth were unblushingly mingled. Reaching the hotel they obtained rooms, ate their dinner, and then strolled out for a walk, visiting Thompson's Falls and the Emerald Pool before they returned to the house. After supper they sat on the piazza until twilight deepened into darkness, admiring the grand summits of the Presidential Range, and watching the shadowy clouds that

WASHINGTON AND MADISON FROM LEAD-MINE BRIDGE.

occasionally flitted across them. Before retiring for the night they engaged a driver and team to take them to Glen Station, and George intimated to Mr. Milliken that a good story-teller would prove acceptable.

The next morning, much to the satisfaction of the party, was pleasant, and after breakfast, the boys, full of enthusiasm, hurriedly

prepared for their trip, and when they reached the piazza, found a light mountain wagon and a pair of horses under the command of a venerable Jehu, who looked as if he had done nothing but drive stages and tell stories all his life. The young fellows clambered up to their seats, bade Mr. Milliken "good-by," who in turn wished them "good luck," and amid the cheers of a few "early birds" who were promenading the piazza, rode away.

The boys gave a parting glance at the hotel as the horses

EMERALD POOL, NEAR GLEN HOUSE.

plunged into the deep forest, and then turned their attention to the scenery along the route. They caught pretty glimpses of the Peabody River, which they followed for two or three miles, and obtained from time to time pleasing views of Mount Washington, Carter Mountain, Wild Cat, and others that form the almost perpendicular walls of Pinkham Notch.

The driver did his part to make the ride entertaining for them; for, no matter what either of the party spoke of along the road, he was always ready with a story in connection with it. When they reached the path leading to the Crystal Cascade, a beautiful stream of water, that comes tumbling down from Tuckerman's Ravine, a deep gash in the side of Washington, the driver pulled up his horses.

ON THE ROAD TO GLEN HOUSE.

"Now, boys, there is the path to the Crystal Cascade, and I'll stop here and have a smoke while you look at it. Take all the time you want, for we have plenty to spare," and the driver pulled out his pipe and began loading it.

"There is no danger of our getting off the path, I suppose," remarked George, with an inquiring look.

"Not a bit. You couldn't lose it if you tried."

"Come on then, fellows," cried George, as he led the way.

The distance was about a third of a mile, and they walked slowly, reaching the fall in fifteen minutes. They were charmed

THOMPSON'S FALLS, NEAR GLEN HOUSE, WHITE MOUNTAINS.

with the beauty of the place, and viewed the cascade from every point of vantage; before they left, a large party of ladies and gentlemen joined them, and the boys entered into conversation with them, and it was nearly two hours before they returned to their team.

"Did you think we were lost?" inquired the Parson, who had made several pretty sketches at the cascade, which he showed to the driver.

GLEN HOUSE, WHITE MOUNTAINS, N. H.

"No; I didn't expect you back for an hour or two. Those pictures are nice; you handle your pencil pretty well. Did the flies bother you any?"

"We saw a few," put in Ned, with a laugh.

Another ride of a mile or more, and they stopped to visit Glen Ellis Fall, thought by many to be the handsomest piece of water scenery in the mountain region. They had quite a difficult climb down to the foot of the fall, but they felt well repaid

CRYSTAL CASCADE, NEAR GLEN HOUSE, WHITE MOUNTAINS.

when they beheld its beauties. The Parson again brought forth his sketch-book, and worked for an hour, when George hurried him away to the wagon.

Beyond here they passed down Spruce Hill, which the boys thought almost interminable, and soon after reached the lower end of the Notch, the valley widening as they approached Jackson. They did not stop here, but continued on through the village, and a few moments before two arrived at Glen Station, in the town of Bartlett, delighted with their ride, but as hungry as tramps; and before the train came they procured dinner, inviting the driver to dine with them, as they had found him a very pleasant companion. They procured seats in the observation car,

LOOKING UP THE NOTCH

and thus had a chance to see all that is possible from a railroad train, while speeding through the grand and rugged Notch of the White Mountains. From Glen Station to Fabyan's they watched the mountains with ever-increasing wonder and delight; the scenery possessing a fascination for them that held them spellbound, and they admired in respectful silence. The innumerable falls and cascades, the Frankenstein Cliffs and Trestle, the Willey House far below them, Mount Webster, Mount Willard, the three great peaks across the valley, the Giant's Stairs, and the Gate of the Notch, were all examined in turn with absorbing interest. As the

GLEN ELLIS FALL, GLEN ROAD, WHITE MOUNTAINS.

party stepped off the train at Fabyan's, George declared that the ride was worth half one's lifetime.

The boys stopped over night at the Fabyan House, and the next morning made the ascent of Mount Washington by rail. It was a bright, pleasant morning, and they enjoyed the trip very much, although Dick said he felt all the time as if he was sliding down hill instead of going up. As they reached "Jacob's Ladder," a cloud passed across the mountain, and for a few moments they were in a fog. The "Gulf of Mexico," in which the Peabody River takes its rise, impressed them with its wildness and depth; and Lizzie Bourne's Monument awakened their curiosity, and from an accommodating passenger they learned the sad story connected with it. The ascent occupied an hour and a quarter, and during that time the boys saw more mountains than they had ever before seen during their lives, and were treated to a succession of such wild and startling views as they had never dreamed of.

VIEW EAST FROM CRAWFORD HOUSE.

After dinner, the weather being favorable, George procured a guide, and the party visited Tuckerman's Ravine, and were highly enthusiastic over the rocky walls of that grand amphitheatre, and the unusual sight of the snow arch. The scramble into the ravine had just enough of hardship and danger about it to furnish a pleasurable excitement, and on their way back they were caught in a snow squall, which greatly added to the romance of their trip. The squall was over before they reached the hotel, and they were fortunate enough to have a charming sunset, with scarcely a cloud in the sky, something that very seldom happens.

Twenty odd years ago the writer, accompanied by his brother, visited the Summit with the avowed determination to see the sun

THE GATES OF THE NOTCH

rise and set from the highest point of land in New England. For three days and nights we stuck to our post, and then from shortness of funds were compelled to descend (board at six dollars per day counting up rapidly), without scarcely having seen the sun while on the summit; rain, hail, and snow, clouds and fog, being the reward we received for our toil and trouble. So damp was the air that the fires would scarcely burn, and at one time we began to think we should have to descend to keep from freezing to death.

Baked beans, dyspeptic biscuit, and roily coffee were the principal articles of the bill of fare, and scarce at that, for there were an unusual number of people on the mountain at that time. One evening we stepped out of the Summit to visit the Tip-Top House, and a gale of wind, with a roar like an angry lion, met us in the face, completely prostrating us. Twice we tried to rise and make headway against it, and finally were compelled to crawl on our hands and knees, and in that undignified position reached the other building. Our room was in the northwest corner of the Summit House, and when we retired at night, the bed was like a cake of ice, and the mat in front, standing upon it even in your stocking feet, seemed made of the same material. Throughout the night we lay and shivered, obtaining scarcely any sleep, the bedclothes and everything else

seemingly chilled with dampness. Outside, the wind howled and moaned, the huge chains and iron rods that secured the building to the solid rock, rattled and creaked, and the building itself shook and groaned, as if each minute it would go to pieces. Once in the night I awoke bewildered, forgetting for a moment where I was, and thinking, from the howling of the wind and the infernal din, which was almost deafening, that I was on a ship in

HARD TRAVELLING.

a storm at sea. A punch in the ribs from my brother's elbow, and a drowsy growl as to whether I wanted all the clothes, dispelled the illusion. I have been on the mountain four times since, and experienced better luck in weather and accommodations, and since the building of the new hotel, with its steam heat and other improvements, it is possible for one to be quite comfortable at night even on the summit of Mount Washington.

The boys arose at four o'clock the next morning, and were again fortunate, obtaining a splendid sunrise view. After breakfast they visited the signal station, and listened to some thrilling experience told by one of the men in charge. The day continuing fine, they concluded to walk down the mountain by the carriage road, and after dinner started, having first arranged with one of Milliken's drivers to send their baggage down by team. They were four hours in their descent, including a half-hour's rest at the Half-Way House, loitering along, and getting views from all the best points

THE LEDGE, MOUNT WASHINGTON.

of observation, and reached the Glen House, after visiting Emerald Pool and Thompson's Falls for the artist to make sketches, about seven o'clock.

In the evening, while sitting on the piazza, and talking over their future movements, they concluded to walk back to Gorham, it being only eight miles, and visit the Copp farmhouse on the way, from which the best view of the "Imp" is obtained. Accordingly the next morning they settled their bill, and made arrangements for their baggage to go over on the stage, and about eight o'clock bade farewell to the Glen.

They walked along slowly, enjoying the landscape before them, and when a mile distant from the hotel reached the path leading to Garnet Pool; and turning to the left, a few rods' walk through the forest, brought them to this picturesque spot on the Peabody. They paused half an hour here examining the work of the water on the rocky bed of the river, and then continued their walk. Two miles more brought them to the road crossing the Peabody River. They turned off here, went over the bridge, and having reached the farm, inquired of a native the best spot from which to view the "Imp," and then walked to the place and gazed at his Satanic Majesty's rocky counterpart to their hearts' content.

Retracing their steps across the bridge, the boys resumed their slow but pleasant march toward Gorham, and reached the Alpine House just before one o'clock, having had a delightful walk. Dinner was the first thing in order, and the afternoon was occupied in writing letters, as they had not communicated with their friends since leaving home.

Saturday proved pleasant and hot, and during the forenoon the boys paid a visit to the Mascot Silver Mine (now abandoned), located high up on the side of a mountain opposite the village on the east side of the river.

HALF-WAY HOUSE, MOUNT WASHINGTON

A letter from Mr. Milliken proved a passport to the entrance of the mine; arrived at the place, the boys climbed the long, steep flight of steps, leading to the top of the dump, coming out on a platform which exposed a long tunnel, leading into the heart of the mountain. They were accompanied by the superintendent, who took them from one gallery to another, and explained the working of the business, giving them many interesting details about its discovery and start, the amount of ore being taken out, and its value.

When they left they were presented with several specimens of the ore, just as it came from the mine, containing silver, copper, and lead in small quantities. The superintendent, who found eager and appreciative listeners in his young visitors, invited them to take dinner with him, which invitation they accepted, and after a thorough inspection of the mine, accompanied him to the large and comfortable boarding-house built by the company at great expense, pleasantly located on the shores of a little pond. After dinner they ascended the mountain above the mine, and obtained a fine view up the Androscoggin Valley. The superintendent went with them, and showed them where he was about to sink a perpendicular shaft, to meet those that were run in horizontally from below.

"NOT DOWN ON THE BILLS."

When they returned to the Alpine, the clerk told them there was to be an amateur dramatic performance at the Gorham House Hall that evening, and asked them if they did not wish to go, informing them that he had some tickets for sale. The boys could think of no pleasanter way of passing the evening, so invested in tickets, and after supper went to the show. The hall was crowded, and George, who was supposed at home to be an authority on such matters, declared it a fine performance for a country village. One incident during the last piece created a great deal of laughter, and was not down on the bills. One of the actors in the farce took a gridiron and piece of

THE MASCOT MINE, GORHAM, N. H.

meat from the fireplace, and lifting the window in the flat, threw out the meat. This was a part of the legitimate business. But it happened that one of the young ladies who took part in the performance was peeping at the audience from behind the window, and when the actor threw out the meat, she had no time to run, and received it square in the face. This was the illegitimate part of the business, and as the audience saw it all, it is needless to say it "brought down the house."

ALPINE CASCADE, BERLIN FALLS, N. H.

Sunday morning the boys attended church, and after dinner started out for a walk. They had not gone over a quarter of a mile when they heard the distant rumble of thunder, and concluding that they stood a good chance of getting wet if they continued on, returned to the hotel and stopped the rest of the day. Having made up their minds to leave Gorham the next morning, they packed their trunks that night.

The boys hired a team from the hotel clerk to carry them to Berlin, it being a lovely drive up the west side of the

Androscoggin River, and sent their trunks up on the train. The distance is only six miles, but the views the entire distance are charming. At Berlin they stopped at the Cascade House, and after dinner walked down the river about two miles, then crossed to the east side, and visited the Alpine Cascades. On the way back they stopped at Berlin Falls, and passed nearly two hours in viewing from different points this magnificent cataract.

BERLIN FALLS, ANDROSCOGGIN RIVER, N.H.

The Parson succeeded in getting a tolerably fair sketch of that part of the fall spanned by the bridge, which we reproduce. It was seven o'clock when the boys reached the hotel, tired and hungry; but a good supper, and pleasant chat in the evening with some of the other boarders, sent them to bed in a contented frame of mind.

After breakfast the next morning they walked up the river two or three miles, and crossing to the opposite bank, obtained the finest view of the three highest White Mountain peaks to be had in this locality. The day was hot, and they loitered along, and it was noon when they reached the house. About two o'clock, accompanied by Mr. Marston, the landlord of the hotel, they drove off several miles to a brook where in three hours' fishing, they obtained a fine string of trout, which they had crisply fried for their supper.

Wednesday forenoon they inspected the mills of the lumber company, and were surprised at the amount of business done, and the speed with which it was accomplished. A log would be drawn dripping from the river, secured on a movable carriage, run on a track to a gang of saws, and "Presto! change!" out it went at the other end of the mill in the shape of inch boards. The mills contained saws of all sizes and kinds; and lumber of all dimensions is sawn here, also plank, boards, shingles, fence-pickets, clapboards, laths, and other articles. A branch track from the Grand Trunk Railway connects the mills with the wharves in Portland, from where it is shipped to all parts of the world, and twenty cars a day are loaded at the mills, and trundled from the forest to the ocean. A planing-mill filled with the requisite machinery for finishing lumber, and a drying-house, are adjuncts of the sawmills. The Berlin Mills Company, who own and run the mills, have also large boarding-houses for their army of workmen, and a store where everything from a jews'-harp to a grand piano, and a codfish to a silk dress, is sold. A schoolhouse, hall, and public library have been built by them, and they have been generous contributors to the handsome gothic church standing on the main street of the village.

In the afternoon they visited a cave Mr. Marston had told them of the day before. It was about a mile and a half from the house, and was called Jasper Cave. The walk led them across some rough ground, and in a north-westerly direction from the hotel. When they reached the cliff where the cave was located, they were in plain sight of the railroad, and but a short distance from it. The boys found the entrance to the cave so small that they had to crawl into it, and dropping on their hands and knees,

ANDROSCOGGIN RIVER, NEAR BERLIN, N. H.

squirmed along through the narrow passage, not without some misgivings in George's mind, who was ahead, that they might light on a bear, or some other wild animal. But the cavern, as silent as a grave, was empty, with the exception of two or three small bats, flying about overhead. Ned struck a match, and lighting a birch-bark torch they had brought with them, they found themselves in an apartment about twelve by sixteen feet in size, and perhaps ten feet high. The walls were damp, and in some places thin streams of water leaked from the rough walls, and filtered down to the bottom. They succeeded in finding two or three fine specimens of jasper, for which stone the cave is noted, and after an hour's exploration in the vicinity, walked down the railroad track to the depot, and then returned to the hotel.

That evening while sitting on the piazza they overheard Mr. Marston talking with two young ladies, who had arrived from Philadelphia the day before, about making the ascent of Mount Forest, and George intimated that if the young ladies were willing, the boys would like to join the party.

The girls expressed themselves as delighted with the idea, and accordingly the next morning, which proved to be all that could be desired, the whole party, with the landlord for guide, started for the summit. The distance from the hotel to the top of the mountain was about two miles, the latter part of the path being very steep, and they accomplished it in an hour and a half, having to stop quite often to give their fair companions a chance to rest. Once on the summit, they felt amply repaid for their climb, the view comprising an extended panorama of wilderness and mountains, and they could trace the Androscoggin River, through all its sinuosities for sixteen miles, a flashing diamond in an emerald setting. Here and there a small village straggled along the river banks for a short distance, suggestive of partial civilization. Two hours on the mountain top, with such a landscape spread out before them, and the fair maidens from the Quaker City for companions, became a part of the past with marvellous rapidity; and it was eleven o'clock before they had any idea of the flight of time, and reluctantly they left the mossy carpet on which for the last hour they had been reclining, and wended their way down the mountain to the hotel and to dinner. A shower of several hours duration came up while they were eating, and the afternoon was passed pleasantly in the house, with conversation and music.

When the boys came out of the dining-room after supper, Mr. Marston told them that a Mormon elder was to lecture that evening at the lower village, and that if they wanted to see some fun they had better go. The boys required no urging, for they scented sport, and accompanied by the landlord, they visited the hall, which was half filled on their arrival, and crowded fifteen minutes afterward. At the farther end of the hall was a small stage, with rather primitive-looking scenery. The curtain was up, and in the centre of the stage stood a small table. About half-past seven the elder made his appearance, and began a harangue in which the beauties of polygamy bore an important part. The crowd listened curiously at first, and then, becoming astonished and disgusted at some of the ideas conveyed, and opinions put forth, began to look at each other in a manner that prophesied mischief.

About this time the boys who sat midway of the hall on the right-hand side, saw a young woman, at the edge of the wings, on the left of the stage, watching the speaker anxiously, while in the next entrance toward the footlights stood two gentlemen, one of whom was laughing, and the other, an angry scowl upon his face, was beckoning the elder to leave the stage. It would have been well for him, had he done so, for the next moment some of the mill-men, who were always ready for a row, and who had left the hall a few moments before, returned with a basket containing eggs, cabbages, and other similar ammunition, and opened such a fusillade on the unfortunate elder, as soon compelled him to stop speaking and leave the stage. A cabbage struck him in the stomach, doubling him up like a jack-knife, and then rolled to the floor behind him. As he straightened up, an egg took him fair on the end of the nose, and broke with a splash, to the no small delight of the younger members of the audience. Several fellows who had been sitting on the front seats, rushed to the edge of the platform, and shouted opprobrious epithets, until the scared Mormon thought his time on earth had come, and he rushed off from the stage, while the curtain rolled down with a bang.

THE WRONG KIND OF APPLAUSE.

This ended the show, and the boys, who had laughed until tears stood in their eyes, left the hall and returned to the hotel. They learned the next day that the mill-men had threatened to ride the elder out of town on a rail, and then treat him to a coat of tar and feathers; but through the persuasion of one of their employers, who learned their intention, they concluded to forego their threats if the Mormon left town in an hour, and under cover of the darkness, the elder and his wife stole away, and Berlin saw them no more.

The boys had intended leaving Berlin on Friday, but they had found such agreeable company in the young ladies, that they changed their plans, and announced their intention of stopping over Sunday, much to the satisfaction of the girls; on Friday, therefore, instead of leaving on the train, they brought out their fishing-tackle, and went off to storm the brooks in the interest of their fair acquaintances, and returned at night with over a hundred handsome brook trout, some of which were served at supper. These were the first trout of the season for the girls, who praised them and their skilful captors in highly extravagant terms. After supper they indulged in lawn tennis until dark, and then went into the parlor, and finished the evening with music. Dick and George were nice singers, and with Miss Van Wyck and Miss Arden, who also had well-cultivated voices, they made a fine quartette, and in chorus were assisted by the Parson and Ned, who had very good voices, but who had not paid much attention to the study of music. After they had been singing an hour, Mr. Marston came in and asked them if they would not sing at church on Sunday.

The girls told him they would not dare, but he persuaded them to try it, as Dick and George had agreed to favor him.

"I suppose we must, then," said Miss Arden, smiling at the boys, "and I think if we are to sing, we should select a quartette. I have one with me that would be just the thing, and my friend Lucie sings the solo just lovely," and she ran up-stairs for the piece.

It proved to be Wondell's "Jesus, Lover of my Soul," the finest music ever written for those words, and Dick and George smiled as they saw it, for they were both familiar with it.

"This is a solo and quartette," said Miss Arden, "and Lucie can sing the first verse, and Mr. Burton the second in the solos, and we will all sing the quartette. Let us try it."

Fred and Ned refused to sing in the chorus, declaring they would only spoil it, and listened while the other four sang. As they finished the first verse, the landlord, Fred, and Ned applauded heartily, and the Parson declared they would take the natives by storm. After singing the second verse, the little party broke up, and retired to rest.

The next morning, after breakfast, George and Dick proposed to their two companions that they should hire Mr. Marston's mountain wagon and a pair of horses, and invite the girls to join them in a ride to Gorham, or the Lead-Mine Bridge, and take dinner at the Alpine House, returning in the afternoon.

"CHAFFING!"

"That is all very well for you and Dick," replied Ned, with a comical look at George; "but what can the Parson and I do," winking at Fred as he spoke, "who don't have a ghost of a chance with either of those young ladies when you two gallants are about?"

"Oh," said George with a blush, "you can go for the ride and the scenery."

"And to help pay the bills, I suppose," with another wink at the Parson.

"Hang the bill," returned George; "I will pay it all myself, only say you will go."

"Oh, George, George! that it should come to this before we have been away from home two weeks!" replied Ned, shaking his finger solemnly at his friend, "you are done for — hooked, played, and landed — as surely as I'm a living sinner" — and with his handkerchief he pretended to wipe tears from his eyes.

"Oh, confound your chaffing," put in Dick; "will you go, or not?"

"Yes, I will, my young bantam, but you are worse off than George. You, with no mamma to look after you, and scarcely out of short clothes."

"Don't plague them any more, Ned. You never know when to stop. I shall be very glad to go, George; but instead of dining at the hotel, suppose we take some grub and dishes along, and have a picnic dinner on the bank of the river."

"Happy thought!" exclaimed Dick, as he rushed off to find the landlord, while George went to invite the young ladies to go on the excursion.

In an hour all was ready. The team was at the door, in which a hamper containing a table-cloth, napkins, and sundry solids and dainties, was carefully packed. The girls were helped to their seats, the boys jumped in, and the spirited horses, under the skilful pilotage of the landlord, were trotting down the river-road. The day passed away like hundreds of others under similar circumstances. The young folks chatted, laughed, and were silent by turns, the gaps being filled with interesting stories by the driver. Every minute was enjoyed, every hour was a feast of pleasure. Ah, youth is the golden age with all of us. What a pity it could not be perpetual! The scenery was duly admired and praised; the dinner in the shade of a mighty elm whose trunk had stood the warlike shocks of many a northern blast, and from under whose wide-spreading branches they could gaze on the silvery river, its rippling waters murmuring a soft lullaby in their ears, all that could be desired; and the ride home, facing the glories of the setting sun, with the golden lights and purple shades alternately caressing the sides of the mountains, was a blissful experience, long to be remembered. When the young ladies had been helped from the carriage, and stood once more upon the piazza of the hotel, they conveyed their thanks in a charming manner to the young gentlemen for the day's pleasure, and declared it had been one of the happiest

ON THE ANDROSCOGGIN, NEAR GORHAM, N.H.

in their lives. What more could the boys ask for? After supper they adjourned to the parlor for music, and the quartette had another rehearsal.

Sunday morning they repaired early to the place where the meeting was to be held, that they might have a chance to practise a little with the young lady organist. It had been noised about that some young people from the cities were to sing that

THE PICNIC DINNER.

morning, and the church was crowded. When the young friends sang they created a marked impression, and the people looked from one to another, and then at the singers, as if they should like to applaud them were it not out of place. At the close of the service, several of the people present, and the minister, thanked them for their singing, and begged of them to sing the following Sunday. George explained that it was out of the question, as his party were to leave town the next morning.

The young people passed the afternoon and evening at home, and the boys gave the young ladies an account of their intended trip. The latter thought it would be delightful, and wished they were going. George learned from Miss Van Wyck that the parents of the two girls, and a party of their friends, were coming to Berlin the first of August, and that the whole party would make an excursion to Dixville Notch, and across Lake Umbagog, before returning home.

This set George to thinking, and he informed his fair companion that the boys would reach Dixville Notch about the 6th of August, and would probably stop a week there, and urged her to get her friends to visit the Notch before the boys left. She promised to accomplish it if possible, declaring that Grace and herself would be very happy to meet the young gentlemen again.

The boys had enjoyed themselves at Berlin; and it was not without a feeling of regret, that they bade the young ladies and Mr. Marston, who had driven to the station with them, farewell, as they jumped on the cars and were whirled away northward.

CHAPTER IV.

FROM BERLIN TO COLEBROOK. — SCENES EN ROUTE. — FISHING FOR BROOK TROUT. — BEAVER FALLS. — A DEER STORY. — ASCENT OF MOUNT MONADNOCK. — AN AMATEUR SHOW.

THEY had left Berlin on the day express, to better enjoy the scenery along the railroad, which between Berlin and North Stratford is well worth looking at. A short distance above the station the road skirts Dead-River Pond, then striking the valley of the Upper Ammonoosuc, follows it down (frequently crossing that erratic stream) to the Connecticut. The Parson, whose eye was ever open to the picturesque, caught a view of a small stream, on which stood an old mill. A little way below a young boy was seated on the bank, indulging in the favorite pastime of many of the country youth, angling for trout. Fred was delighted with this view, and quickly transferred the salient points of the picture to his sketch-book, to be worked up at his leisure. Milan and West Milan were soon passed, and the boys were surprised to see the rocky character of the land. A countryman who sat near, overhearing their talk, told them it was "strong land," and added, with a grin, that "it must be, to hold up all the rocks there were on it." A little beyond Stark, the next station, the train dashed through a frightful gap in the mountains.

Of the scenery along this part of the road, Farrar's "Androscoggin Lakes Illustrated" says: —

"A short distance from Stark, we pass by a tremendous circular precipice, called the 'Devil's Slide,' whose perpendicular walls, shattered and torn apparently with some mighty convulsion, rise to the height of five or six hundred feet. The Indians, in their mythology, peopled all these mountain regions with invisible spirits, who controlled the winds and storms, and in their quarrels hurled the gleaming thunderbolts at each other, the effects of which were seen in the splintered trees and shivered rocks; and they have a tradition that in a remote age a huge mountain barred the valley where now the railroad passes, and that on a time when the heavens were convulsed, the earth reeling, and the atmosphere blazing with the terrible warfare of these invisible powers, onehalf of the mountain sank down into the bowels of the earth, leaving the precipitous sides of the other, bare and shattered, as they have remained to the present day. Just beyond this locality you open on a fine view, off to the right of those remarkable twin mountains, the Percy Peaks, — generally considered to be the most symmetrical elevations of the whole mountain region. Standing aside from the dark mountain ridges which swing away northerly, their white cones clearly defined, the tourist cannot mistake them, from whatever point viewed; they are the admiration of all who behold them. Having these peaks in sight almost constantly for six miles, we next find ourselves at Groveton. Half a mile above here is a station known as Groveton Junction, the terminus in this direction of the Concord and Montreal Railroad, whose trains connect with those of the Grand Trunk."

At the junction the boys left the train a few moments, and were rewarded for their trouble with a beautiful view of the mountains to the southward. A short distance above here, as the train flew onward, they caught their first glimpse of the Connecticut River, which kept them company on the left. They

DEVIL'S SLIDE AND STARK VILLAGE, ON LINE OF GRAND TRUNK RAILWAY.

soon passed Stratford Hollow, and Beattie's, two small stations, at neither of which the train stopped, and in about thirty minutes the conductor called out "North Stratford!"

"That means me," said George; "grab your grips, fellows;" and suiting the action to his words, he took his valise, and followed by his friends, jumped off upon the platform. Directly opposite was the hotel, and a clerk from it hailed them, and inquired where they were going. George nodded to the house across the street, and the clerk took his checks, and went after their baggage, while the boys walked over to the hotel. They found the landlord, who proved to be pleasant and affable; he conducted them to a couple of nice rooms on the second floor, and the boys retired to attend to their toilet, for it had been very dusty on the railroad.

PERCY PEAKS.

When they returned to the office below, George asked the landlord what there was in the vicinity worth seeing, and to suggest a pleasant way of passing the next day. He told them an excursion to Maidstone Lake, seven miles distant, where they would find good fishing, would use up a day very nicely.

"Are we not quite near Vermont, landlord?" asked George.

"I should say you were," smilingly replied Mr. Moses. "The river is the boundary line between the two States. You have

PILOT RANGE FROM GROVETON JUNCTION

only to walk across the bridge to be in the Green Mountain State."

"I guess we'll take a trip into Vermont, then, before supper," remarked George, laughing, and added, "By the way, was it not

ON THE CONNECTICUT RIVER, NEAR NORTH STRATFORD, N. H.

somewhere in this vicinity that Boyton took to the water, when he floated down the Connecticut?"

"He went in just below the bridge."

"Suppose we take a walk over that way, boys," proposed George, and the party started toward the river.

The next day they made an excursion to Maidstone Lake in Vermont, and "had a bang-up time," as the Parson expressed it, returning to the Willard House at night, well tired out. Wednesday they visited a trout stream, that was well recommended by the village fishermen, accompanied by one of them as guide; they carried their dinner, and at night returned with over sixty trout, part of which the landlord had cooked for their supper.

Thursday morning they suddenly concluded to go on to Colebrook, and, as they did not wish to wait for the stage, hired the landlord to carry them up in an open wagon,

WHERE BOYTON TOOK TO THE WATER.

which gave them a good chance to see the country. They enjoyed the ride up the Connecticut Valley very much, the river being in sight on their left nearly all the way. The view of the intervales was charming, and the dark-browed peak of Monadnock during the latter part of the ride was ever before them. They put up at the Parsons House in Colebrook, it having been recommended to them, and they found it all that could be desired, in a country inn. There were some thirty people in the house from Boston, New York, and Philadelphia, among them some young fellows about their own age. .

Mr. Moses went back after dinner, and the boys walked out to see the town, and "get the lay of the land," as Ned expressed it. The hotel was pleasantly situated, commanding a view of the intervale, cut in two by the sparkling river, with the thickly wooded mountains beyond. During the evening the boys had some talk with Mr. Bailey, the proprietor of the hotel, about the best places in the vicinity for fishing, and as he had nothing especial to do the next day, he promised to go with them.

The following morning after breakfast, accompanied by their host, they drove some five miles to a stream that had the reputation of being a good trout brook. They put up their horses at a farm near the brook, and with their fishing-tackle and lunch, plunged into the woods, following up the stream for three miles, and then began fishing down. They met with good success, capturing about fifty before dinner-time, and when they stopped to lunch, Mr. Bailey, who had brought a frying-pan, pork, potatoes, salt and pepper, along with him,

MOUNT MONADNOCK, AND COLEBROOK, N.H.

made a fire, and the party had some of their trout, fresh from the brook, and crisply fried, as the *pièce de résistance* of the meal. The boys all declared it was jolly, it seemed so like camping out, and George remarked that it was only a foretaste of what was to come when they reached the Androscoggin Lakes. After dinner they resumed their fishing, following the brook down to the house where they had left their horses; they carried home about two hundred trout, and the other guests of the hotel complimented them on their good luck.

When the boys arose the next morning, they found it raining, and saw from the piazza that the top of old Monadnock was buried in the

LUNCH IN THE WOODS.

clouds. Lounging about the house after breakfast, they became acquainted with a guide and hunter by the name of Norton. He also paid a good deal of attention to taxidermy, and the fellows, becoming interested in his talk, at his invitation went to his shop near the hotel, and looked over his stock of stuffed owls, ducks, partridges, eagles, etc. He had also on hand several fine deer and caribou heads, some with very handsome horns. Ned told Mr. Norton that if he shot a deer or caribou, he would send the head to him to be mounted.

The weather cleared during the night, but as the following day was Sunday, the boys went to church in the forenoon, and for a short walk in the afternoon, passing the rest of their time at the hotel in reading and writing.

Monday forenoon they made a trip to Beaver Falls, which they pronounced one of the prettiest cascades they had ever seen. The ride going and returning was also enjoyable, in spite of the mud caused by the recent rain, for the day was delightful overhead, and the scenery along the way worth noticing.

BEAVER FALLS, COLEBROOK, N. H.

After dinner, while talking over their trip to the Falls, a young fellow who was boarding at the house came out on the piazza and spoke to them. After talking a short time, he informed them that some of his friends had been working with him to get up a variety show to be given at the town hall the following Friday evening, and inquired if they had ever done anything in the amateur theatrical or minstrel line, and when told that they had, he immediately importuned them to take part in the performance. He said he was going over to the hall in a few minutes to rehearse some acts, and invited them to go ; as the boys did not wish to appear churlish, they went, and the result was their promising to take part in the performance.

Tuesday morning after breakfast they strolled into Norton's place again, and began chatting with him about his experiences in the woods, and Dick asked him to tell them a story. He laughingly replied that he was not much of a story-teller, but he would tell them about a little scrimmage he had with a deer once that might interest them. Asking them to sit down, and make themselves at home, he related the following narrative:—

"During the month of October a few years ago, I was camping at Lincoln Pond, over on the east side of the Magalloway. Deer signs were thick in the vicinity, but as I had been there only a week, and was busy all the time in building a camp and setting traps, I had not obtained a shot at one.

"Taking my rifle one morning after breakfast I started for Flint's Camp at Sunday Pond, and had followed the trail leading to the Magalloway River, scarcely a mile, when I came upon the largest deer track I had ever seen.

"Stooping down, I examined the prints of the animal's hoofs, and found the tracks fresh — in fact, he must have passed along within an hour. He was heading down river, and without another thought of Spoff, I followed the tracks.

"At first I walked rapidly, stopping occasionally to see that I was on the trail, and after following it for half an hour, I moved more cautiously, as I had an idea I was nearing the game.

"Half a mile below where I was at the moment, a lagoon made in from the river, and at the head of this was a good feeding-ground for deer. I was confident that if I did not overhaul the deer before reaching the lagoon, I should find him there, and such proved to be the fact.

"I covered the last half mile slowly, as I crept carefully most of the way, and as I approached the water, I saw between the trees the deer standing at the edge of the lagoon feeding.

"As yet, he was unaware of my presence. But as I changed my position a trifle, to secure a better aim, I stepped one foot on a dry limb, which broke under my weight. The deer heard the noise, and raising his head looked suspiciously around him.

"Then I noticed it was the largest buck I had ever run across in this part of the country, and he carried a splendid set of horns. For a moment I was so excited I did not dare trust myself to fire, for fear of missing my mark, but after a few seconds, feeling cooler, I took careful aim and blazed away.

"The deer dropped, and, not doubting but what he was dead, for I never had a better shot in my life, I rushed out of the woods, set my rifle against a tree, and drawing my knife, walked up to the buck to cut his throat. When within six feet of him, I stepped into a hole, my right leg going down clear to my knee, throwing me forward, and shaking the knife out of my hand, which flew beyond my reach.

"Just as I had succeeded in getting my foot out of the hole, the animal, which I had not killed but only wounded, came at me with a rush. I dodged him by a hair's breadth, and sprang for my knife, which I had just caught sight of.

"I grabbed it by the handle, and arose to my feet just in time for the deer to catch me between his horns, and throw me over his back six feet behind him, as easy as a terrier would shake a rat. I lit on all fours, feeling a good deal, I imagine, as a man would if an elephant had struck him; but I knew it would not do to lie there, although I felt as if every bone in my body was broken, and scrambling to my feet, I dodged behind

FIGHT WITH A DEER.

a spruce tree, about two feet through, just as Mr. Buck charged on me again.

"In his blind fury he struck a large spruce tree with such force that it staggered him, and whipping around to one side, I plunged the knife into his neck, and giving it a rip, killed him almost instantly. Then I sat down to rest, for I felt about used up."

"I think you must," remarked George.

"After sitting awhile, I stood up, slipped a fresh cartridge into my rifle, and then whipped off the deer's hide. I dressed the carcass and cut it up, then taking the head and horns, and a quarter of the meat, I put for camp. In the afternoon I made two trips to the place, although feeling bruised and sore from my shaking up, and sacked the skin and the rest of the meat to camp.

"That was my first deer that season; and although I never could tell just what he weighed, not having any scales, I think he must have run up to nearly two hundred. Before the first of January, when I broke camp, I had shot five more."

"I suppose you call that pretty good luck," said Dick.

"Yes; and besides, I took from my traps over two hundred dollars worth of fur. But it is most time for dinner; let's go over to the house."

In the afternoon the boys went to the hall with the other young fellows who were to give the show, and passed the time until supper in rehearsing.

The next day, taking their guns and a small spy-glass belonging to Ned, they started to ascend Mount Monadnock. The morning was clear and bright, and they expected to get a fine view. From the hotel to the summit of the mountain, Mr.

Bailey had told them was about three miles. They crossed the river over the toll-bridge, then struck into a field directly opposite, passed across the cleared land to the edge of the woods, where they found a logging-road. This offered very fair walking, except for the windfalls, which obstructed their path frequently. Half-way up the mountain the road ended, but they kept on over a rather blind path, that was supposed to lead to the top. After following this for a time, they lost it, and after a few minutes useless search to regain it, they struck through the forest. For two hours they scrambled through the woods, which in many places contained thick underbrush, coming out by accident upon the barren ledge, from whence the best lookout is obtained, and sat down to rest.

The view from this point they found to be picturesque, wild, and extensive, and they passed nearly an hour there. Before leaving the place they ate their lunch, washing it down with draughts of cool water from a sparkling spring near them.

Norton had told them the night before, that if they went down on the back side of the mountain they might possibly find a deer. After eating they started over the summit, and took a long tramp on the other side; but although they ran across many tracks, some of which were apparently fresh, they did not see any animal larger than a squirrel. At three o'clock they were nearly at the foot of the west side of the mountain, and as they had a steep climb before them, before they could hope to descend the east side, George advised moving toward home. Their course was rather irregular, and it was after six o'clock before they reached the hotel, completely tired out, and hungry as bears that have just left their den in the spring.

Thursday, much to their disappointment, they had another rainy day, and were compelled to stay in-doors. Friday forenoon they went out to a point on the Mohawk stream some distance from the village, and caught about twenty trout, returning to the hotel in season for dinner. The afternoon they passed at the hall in rehearsing, and assisting their new friends in putting up scenery.

After an early supper, they returned to the hall, and went behind the scenes. The show was to begin at eight o'clock, and as it was free, the young men only giving it for fun, at half-past seven every seat was filled, and every available foot of standing room occupied. The bill embraced music, singing, dancing, banjo and bone solos, negro acts and farces. The performance went very smoothly, and everybody and everything was applauded to the echo. But an incident occurred on the stage that was not down on the programme.

Dick, who had not forgotten the chaffing he and George had undergone from Fred and Ned at Berlin Falls, on the occasion of the ride to the Lead-Mine Bridge, determined to get even with his tormentors, and as Ned was to black up and play a banjo solo, Dick watched his chance, and fixed a small carpet tack, point upwards, in the stool on which his friend was to sit while manipulating the banjo. The curtain was down to change the scene just before Ned went on, and Dick, who was busy helping set the scene, carried on the stool for his unsuspecting victim. The curtain was rung up, and Ned walked leisurely on, bowing right and left to the applause that greeted him, and then carelessly threw himself down on the stool, and with a yell that would have done credit to Forrest in Metamora, went about six feet into the air. As he came down he pulled the tack out of his pantaloons, and then looking the stool carefully over, to see if it was all right, he cast a savage glance at the wings, where some of the company were watching him, convulsed with laughter, and sat down and went on with his playing. The audience had supposed Ned's freak was a part of his business, and had laughed themselves hoarse at the queer antics he cut. When he left the stage he savagely interviewed every one who had taken part in the performance, about the tack; but not a soul knew anything about it, although they all "saw the point."

Later along in the evening, George and Dick were standing at one of the entrances, listening to two young ladies who were singing a duet, when George asked his companion if he had ever thought what a difference there was in the appearance of things in a theatre before and behind the curtain.

"Not particularly; but I have no doubt if the curtain should rise suddenly, when the actors were unprepared, and reveal what was going on behind it, it would be better than the play."

AN UNCOMFORTABLE SEAT.

"You are right, Dick. One night about a year ago, I was behind the scenes on the Boston Theatre stage. It was between the acts. I had just peeped at the audience, and noticed the expectant look on the crowd of upturned faces, and the air of business with which the musicians were playing a medley, when I suddenly turned and took a glance at the stage, and the difference struck me as being so ludicrous, I could not help laughing. Down in the centre of the stage a lady and gentleman of the company were trying to waltz to the music of the orchestra; off to the right of them, two others were rehearsing a love-scene that came in the next act; behind them on one side, an actor was conning his lines, and two others were indulging in a boxing-bout with gloves on; and at the rear of the stage one of the carpenters was at work on a flat. I thought

THE DIFFERENCE.

to myself, if the curtain should rise suddenly, it would be as good as a circus to see those people scatter, and I really itched to run it up."

"You would have brought down the house," said Dick, laughing at the contrasted picture.

A farce wound up the performance, and it went well, giving satisfaction to both actors and audience, and the show was over. The boys had all enjoyed it, and had had a good time, and their last night in Colebrook would always be green in their memory.

CHAPTER V.

COLEBROOK TO THE DIX HOUSE. — CATCHING TROUT WITH A SILVER HOOK. — DIXVILLE NOTCH. — A DAY'S FISHING. — LOST IN THE WOODS. — SHOOTING A DEER. — CAMPING OVER NIGHT. — THE RESCUING PARTY. — RETURN TO THE HOTEL.

SATURDAY they were up bright and early, and packed their trunks before breakfast. It was a lovely morning, clear as a bell, with but very little air stirring. At eight o'clock they left the Parsons House in one of Mr. Bailey's mountain wagons, with four good roaders in front of them. It was ten miles to the Dix House, the road following the Mohawk River nearly the entire distance. The highway led through a valley, walled on both sides by mountains, which gradually increased in height as they neared the Notch.

For the first five miles the view although charming was quiet and pastoral, but on the latter half of the ride it became wild and grand; the irregular peaks that shut in the Notch, cleaving the sky with their sharp minarets and towers, called forth exclamations of surprise and delight from the boys, who had read considerable about this romantic place.

After a few miles drive the knight of the ribbons hauled up at a watering-trough beside the road to water his horses; and while they were drinking, two young urchins came along the road, each with a fine string of trout.

"Where did you get those trout, bub?" asked George, addressing one of the boys.

"Over 'n the river."

"What river?"

"Mohawk."

"Will you sell them?"

"Dunno," with a look at his companion, as if to see what he thought of it.

"I will buy them if you wish to sell. Now what will you take for them?"

"Dunno. What'll yer give?"

"A regular Yankee," said George, smiling. "Answers one question by asking another. I will give you a dollar, — fifty cents each."

The two boys now whispered together for a few moments, and then announced that they would trade. The trout were accordingly placed in the bottom of the wagon, and covered up, and George passed the boys fifty cents each, and their eyes opened like full moons as they turned the silver over in their hands.

"You've made them little chaps happy," said the driver, chirruping to his horses, and starting them along.

"I'm glad of it," returned George. "They don't look as if they had much money to spend."

"They never had so much before in their lives," declared the driver confidently. "They're brothers, you know, and their father is a regular out-and-out guzzler, and spends every cent he can earn for whiskey. I hope the boys will give that money to their mother, for if the old man finds they've got it, he'll take it away from them, and keep drunk a week on it."

"Then I hope he will not get it," replied George with energy.

"So do I, blast his pictur!" and the driver looked fierce, as if thoughts of the drunken man awakened unpleasant memories.

They passed through two small villages on the way, both of which

FISHING WITH A SILVER HOOK.

clustered around mills, but the greater part of the distance the houses were a long way apart, and when they were within two miles of the Dix House they passed the last cottage. The driver informed them that many of the farms along the route had been partially or wholly cleared up within the last five years; and the numerous stumps standing in most of the fields confirmed the driver's story.

"Do they cut much lumber around here?" asked Dick of the driver, as he gazed on the thick forests which covered many of the mountains to their summits.

"Wall, no, not much. But over on the Connecticut, I tell yer they put in a raft of it last spring; there was a hundred million went down that river, and all owned by the Connecticut River Lumber Company."

"What a pile of logs that must have been!"

"Yes," returned the driver, "that was a grist of logs. But I didn't mean there was a hundred million logs," he continued, for he had seen the mistake the city boy had made, and, with more honesty than most of his class would have shown, hastened to correct Dick's error. "When I say a hundred million, I mean that is the number of feet, board measure, that can be sawed out'n logs; and whenever yer hear men talking up here about thousands or millions in connection with logs, you can know it isn't the number of logs, but the number of feet of lumber they can get out of 'em, that they mean."

"Thank you for the explanation; I understand it now."

"I should judge we were near the Notch," said George, as he caught a glimpse, through the tops of the trees, of some seamed and ragged peaks looming high above them.

"Only half a mile from the house," returned the driver, and added, "Do you see that big rock'n the left of the road?" pointing at a good-sized boulder that stood just outside the wheel ruts. "I was coming along here on my way home one day last week with a single hitch,

FRIGHTENED DEER.

and right opposite that rock I saw two deer standing in the middle of the road, and darned if they didn't frighten my hoss, and he like to run away with me."

"Did you have a gun with you?" inquired Ned eagerly.

"No, I didn't; but if I had, I couldn't of used it, for I had all I wanted about that time tew take care of my animil. And besides, it frightened the deers as much as it did the hoss, and they streaked it on the clean jump."

"I hope we shall run across some," said Ned; "if I can only get a good shot at one, I'll fix him."

"Perhaps yer will," said the driver doubtfully. "Did yer ever shoot a deer?"

"No."

"Wall, the proberbility is that the first deer yer see, you'll have the buck fever, and 'll miss him by a rod."

"Don't you believe it," replied Ned indignantly.

"Bet a quarter I'm right," chuckled the driver, who had not a very high opinion of city Nimrods; "but there's Parsons's," as the wagon reached a cleared space, "and you'll soon have a chance to stretch your legs."

The horses were reined to the left, and soon covered the short distance between the main road and the hotel. A few people were sitting on the piazza, and they gazed curiously at the new-comers, as the boys jumped out of the wagon. A tall gentleman, old and somewhat wrinkled, with bushy whiskers, now came forward and welcomed them, and the driver introduced him to the party as the landlord. George asked him to show them some rooms; he took them up-stairs, and they selected apartments that looked out on Table Rock. They followed the landlord down, and the driver, who was awaiting them on the piazza, asked George what he should do with the trout.

"Have part of them cooked for our dinner, and the rest for supper," put in Dick, who was very fond of fish, and Mr. Parsons ordered a man to put part of them in the ice-house, and carry the remainder to the kitchen.

"I say, Parsons, the boys had pretty good luck, didn't they?" and the driver winked at George. "They caught all those trout this morning between Colebrook and here."

"They did! They must be lucky fishermen. That is more trout than I have seen at once before this summer."

"Yes, we are always lucky," chimed in the Parson. "Might have shot a deer back here a mile on the road, but did not wish to break the law."

"Is that so?"

"Yes, we might have shot one, if there had been one to shoot;" and the rogue laughed, and looked saucily at Mr. Parsons, who only said, "Ah, um, I see," but could not repress a smile, as the joke dawned upon him.

After the baggage had been carried to their rooms, the boys removed the stains of travel from their clothes, and then came down to look about them. They found the house stood on a slight eminence, a few rods from the road, close to the Gate of the Notch, entirely surrounded by mountains, which formed an irregular amphitheatre, with the road toward Colebrook the only ostensible outlet. Toward the Notch the road was seen a short distance, until it disappeared among the cliffs, entirely lost in that direction. Some of the loftiest and most romantic peaks of the pass were in sight of the hotel, and but a short distance from it.

Just before dinner George inspected the register to see if their friends from Berlin had been there, but he did not find their names.

In the afternoon the boys asked Mr. Parsons if the path leading to the top of Table Rock was easy to follow. He assured them it was, and from the piazza pointed out the place where they should leave the road. With this information they started to climb the mountain, but they found it a hot day for such violent exercise. Once on the way, however, they would not back down, although they soon discovered that it was the steepest piece of mountain climbing they had ever undertaken. The last few rods to the summit, called "Jacob's Ladder," severely tried their muscles, and in the hot sun they "sweat like beavers." After thirty minutes' hard climbing they reached the

WESTERN ENTRANCE TO DIXVILLE NOTCH.

top, and walking across the giddy path that led to the verge of the cliff they sat down to rest. Looking about them they saw Mount Monadnock, on whose summit they had so lately stood, and mountain upon mountain beyond it, many of which were in Canada. They could see nearly the whole of the Mohawk River Valley, which lay spread out before them as on a map, and toward the south they could look over into Maine, until the view was barred by Speckled and Saddleback Mountains, the gigantic sentinels of Grafton Notch. All was wildness and desolation around, the only sign of civilization in the immediate vicinity being the hotel, far below them, dwarfed to Lilliputian size.

"I should think it would be a hard climb for women up here," said Dick, finally breaking the impressive silence.

"Probably it is," returned George. "I did not find it any too easy. But Parsons says that a great many ladies come up here."

"Where is the Snow Cave?" queried Ned: "let us see if we can find it."

"Mr. Parsons said it was back of this ledge somewhere," remarked Fred. "Come on, and we will hunt it up;" and suiting the action to the word, he walked carefully back over the narrow path, followed by the others, and after fifteen minutes' diligent search they found the place.

SUMMIT OF TABLE ROCK.

It was an immense split or rift in the mountain, how deep they could not tell, into which the snow had blown, and was now full to within about six feet of the top.

"The idea of finding snow or ice, whichever it is, the sixth day of August!" said George, shrugging his shoulders; "I should think the people up here would freeze to death in winter."

After looking at the cave they tramped along the edge of the cliff for almost a mile, obtaining different views all the time, then retraced their route to Table Rock, and thence to the road by the same path. From the highway they obtained a good general view of the Notch, and feeling tired from the heat and their climb, they returned to the hotel, and lounged away the rest of the afternoon on the piazza; that is to say, all but the Parson, who busied himself in making a sketch of Table Rock.

After supper the boys brought down their hammocks and hung them in the grove near the house, and turning into them, lay chatting while they watched the daylight fade to twilight, and the twilight deepen into darkness.

" How still it is here," said Dick, during a lull in their conversation; " one can almost fancy he is out of the world."

" It comes pretty near it," replied George, " when in a place like this, dropped down in a hole scooped out of these mountains, and not another house within two miles of you. What a place for a person who wanted absolute rest and quiet! If one could not find it here, I don't know where you would go for it."

The evening was hot and sultry, and about nine o'clock it began to thunder, accompanied by lightning. Then came a gentle sprinkle, which soon degenerated into a down-pour, and the rain fell in torrents. The peals of thunder grew heavier, and the flashes of lightning sharper, until it seemed almost as if the heavens were on fire, while the salvos from heaven's artillery became absolutely terrific, echoing back from cliff to cliff, on each side of the narrow pass. The very ground beneath the hotel seemed to tremble with the concussion. The clouds black as ink hung low down, entirely concealing the tops of the mountains, while the darkness was so profound, you could almost seem to touch it; with each flash of lightning the ragged walls of the Notch were illumined for a moment, but so short was the flash, that everything appeared confused to the eye, and you fancied the pinnacles gigantic goblins, threatening to descend from their rocky foundations and devour you. A weird feeling was in the air, and its supernatural influence stole over the boys, giving them a decidedly unpleasant and unnatural feeling. The storm lasted an hour, which seemed an age to the party, and when it was over, the boys concluded that it was a little ahead of anything in the shape of a thunder-storm that they had ever experienced.

PINNACLES OF DIXVILLE NOTCH.

" Do you have many such thunder-storms as that here in a season, Mr. Parsons?" asked Ned, after the last mutterings of the storm had ceased, and the party had recovered from the uneasy influence which had held them spellbound for a while.

"Well, no, no, not many." replied the landlord; "that is about as heavy a one as I ever remember."

"I am glad you don't. There was a little too much sublimity about that to suit me. I came about as near being frightened as ever I did in my life. I never heard such a racket during a thunderstorm before."

"Nothing like getting used to it," said Mr. Parsons.

"Very true. But you might as well kill a person as scare them to death. What time do you have breakfast in the morning?"

"About eight o'clock. But you can have yours earlier if you wish."

"No, thanks. Eight o'clock Sunday morning is early enough for us," and bidding the landlord good-night, the boys retired.

After breakfast Sunday morning, the boys gathered on the piazza, where they amused themselves for an hour, and then started off for a walk, George leading the way. They followed the highway nearly to where the path turned off to Table Rock, and then George proposed that they should try and scramble to the top of the mountain on the opposite side of the road. This was no easy task from the fact that there was no path, and the footing was precarious. When they had ascended twenty or thirty feet they reached a spot where the carriage road had formerly run, but a slide had destroyed it.

"I should like to know who keeps this road in repair," said Dick, as the party stopped a moment to take breath; "it looks as if the rocks were tumbling down here all the time."

"The State," replied George, "and it must require quite a sum to do it."

Climbing over the ruins of the former road, they picked their way carefully to the summit, but not without two or three slips which threw them down, and caused miniature slides to roll down the mountain. Gaining the top, they followed the edge of the cliff for some way to the east, obtaining excellent views of the opposite side of the Notch. Some way beyond where they had climbed up, they came upon Columnar Rock, a curious column of seamed and scarred rock, its sides nearly square. It towered to a height of from thirty to forty feet, and Dick thought he would like to climb to the top of it, but his friends would not let him make the attempt, as it seemed a very dangerous if not impossible thing to do. It was very tiresome walking in this vicinity, and they suddenly came to the conclusion that they had taken all the exercise they needed, and, descending carefully to the road, returned slowly to the hotel.

"There is one good thing about this Notch," said the Parson; "there is always a breeze here. It would be a fearful hot hole, were it not for this wind."

"That is so," acknowledged Dick; "but I will bet it blows hard enough here in the winter to take the hair right off of a man's head."

"Oh, the natives up here glue it on in winter," grinned Ned.

After dinner Dick proposed that they should go a-fishing;

COLUMNAR ROCK, DIXVILLE NOTCH.

but George told him it was Sunday, and he had better content himself in the house, and flatly refused to go. As Dick was not anxious to go alone, he stopped at the hotel with the others, and they devoted most of the afternoon to music.

As the boys gathered on the piazza in the evening, Dick asked

George where he supposed the girls were, meaning the young ladies whose acquaintance they had formed at Berlin.

"I think they are at the Cascade House," answered George.

"Did you not expect them here last night?"

"Hardly. You know, it all depended on their folks whether they came or not, and perhaps their party have not reached Berlin yet."

"I looked for them Saturday night, and thought sure we should see them to-night."

"Oh, don't worry, Dick. If they come we shall know it, and if they don't we cannot help it. I do not imagine their parents are the kind of people who travel Sundays, unless it were absolutely necessary, so I did not expect them to-night. If I were you, young man, I would not build my hopes too high on their coming, and then if they don't come, you will not be so badly disappointed."

"You talk cool enough, I hope," replied Dick with a comical look. "I thought you were very anxious to have them come here. I thought you were smashed on Miss Van Wyck."

"Oh, not so bad as that," declared George, blushing and laughing. "I think she is a nice girl — yes, a very nice girl — and in fact she takes the cake."

"Takes the cake, does she? Well, then, if I know anything, Miss Arden takes the whole bake-shop."

"That may be your opinion; but there, we will not argue the case further, and let us hope the girls will come to-morrow."

Early the next morning George ran across Mr. Parsons, and questioned him about the fishing in the vicinity; and the old gentleman informed him that he could get some trout over to Nathan's Pond, three miles from the house, or on the Diamond Stream, about five miles distant. At the breakfast-table George acquainted his friends with what he had learned from Mr. Parsons, and asked them if they would not like to try their luck at fishing.

They were all ready for anything that promised sport, and accordingly went from the breakfast-table to their rooms, and unpacked their guns and fishing-tackle, and changed the clothing they had on for their hunting-suits.

"Suppose," proposed George, "that two carry their guns, and the other two fishing-rods; that will be better than for every fellow to take both his gun and rod, for when the two who have rods become tired of fishing, they can change with those who have guns. We will take some matches and Dick's light axe, and I will carry my drinking-cup. Now for the lunch."

George found the landlord, and asked him to order a lunch put up for the party, and then brought down his fishing-rod. Ned also carried an angler's equipment, and Fred and Dick their guns, the latter also taking his axe.

The landlord now returned with the lunch, handing it to George, with the suggestion that they had better take a few worms. The Parson thought it a good idea, and went out by the stable and dug several handfuls which he imprisoned in a tomato-can.

"A bridle-path leads to the pond, Mr. Howe," remarked the landlord, "and you can ride there on horseback if you choose."

At this the boys laughed, considering it a good joke.

"I don't think we care to go fishing or gunning on horseback, Mr. Parsons," replied George when he could speak; "at least, not while our legs are all right; but it is very kind in you to make the offer, and we thank you for it."

"Some of our boarders will not go over there, unless they can ride," added Mr. Parsons.

"Yes, I suppose you have some lazy fellows visit you," answered Dick, "but we don't belong to that breed of cats. I never require anybody to help me draw my breath, or my salary either."

"No," put in Ned, giving his friend a poke, "the only time Dick requires any help, is when he is clipping the coupons from his bonds."

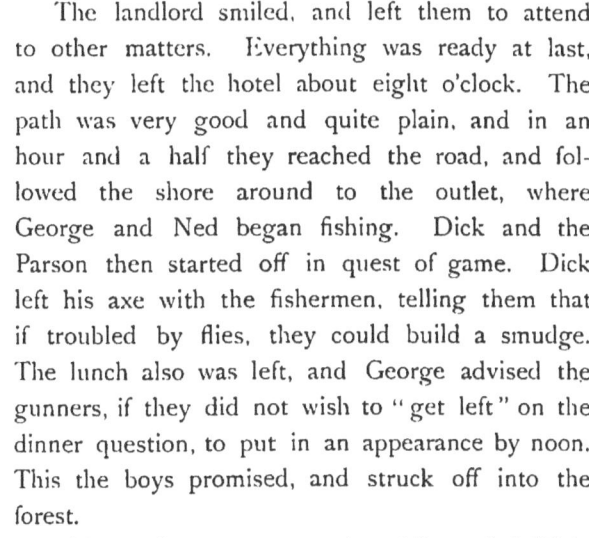

The landlord smiled, and left them to attend to other matters. Everything was ready at last, and they left the hotel about eight o'clock. The path was very good and quite plain, and in an hour and a half they reached the road, and followed the shore around to the outlet, where George and Ned began fishing. Dick and the Parson then started off in quest of game. Dick left his axe with the fishermen, telling them that if troubled by flies, they could build a smudge. The lunch also was left, and George advised the gunners, if they did not wish to "get left" on the dinner question, to put in an appearance by noon. This the boys promised, and struck off into the forest.

"Now, what are we to shoot?" queried Dick, as he and Fred left the pond. "Anything we come across?"

"Yes, anything we can eat, except squirrels or rabbits. I don't like to shoot rabbits, because, if you only wound them, they will sit up on their haunches

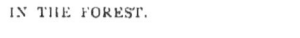

IN THE FOREST.

and cry so piteously. I popped at one with a revolver once, and only wounded it, and had to fire three or four times more before I killed it. I would not shoot another unless I were starving. Squirrels we probably should not eat, as the only kind about here are chipmunks; and between you and me, Dick, I don't care to shoot a squirrel just for the purpose of killing it. I think it's mean."

"So do I," assented Dick; "and the little rogues are so cunning, I like to see them playing in the trees."

"I tell you what we will do; make the circuit of the pond, a short distance from the shore, and we may come across some partridges or deer. I should not wonder if deer came into this pond some time."

"All right; go ahead."

The two boys now made their way carefully through the woods, keeping at a distance of about four rods from the pond. Occasionally they stopped and inspected the ground in search of deer tracks, and when they had travelled about a mile they found two or three prints of deer's hoofs in a path which intersected their course, and following these closely, they soon reached the pond. But no deer were in sight, and they heard no noise but the buzz of the mercantile mosquito, ever ready to present his bill, and the chipper and chatter of squirrels among the trees.

Retracing their steps from the pond, they continued their course, and shortly came to a place almost impassable from the effects of some hurricane. Twenty or thirty trees had been blown over, some uprooted, others torn and twisted off, and the whole lay piled up in every direction in inextricable confusion. Making a *détour*, the boys passed around this obstruction, and just as they reached the farther side a partridge, an old cock, flew up ahead of them, and Dick let drive at it, shooting it through the head.

"That's a good shot for a rifle," said the Parson, who carried a double-barrelled shot-gun; "you have bagged the first game, Dick."

"Let us hope it won't be the last," answered Dick, as he threw the empty shell away, and put a fresh one in his rifle. Then, picking up the partridge, they went on.

In some places the underbrush was very thick, and they progressed slowly. But at half-past twelve they reached the outlet of the pond, and joined their friends, without having increased their bag.

THE FIRST BIRD.

"What luck, fellows?" cried George, as the gunners came up.

"Poor," answered Fred. "We have only a cock partridge, and Dick shot that. But we saw deer tracks on the other side of the pond, and that proves they come in here sometimes."

"I wish one would show up now. But let's have our dinner. I feel hungry."

"All right; how many fish have you caught?"

"About fifty," returned Ned, "but they are all small."

George now overhauled the basket, and taking out its contents, spread them on a flat rock near by, inviting his friends to "pitch in." No one required second urging. When they had eaten all the food, and Dick had even squinted into the basket to be sure nothing had been overlooked, they interchanged experiences of the forenoon, which, however, had neither been exciting nor particularly interesting. For an hour they talked over their plans for the future, when suddenly Dick jumped to his feet, and, pointing to the shore of the pond on their right, exclaimed in an excited whisper, —

"I see a deer!"

"Where, where?" softly queried the others.

"There in the water; don't you see? he is either drinking, or going to swim across the pond," and Dick pointed along the shore, some distance away.

"He's ours!" declared Fred, snatching up his gun.

"Don't count your chickens until they're hatched," warned George with a low laugh; "but you and Dick try and stalk him, and Ned and I will unjoint our rods, and follow you."

"Yes, we wish to be in at the death," grinned Ned.

Fred made no answer, but picked up his rifle and followed Dick, who was already making his way swiftly, and with but little noise, toward the deer.

Before the boys were within good shooting distance, the animal turned and came out of the water, and stood still, apparently listening. In a few moments he started again, and Dick, who was yet ahead, afraid of losing entire sight of the game, as he would the moment the animal entered the thick woods, threw his gun to his shoulder, and fired both barrels in rapid succession. The deer leaped forward and fell; but rising quickly to his feet, started on the run, and was out of sight before the Parson could get a shot.

"Confound it! why couldn't you wait until I came up?" asked Fred excitedly; "we have lost him now!"

"I am not so sure about that," returned Dick coolly, as he threw the empty shells away, and slipped two loaded ones into his barrels; "besides, I couldn't wait. He was starting to run, and if I had not let him have it then, I should have lost my own chance for a shot. I'll bet ten dollars I hit him, too. I had him covered fair, and although it was a long distance, you know my gun is a mighty close shooter. I brought him to the ground anyhow, and I must have hit him, or

A DEER CHASE.

he wouldn't have fallen."

"Stumbled over something probably," said Dick.

"Yes, over your grandmother, I guess," returned the Parson indignantly. The boys had now reached the spot where the deer was when Dick fired; and, looking round, he discovered some blood on the grass and bushes, and shouting with triumph, pointed it out to Fred.

"Perhaps we can track him by the blood, and may get him yet," said the Parson with animation.

"We'll try it anyway; but let us wait until George and Ned come along. We ought not to run away from them."

The two fishermen soon arrived, and when they saw the blood stains were unanimous for following the trail, and running the game down if they could. Careful search soon revealed blood on the ground in the direction the deer had taken, and they hurried onward. The trail led parallel with, and near, the shore of the pond for some distance, finally intersecting the path leading to the hotel. Here they left the fishing-rods and basket until they should return, not expecting to be gone from this point more than an hour.

The pursuit was now taken up in earnest. Half a mile from the bridle-path the trail turned to the left, and skirted the south end of the pond, and then led straight into the forest. Several times the boys stopped and listened, thinking they heard the deer. But a few seconds' anxious waiting served to undeceive them, and again they pressed forward. Occasionally they would lose the trail, and would spend sometimes half an hour in searching, before they would strike it again. Over hills and through valleys, across brooks, then through some cluster of windfalls, or over a piece of ground covered with huge boulders, they persistently followed the wounded animal, and after several hours' hard tracking, they reached the foot of quite a high mountain, and stopped a moment to rest, and wipe their heated faces.

"I should not think there would be a drop of blood left in that deer by this time," cried Dick, panting; "he can't be a great distance ahead."

"I hope not," said Ned. "I never was so tired in my life."

"I guess he don't intend to stop this side of the Magalloway," laughed George.

"Come on! come on! don't talk here any longer," urged the Parson, "we must sight him soon;" and he took the lead up the mountain.

Climbing this they found to be anything but fun. The ground was as rough as the sides of the mountains in the Notch, and was made up almost entirely of huge boulders, with but a slight covering of soil or moss, and between them the roots of the trees had struck down, and obtained a little sustenance. Their pathway was full of holes, and they had to be very careful where they placed their feet to avoid falling.

"RUN TO EARTH."

Huge ledges and overhanging cliffs, sometimes fifty feet in height, rose before them and barred their progress, and almost invariably in such places they lost the trail, and had to hunt some time before finding it.

At last as they reached the top of a cliff, so steep that they had been compelled to boost and pull each other up, they came suddenly upon the deer lying on the ledge. One glance was enough to convince them that they did not need to waste further ammunition.

Dick's buckshot had done their work. It was a buck, with a splendid pair of antlers, and he was fat as a pig. The boys looked him over for a few moments, and then George said they had better bleed and skin him.

"I don't believe there is any blood in him," said Ned.

"I shall send the head out to Colebrook to Norton," said Dick, "and have him preserve and mount it."

Dick and George pulled off their jackets and rolled up their sleeves and went to work. With the axe, they cut the head carefully off, and then used their knives in taking off the skin. While they were doing this, George asked Fred and Ned to hunt up some water if there was any in the vicinity, for he was half-choked.

After skinning the deer they opened and dressed it, then cut it up into quarters to make it easy to carry.

"How much do you think it will weigh, George?"

"I don't know, Dick; it is something I am not used to estimating the weight of, but by comparing it in size with a man I should judge it would have weighed one hundred and fifty pounds. Just lift that hind quarter I laid down, it is about all one of us will care to carry to the hotel."

At the word "hotel," the boys looked at each other earnestly, and simultaneously they pulled out their watches.

"Seven o'clock!" both at the same moment.

"Where in the name of Heaven has the afternoon gone to?" asked George.

"That is what I should like to know, and how we are going to get back to the hotel. The Lord alone knows where we are, and it will be dark in the woods in less than an hour," and Dick gave utterance to a profound whistle.

Just then the two friends returned, bringing a cup of water.

George drank half, and passed the cup to Dick, who finished its contents.

"Look here, George, is it not about time we were getting back to the hotel?" and the Parson peered at his friend earnestly.

"Yes, it is, if we only knew the way, or could have daylight to go back in."

"You don't mean to say we are lost?" queried Fred anxiously.

"That is about the size of it, for to-night at least. If it were noon, I don't think we should have any trouble in finding our way back to the hotel, and no doubt we can to-morrow. But we cannot travel through this forest in the dark, and the sooner we get down this mountain and find some decent place to camp, the better. I have no notion of sleeping on the soft side of one of these rocks."

"Camp?" said the others in a breath.

"Yes, camp, and we are losing valuable time now. Where did you find your water, Ned?"

"Down below, a short distance off to the left. A brook runs down the mountain."

"That is a piece of luck to begin with. Let us strike the brook and follow it down. I will take one of the quarters of the deer, and the skin, and the rest you can divide between you."

Dick picked up the axe and his rifle in one hand, and the head, which he wished to reach the hotel without injury, in the other, and the Parson and Ned tackled the other three quarters of the meat, and the latter leading the way to the brook moved on. After reaching it they followed down the mountain, a distance of half a mile, and there stopped a moment to rest.

"Now," said George, "it will not do to get a great way from this brook, for we must have water. Dick, you and the Parson cross the brook and see if you can find a decent camping-spot while Ned and I hunt on this side. The proper spot is a dry knoll or hummock if we can find one, with a little hard wood in the vicinity."

Leaving their burdens the boys scattered, and began their search for a suitable place to camp on. George, who had read more about wood life, and heard more of it, than the other boys, soon found a suitable place, and giving a shrill whistle, returned to where they had dropped their things. The others came hurrying along, and George requested them to pick up the things and follow him.

"I don't believe we could find a better spot if we hunted a week," said George. "Close to the bank of the brook, I ran across an immense boulder, perpendicular on the water-side, but shelving on the other. The top of it is about ten feet from the ground, and overhangs so far, that a plumb-line dropped from the top would touch ground seven feet from the base. All we need do is to put up a few boughs on each side, build a fire in front, and we can get along nicely."

"We shall not need much fire," said Dick; "it is not cold."

"You will change your opinion before morning; and you know we have neither overcoats nor blankets. A good fire, well attended, is all that will keep us from suffering with the cold."

Dick looked incredulous, but George did not argue the point further. He had read enough to know what nights were in the mountains and northern wilds, and meant to govern himself accordingly.

When they reached the rock the party were delighted with the place, and at once set about their work, for daylight was nearly gone.

"Give me the axe," said George, as they dropped their burdens to the ground. "It is a pity we have not another axe, but we shall have to make this one answer. Luckily we have no clearing out to do. But we must work quick and work together; and while I am, cutting poles, do the rest of you procure a lot of small cedar, spruce, or hemlock boughs for us to lie on, and put them under the boulder; get plenty of them while you are about it."

Then George began searching for poles, and soon found what he wanted. He cut four with crotches in the tops, and two straight ones, then cut down a large spruce and trimmed off the limbs. After stripping it he carried the axe and poles to the rock. The crotched ones he sharpened at the opposite ends, and drove two on each side about four feet apart, one on each side being close to the rock. Then taking the two straight poles, he laid them in the crotches one on each side. Returning to the felled spruce, he obtained an armful of limbs, carried them to the rock and spread them across the poles, thus finishing the roof of the camp, the greater part of which was formed by the boulder. After this he cut down a number of small spruces, and dragging them to the camp stood them up on each side, leaning them against the horizontal poles. The remainder of the long limbs from the large spruce he also stood up at the sides, thus giving them a camp which would answer very well for a pleasant night.

By this time his companions had collected a huge pile of limbs, and asked him what next they should do, for they acknowledged him as their leader, he being the oldest in the party.

" Build a fire now, and then we'll have our supper," said George cheerfully.

" Supper ! " yelled Ned, looking at George with staring eyes. " Where in creation shall we get it ? "

" Right behind you. Are we going to starve with four quarters of venison in the larder? Not if I know myself. Now, if some of you fellows will start a fire directly in front, and about six feet away from the camp, I will arrange our bed. Fred, hunt up some birch bark; Dick, gather some small, dry limbs ; and Ned, you tackle that old pine

CAMPING OUT.

stub yonder, and see if you can hack it down; that is about twenty feet long, and with a few sticks of white birch will make wood enough to last us all night."

"When did you learn so much about forest trees, George? I can scarcely tell one from another."

"Reading and observation, Ned. Keep your eyes and ears open as you go through the world. You will find it a great help to you."

Ned started for the pine stub, muttering something about being "wiser than Solomon," as he went. But George did not hear him; he was busy arranging the boughs the boys had brought, under the rock for them to lie on. He laid them in a square of six feet, and about six inches deep, and then threw himself down to see how it lay.

"A bed fit for a king," he remarked after trying it; "if we only had a couple of blankets we should be pretty well fixed. But we shall have to take turns watching in order to keep up a good fire. Now for a pillow," and taking more boughs he laid a row across the inner end of the bed about six inches high and a foot deep.

"Here's your bark," said the Parson; "And your dry limbs," chimed in Dick, as they returned, and threw down the material they had gathered.

George went out, and taking a little of the bark, and a few of the smaller limbs, soon had a fire started, which grew fast as he piled on the fuel, until it reached a respectable size, sending forth plenty of heat, and a bright light. At this moment the old pine fell, the upper end of it nearly reaching the camp.

"That pine is just what we want," remarked George, taking the axe from Ned, and telling him to rest a few moments, he chopped off several large pieces which Ned placed on the fire. It was now dark, and the boys, after cutting up the old pine into moderate-sized junks, gathered around the fire, and waited for George to get supper. They had not long to wait. Taking his knife, he cut four generous slices from one of the hind quarters of the deer, and brought them to the fire.

"Now, each fellow must be his own cook, and you can all watch me." George went off with the axe a short distance, but soon returned with four small maple limbs, each almost four feet long. He distributed these to his friends, then peeled the bark off from one end of the stick he had kept, sharpened that end, then stuck it through his slice of venison, and held it over the blaze. His companions, who were watching him closely, quickly took the hint.

THE WOODCHOPPER.

"I wish we had some salt," remarked Dick, as the meat began to broil, sending forth a fragrant smell, that sharpened the appetite of every boy around the fire.

"Don't you remember that paper of salt that was in the basket? You said it was not worth keeping, and threw it away," and George gazed at his hungry young friend with a sarcastic smile.

"Yes, I do. And I was a fool for throwing it away."

"Just what I thought at the time, so I picked it up," and George drew the paper of salt from his pocket, adding: "Never throw away a thing in the woods; you can't tell how soon you may need it."

"You are a brick, George; that will make the meat relish a great deal better."

When the boys had broiled their venison sufficiently, they sprinkled it with salt, and it tasted very nice. It was much better than being entirely without food. Dick declared it to be the best meat he had ever eaten in his life; but the fact that he had eaten nothing but a slight lunch since morning, and had tramped all day, had a great deal to do in forming his opinion. There is no sauce like hunger.

It was nine o'clock when they had finished their frugal supper, and George threw several sticks of wood on the fire, sending out a brilliant blaze, lighting up the woods some thirty feet away.

COOKING VENISON.

"We must have more wood," remarked George, "and each one must chop down one of those white birches, cut it up into lengths three feet long, and bring it to camp. That will give us wood enough for the night, I think.

Here goes for the first tree;" and taking the axe, he walked to a clump of white birches close at hand, and attacking one valiantly, soon brought it to the ground; then cutting it into the proper lengths, carried them to camp. The other boys followed his example, and at ten o'clock had all the wood they needed.

"This fire must be kept up," declared George, as they threw themselves down on their bed of boughs to rest. "It is now ten o'clock," looking at his watch by the firelight, "and I think we had better divide the night into four watches of an hour and a half each. The first would run until half-past eleven, the second until one, the third until half-past two, and the fourth until four o'clock. By that time it will be light enough for us to travel, and we ought to reach the hotel at the earliest moment possible; for of course the people there will be anxious about us, knowing we are strangers here."

"I'll take the first watch," said Dick.

"Don't you be in a hurry," remarked George dryly. "The first watch, of course, is the most desirable, and, as we can't all have it, I propose we draw lots to see who shall."

"That is fair," observed the Parson. "How shall we do it, George?"

"I will get four small sticks of unequal length, and hold them in my closed hand, leaving the ends sticking up evenly. Then you shall all draw one. The fellow who gets the shortest shall have the first watch, the one the next longest, the second, and so on. That will give us all an equal chance."

"But you will know which is the shortest stick," said Dick, with an air which conveyed the idea that he was a little too smart for the leader of the party.

"What of that, stupid? I don't draw myself."

"That's so," acknowledged Dick, while his friends joined in a hearty laugh at his expense.

George then selected his sticks from two to four inches long, and, arranging them in his hand so the boys could only see one end, told them to draw. When each had selected his fragment of wood, it was found that Ned had secured the first watch, the Parson the second, Dick the third, and George the last.

"Now, remember, fellows, there must be no sleeping on duty. And I move that any one who goes to sleep on guard be fined five dollars, said sum to be expended for the benefit of the crowd when we return home. What do you say?" and George looked from one to the other.

The boys laughed at the proposition, but all agreed to it.

"Well, Ned, my dumpling, you can go on guard, and we will turn in. Keep up a good fire, for it is beginning to grow chilly now. I think you had better put all our things in camp, then the meat will be out of the reach of any prowling animals."

"All right, boss," replied Ned facetiously, "only I will keep the rifle and gun where I can get at them handily; we may have a visit from a bear in the night."

"I will insure you against all the danger from bears, only don't let the owls frighten you;" and George, Dick, and Fred threw themselves down on the boughs. It was half an hour, at least, before they could get to sleep. The strangeness of their situation (for none of them had ever passed a night in the forest before), the solemn stillness of the woods, relieved only by the rippling of the brook behind them, or the crackling of the fire, and an occasional movement on the part of Ned, who had a vague idea that bears or some other wild animals were about, served to keep them awake; but gradually they yielded to the unusual fatigue through which they had passed, and first one and then another fell into the arms of Morpheus, and all became a blank to them.

After his friends had quieted down, Ned began to think it rather dull, and for want of something better to do, laid all the wood scattered about the camp in a solid pile near the fire, and sat down on it. He had sat hardly a minute, when he heard a noise that startled him; and listening carefully, off to his right he heard, "Tu whit, tu whit, tu whoo-o-o," repeated half a dozen different times. He arose to his feet, and peered intently off through the flickering firelight into the darkness.

"Confound it!" he muttered half aloud. "It is nothing but the owls. I suppose the light of the fire bothers them. However, I will throw on a few sticks more, for it is growing colder. George was right; if we had been without matches, and consequently without fire, we should have suffered from the cold."

He sat down again on the woodpile, but he could not rest comfortably. Every moment or two he heard some unusual sound, the least noise seeming painfully audible. An undefined fear was creeping gradually over him, which he felt he must shake off, and stepping softly into the camp he procured George's drinking-cup, and started for the brook; not that he was particularly thirsty, but that he felt better when he kept moving. The brook was just within range of the firelight, and he could see sufficiently well to make his way along without stumbling. He reached the stream, and drank a cup of the pure water, now changed to the ruby color of wine, from the reflection of the camp-fire. Filling the cup a second time to carry with him, he turned to go back. The distance was perhaps a couple of rods, and midway grew a large sapling pine, under whose wide-spreading branches he had to pass. As he went by the tree, from its topmost branches came a sound, that for a moment paralyzed, and then started him, as if he had felt the full force of an electric battery. Rushing to the camp, and throwing down the cup, he grasped the rifle, and sang out for the sleepers to awake.

"What's the row?" inquired George. He was only half-awake, and had an idea that it was his turn to go on guard.

"Yes, what is the matter?" asked his other friends, as the three sprang to their feet, and gazed at Ned, who stood just outside the camp, rifle in hand, his eyes glaring in the direction of the pine.

"I heard either a wildcat or the evil one; I don't know which."

"Of the two," replied George, laughing, for he was now thoroughly awake, "I should say the chances were that you heard a wildcat, or a "lucivee" as they call it up here. Where do you think the animal is?"

"In that large pine. Perhaps he will yell again."

George stepped into camp, and brought out Fred's gun, which

SCARED BY AN OWL.

was loaded with buckshot, and the four friends stood in earnest expectation.

"Throw some more wood on the fire, Dick," requested George.

Several large sticks were added, and the flame shot up five or six feet in the air, and shortly after, the same blood-curdling noise, half way between a screech and a yell, broke forth from the top of the pine. The boys jumped, and Ned fired in the direction of the sound. The bullet was heard to strike the tree with a thud, showing it had not touched the unwelcome tenant, whatever it might be.

"Don't fire again," cried George, as he noticed Ned slipping another cartridge into his rifle, and beginning to laugh, "it is nothing but a screech-owl."

"Screech-owl?" queried Ned contemptuously, "and make such a noise as that! I half-thought it was a panther."

"All bosh!" continued George. "One summer when father was at Moosehead Lake, old Masterman, one of the oldest and best guides and hunters there, told him that he was never frightened in the woods but once in his life, and that was by a screech-owl."

"How was it?" asked Dick.

"Father told me that Masterman was out trapping, and one night he camped under a large pine. He was awakened from a sound sleep by a fearful noise, and jumped into the air more than six feet, with his hair standing straight all over his head. He grasped his rifle, and soon heard the noise, then he knew what it was, and he was so mad he shot the owl. He had heard them hundreds of times, but had always been awake; but this one screeching in the night, and being directly over him, and his quick awakening from a sound sleep, rattled him so that he did not recognize the owl's noise, and was badly frightened. The old man used to laugh at the end of his story, and say he had heard people tell 'they were not brought up in the woods to be scared by an owl,' but he acknowledged that he was brought up in the woods, and that an owl gave him the worst fright he ever had in his life. But it is quarter to twelve; it is your turn, Fred, to keep up the fire; and don't be scared by the owls," and laughing, George went into camp, followed by Ned and Dick, and in spite of their fright they were soon sound asleep.

When the Parson was left alone, he began pacing back and forth in front of the camp, to keep awake; for now that the excitement was over, he began to feel sleepy again, and it did not seem to him that he had slept five minutes when he was awakened by Ned's outcry. For three-quarters of an hour, nothing occurred to trouble him, and he only discontinued his lonely march, when it was necessary to replenish the fire; but becoming tired he sat down on the woodpile to rest. In this position, with the heat of the fire casting its soothing influence over him, he began to nod, and would surely have fallen asleep had he not heard a noise in the forest beyond the fire, to his right. Instantly he was wide awake, with every nerve strung to its fullest tension, and seizing the rifle and cocking it, he watched and listened. He heard slow footsteps, evidently approaching the fire, and in about ten minutes caught the glare or shine of some animal's eyes, opposite to him. Whatever the animal was, its body was so concealed by the gloom of the forest, that Fred could not make it out. Hesitating about firing, for he did not wish to unnecessarily alarm his companions, the fearful note of the screech-owl sounded on the stillness of the night once more, and involuntarily he jumped and shouted, the rifle going off at random. Then he heard a crashing in the underbrush, and the sleepers again turned out with alarmed inquiries.

"Have you shot another wildcat?" asked George. "You fellows seem bound to keep me awake all night."

"No. I heard a noise in the woods opposite, and I stood on the watch to see what it was, when that infernal owl gave one of his confounded screeches again, and it startled me so that

I jumped, and the rifle went off without any intention of firing on my part, and something, I should say a large animal by the sound, went crashing away through the bushes. I have half a mind to pepper away at that owl till I kill him," and the Parson gazed up threateningly at the pine, whose thick upper branches yet concealed the owl.

A NIGHT ALARM.

"Nonsense! Let the bird alone. He's only a little sociable," returned George, winking at Ned.

"Too sociable by half," grumbled Fred; "but it is one o'clock, so, Dick Burton, you can take your turn with the owl."

"And see," said George, as the boys lay down again, "if you can get through your watch without waking everybody up. We are getting nothing but cat-naps, any of us, and we shall all be as sleepy to-morrow as our friend the owl, who is undoubtedly wondering what kind of a racket we are carrying on down here."

For an hour Dick, who was a regular sleepy-head, resorted to various devices to keep awake, and as he would occasionally catch himself nodding, would get up and stir the fire, and wish the owl would screech again, if for nothing more than to keep him awake. Sitting down again, after a few moments' pacing before the camp, he began to nod, and in a few moments more he was sound asleep, and snoring like a major. And soon his restless brain began to work, and he dreamed he was chasing an owl, which was flying through the air; before he could catch it, the bird suddenly changed to a deer, upon which rode an Indian maiden, who, as she turned her head towards him, disclosed the features of Miss Arden. Startled by this discovery, he half awoke, and his fancy took a new turn. He imagined himself camping alone on the shore of a lake, with only his dog for a companion. He had just shot a brace of partridges, and hung them up in a tree. As he felt thirsty, he leaned his gun against it, left his game-bag lying on the ground, ordered the dog to keep watch of his things, while he went to the lake to procure a drink. His mouth was dry, and his tongue parched; as he lay down and bent over the water, it appeared like nectar to him. He had only taken a few swallows, when some one from behind gave him a push, and in he went all over. Struggling to get out, he awoke to find George shaking him, and the Parson and Ned standing by laughing. For a moment he was confused, but soon realized what had happened, and knew he was in for the five dollars.

"Supper at Young's for four," cried Ned delighted, as Dick with a gape and a stretch arose to his feet.

"All right, when we get home I'm your man. I fell asleep before I knew it. I had two funny dreams, though, and thought I was just scrambling out of a lake when George awoke me. What time is it?"

"Quarter of three," answered George; "and now lie down and get what sleep you can, for I shall call you promptly at four, for we must try and get back to the hotel before they send out a searching party after us."

Quiet again reigned in the camp, broken only by the heavy breathing of the tired sleepers, or George throwing more wood upon the fire. George's watch was an uneventful one, and he passed the whole of the time in carefully thinking over the way they had travelled the day before, and of the crooks and turns they had made. Although not a woodsman, George was level-headed; and if he was a city boy, would perhaps be better able to take care of himself, under the circumstances in which the party was placed, than some country boys, for he was particularly observant of men and things, and had read very extensively for a boy of his age, besides having a remarkable faculty for remembering what he had heard, and what he had read. After carefully reviewing in his mind their course of the day before, George came to the conclusion that he could find his way back to the hotel. At four o'clock daylight had dawned, and he awoke his friends, who quickly made ready for departure.

"I wish we had something to put this fire out with," remarked George, as he scattered the burning brands about, so they would deaden quicker.

"What for?" asked Dick. "What harm will it do to leave it?"

"It might do a great deal, if there should come up a heavy wind, and the woods catch fire."

"True enough. I didn't think of that. But as we have nothing to bring water in, you have taken all the precaution in our power."

"Yes, I have, and now we will be moving."

With their load as equally divided as possible, the boys started off, George in front. Avoiding the underbrush all they could, without going too far from what he considered the right course, he led the way at a rapid pace for about three hours, when he stopped to rest.

"Does any fellow remember what time it was when we passed the end of the pond yesterday, while on the track of the deer?" and George threw an inquiring glance at his friends.

"I think it was about two o'clock," said Dick.

"And it was seven when we found the deer. Then we camped three-quarters of a mile this side of the spot where he lay. We have now been travelling three hours, and a great deal faster than we did yesterday. According to my calculations, this ridge we are on was the first hill we crossed after leaving the pond, and nearly as I can recall, it is about a mile from the pond. If we can find that, we are all right. Dick, you are the youngest and lightest, and the best climber in the party; see if you can get to the top of that spruce, which seems to be the highest tree in this vicinity, and tell us what you see. Come along, and I will give you a boost."

Dick followed George to the spruce, which was about a foot in diameter, with limbs reaching to within twelve feet of the ground. Grasping the trunk as far up as he could reach, he gave a spring, and then George caught his feet and pushed him higher, and this aid enabled Dick to catch hold of the lower limb. From that moment it was child's play to him, as he was one of the best gymnasts in the Young Men's Christian Union, and he rapidly made his way to the top. Seating himself on a limb, he looked about him, and much to his joy, for he was beginning to feel hungry, he discovered the pond off to the right, but some way beyond them. It lay diagonally from the tree.

"I say, up there," hailed George. "Can you see anything you recognize?"

"Yes, sir! I 'see the pond, a mile or more away."

"In which direction?"

"Off to our right, in a diagonal course from here."

"Point exactly where it lays," and George pulled out a small pocket-compass he carried, which he had not thought of before, but which now came to him like an inspiration.

Dick did as requested, and George, stepping back a few feet from the tree, so that he could see better, took the point by compass.

SPYING THE COURSE.

"North-west by north. Come down, my boy, we are all right now. I'll bet a hat on it."

The moment Dick reached the ground, they all resumed their march, George watching the compass carefully. In half an hour they struck the pond, and then, knowing they were out of danger, they gave three hearty cheers to vent the exuberance of their feelings. Keeping along in sight of the water, they soon reached the path, finding their basket and rods just as they had left them the day before. Here they rested a few moments, and while they were congratulating each other on "finding themselves," as Dick jocosely put it, they heard the report of a gun a short distance beyond, from the direction in which the path led.

TO THE RESCUE.

"That is somebody after us, you may depend," said George. "Fire one barrel of your gun, Fred."

Pointing his gun in the air, the Parson pulled the trigger, and as the report and echo died away, they heard a second report from the same direction as the first. Picking up their loads once more, they started along the path towards the hotel, and in about fifteen minutes met the clerk and hostler of the hotel, who had been sent out to look them up. When they saw the venison, and the skin and head of the deer, their eyes opened wide with astonishment, and the clerk thought the boys rather smart to shoot a deer on their first trip away from the house. He felt relieved also that he had found the young fellows so readily, and that they were to all appearances safe and uninjured.

CHAPTER VI.

RETURN TO THE HOTEL. — OLD FRIENDS. — CLIMBING TABLE ROCK. — A PEEP AT THE SNOW CAVE. — VIEWING THE PROFILE. — A RAINY DAY. — A GLANCE AT PULPIT ROCK. — INSPECTING THE FLUME. — THE LOWER AND UPPER CASCADE.

"CHRISTOPHER COLUMBUS! I should like to know what has brought you out here at this time in the morning," said Dick jauntily,. as the two parties stood eying each other.

"You are pretty fellows to stay away all night and frighten everybody," said the clerk. addressing George as the eldest of the party; "we thought you were lost."

"Not exactly lost, but pretty near it," and George told him their story.

"You've had good luck anyhow. That is the first deer that has been shot around here this season to my knowledge, and you have some trout beside."

"Yes, sir, but I wish they were cooked. We are as hungry as bears."

"Perfectly wolfish," added Dick.

"Then the sooner we reach the house, the better for you;" and the clerk turned toward the hotel. "By the way," looking back at George and winking to him, "there were some friends of yours came to the house last night, and they seemed to feel very bad about your being lost."

A REUNION.

"Who are they?" asked George carelessly, although the gathering color in his face told his friends that he knew very well.

"A party from Berlin. Said they met you there at the Cascade House. Marston drove them up."

"How many are there in the party?" inquired Ned.

"Three gentlemen and their wives, and four young ladies."

"That gives us a chance, Ned," said the Parson, punching his friend in the ribs.

An hour more, and they had reached the hotel, but felt a little bashful when they found the piazza full of people. Miss Van Wyck and Miss Arden were among the number, and greeted them cordially, and then introduced them to their parents, also to Mr. and Mrs. Brown and their two daughters. Mr. Brown was a brother to Miss Arden's mother, and consequently the fair Grace and the two Miss Browns were cousins. Mr. Marston, who was among the party, greeted them cordially, and told them he was very glad they had returned safely.

George then begged they would excuse his party, that they might attend to their toilet and get some breakfast, confessing that they stood sadly in need of the latter.

"You are very excusable. Do go," said Miss Van Wyck, "you must be awful hungry."

The boys retired to their rooms, changed their clothes and washed; then repairing to the dining-room, ate such a breakfast that the cook was frightened, and she told the table-girl she hoped those fellows would not get lost again while they were at the Notch.

When the boys had appeased their appetites, they adjourned to the piazza, and were soon relating their story to the young ladies, who, with the old people, were attentive listeners.

Mr. Van Wyck complimented the boys highly on the faculty they had shown in finding their way out of the woods, and the young ladies thought the whole affair very romantic, and probably wished they had been participants.

After dinner the whole party walked to the Notch, and viewed the Profile and Pulpit Rock; then the old folks returned to the hotel, while the young people climbed the mountain on the north side to Columnar Rock, and spent an hour in that vicinity very happily. Ned early showed a partiality for Maud, the elder Miss Brown, while the Parson seemed quite contented to play cavalier to Miss Nellie, the younger, and this arrangement was very pleasant for the young people.

ON THE CLIFFS, DIXVILLE NOTCH.

The young ladies, when leaving the house, had expressed their intention of ascending to Table Rock, but after climbing up to Columnar Rock and scrambling back to the road, they concluded they were too tired to do any more sight-seeing until the next day. On their way back to the hotel Lucie informed George that she thought her folks would stop two weeks in the vicinity, and that they would visit the lakes in company with the boys; all of which was delightful news to George, and was received with pleasure by his three friends, when George told them. That evening the lads retired early, and Ned told the girls they were going to make up for the sleep they had lost the previous night. Just before dark Mr. Parsons started for Colebrook on some errand, and Dick asked him to take the skin and head of the deer, and wrote Norton a letter, in which he directed that the skin should be tanned and the head properly set up.

PROFILE, DIXVILLE NOTCH.

The next morning when the boys came down, they found the young ladies on the piazza, all looking more or less disappointed. A glance around showed the reason. The Notch had vanished, or, in other words, was enshrouded in a mantle of heavy clouds, which were even then weeping fine mist. Before breakfast was over, a steady, drizzling rain had set in, and although the clouds lifted partially toward noon, the rain continued all day with an exasperating steadiness. The young people made the best of the situation, and between reading, conversation, and music, worried through the day. Thursday morning was fine, and during the forenoon the whole party, young and old, made the ascent of Table Rock. The girls, as before, proved themselves good climbers, although the young gentlemen found several opportunities of rendering their fair companions assistance, which was accepted with becoming graciousness, accompanied by a fusillade of glances, that, as Ned roguishly asserted, "tore his heart to tatters." The Snow Cave was also visited by the party, and as they were quite moderate in their movements on account of the elder ladies, it was nearly noon when they returned to the hotel.

THE FLUME, DIXVILLE NOTCH.

The afternoon was passed at the house, most of it being devoted to croquet and lawn-tennis out of doors. In the evening, while they were gathered on the piazza, the elder people began speaking of the attractions of the Notch, and Mr. Arden declared that the scenery in the vicinity far surpassed, in alpine characteristics, anything he had seen in the White Mountain region.

Friday morning the whole party visited the Flume, at the eastern

DIX HOUSE, DIXVILLE NOTCH.

end of the Notch, the path leading in from the end of the road. The young people took a luncheon with them, intending to visit the Huntington Cascades, and return over the mountain. After stopping an hour at the Flume the party separated, the elder gentlemen telling the younger ones to look carefully after the young ladies, and not take them into any dangerous places. The old people returned to the hotel, the younger continuing on along the road through the Notch. Beyond the pass, on the left-hand side of the road, are the graves of some former residents of the valley, with tombstones giving their names and ages. The young people visited this miniature cemetery, and their laughter was momentarily hushed while reading the inscriptions of those whose crumbling remains reposed below.

Leaving the wayside graves the young people crossed to the other side of the road, and, passing through a charming grove of maples, reached Huntington Falls, a series of cascades that come laughing and tumbling down from the mountains above.

After enjoying a short rest at the foot of the Lower Cascade, they commenced to follow the stream up, climbing along the right-hand bank. There being no path, this was a work of labor, bordering very nearly on danger; for several times they came to places where the boys were put to their best

LOWER CASCADE, DIXVILLE NOTCH.

judgment to get the girls over, but by careful perseverance they succeeded without accident. Having stopped to inspect the Upper Cascade, and several times to rest, it was one o'clock when they reached the top of the mountain. On the summit they discovered a pretty spot, where the stream was nothing but a tiny rivulet issuing from a sparkling spring, surrounded by moss, under the shade of a large tree; and here they took their lunch. Their hunger appeased, they made their way slowly over the mountain, and veering toward the edge of the pass, soon came in sight of the road below, along which a carriage was passing. Dick called the attention of the others to the horses, which appeared no larger than rats. Following on until they came to Profile Cliff, they tried from the top to trace some resemblance to the huge stone face, serious and solemn, that looked down upon them when they had stood in the road. But they could not discern a single feature, and after fifteen minutes delay here they continued their course. In some places the top of the mountain was gullied back for several hundred feet, and they were obliged to make long detours to avoid these chasms. Not unfrequently, also, they found some deep holes among

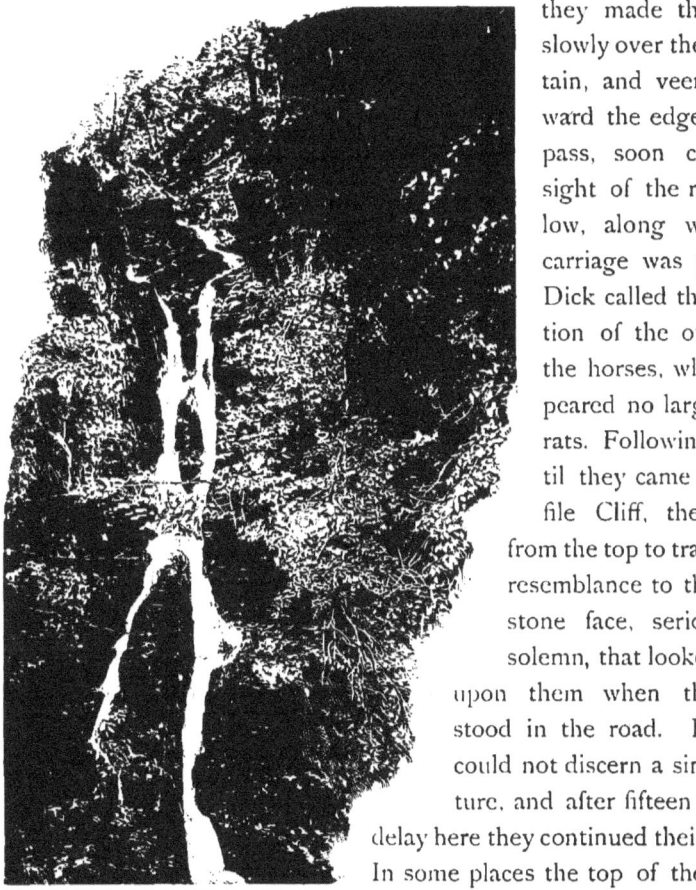

UPPER CASCADE, DIXVILLE NOTCH.

the uneven rocks forming the surface, and they had several narrow escapes from dropping into them. But the boys watched sharply, and thoroughly inspected every foot of the way, and they reached Table Rock without mishap, and descending to the road at this point, were soon at the hotel. It was five o'clock when the party reached the house, and they were all quite tired. The girls went up to their rooms to obtain a little rest before supper, and the boys turned into their hammocks for the same purpose.

Saturday, the young fellows, accompanied by the older gentlemen, went over to the pond for a day's fishing. They returned at night with over two hundred trout, well satisfied with their sport. During the evening it was arranged between the two parties that on Monday they would leave the Dix House, drive to Errol Dam, and take the steamer on the Androscoggin. Sunday was a day of rest with all, and a few short walks near the house was all the recreation they had out-doors. In the evening all the guests gathered in the parlor and had a praise meeting, and the music was enjoyed by all.

Monday morning Mr. Parsons had three teams harnessed and driven to the door. The large mountain wagon was occupied by the young folks, a smaller one by the old people, and the third vehicle was filled by the baggage. The moment the party were seated, the drivers started their horses, and the wagon containing the young folks took the lead. They had their last view of the crumbling cliffs, now wearing a familiar look, as they passed through the Notch, and were soon beyond its rocky portal, and out on the Clear Stream Meadows. Here there had once been a farm; but the former tillers of the soil had either died or moved away, and the cleared fields were fast returning to their original state of wilderness. Beyond the clearing they entered a piece of woods, and while passing through this forest, George called the attention of the girls to an eagle that stood poised on the edge of its nest, on a ragged limb, at the top of a high yellow birch standing on the side of the mountain.

"That is a bald eagle," observed the driver, "and a big one too, by mighty."

"I wish we were near enough to get a shot at him," remarked Dick.

"You will see plenty of them over on Umbagog," said the driver, "and probably you will get within reach of one of them."

Along their route the houses were widely scattered, and most of the farms showed evidence of having been reclaimed from the forest but a few years. Some were nothing but shanties built of odds and ends, old boards, poles, sawed and hewn timber all entering into their construction, while others were built of logs, mostly cut on or near the spot where the cabins stood. This primitive architecture greatly interested the young people, and they asked the driver many questions in regard to their construction. One especially attracted their attention, from the fact of a bear's skin being stretched upon it to dry, and turned the conversation on bears.

THE EAGLE'S NEST.

"Are there many about here, driver?" asked Miss Van Wyck.

"The woods are full of 'em."

At this startling announcement, which the girls took literally, they turned pale and looked somewhat alarmed, no doubt expecting to see some monstrous Bruin rush from the forest each moment and attack them. The boys, however, winked at each other and smiled.

"We did not see one while in the woods," dryly remarked George. "I guess this is not the right time of year for them."

"They generally keep out of a man's way when they can," declared the driver; "but all the farmers about here have lost sheep by bears killing them."

"Now, upon your word of honor," questioned Ned seriously, "did

ALONG CLEAR STREAM.

you ever know of one single bear being killed anywhere in this section of the country?"

"Did I?" returned the driver with an indignant look, and as a salve to his feelings, which were hurt by Ned's question, bringing his whip-lash down on the off leader's ear, on which a large moose-fly was feeding, and sending the fly to Jerico; "did I? Well, I should rather say I did."

"Tell us about it," urged Miss Arden.

"Why, a year ago, yes, less, only last November, the biggest black bear I ever heard of was started up, right here in this township, through which we are now driving, Millsfield, by a fellow who followed it all day, and tracked it into Errol. The next day he made up his mind that he would not follow Bruin any longer, and sold his chance in the animal to a fellow down there for a quarter. The second man, with his rifle and a box of cartridges, started after the bear, found the trail, and followed it. The animal had left an awful big track, and the fellow made up his mind that it was a Jumbo, and determined to have it. He followed the track about half an hour, and then came to a place where there was a lot of windfalls tumbled over. By the tracks in the snow, he knew that the bear had climbed over the tree trunks, and as it was hard getting around them or through them, he went the same way. He climbed across the trees, and reaching the last jumped down into a little hollow, and the bear reared up in front of him. The fellow was frightened just about to death, and he told Bill Bragg afterwards, he could feel his hair standing right up straight, and lifting his hat off his head. He knew he was in a tight place, and just as the bear, with an awful growl, was going to freeze to him, he lifted the rifle and pulled the trigger. And he was so near that the muzzle of the piece touched the bear when he fired. I tell you, 'twas a close call."

"Did he kill him?" asked George, breaking in.

"Yes. He happened to make a lucky shot, and killed him instantly. Couldn't done it hardly once in a hundred times. Then he skun him, and carried the hide to the hotel, and raised some help, and they went back and cut the bear up, and brought the meat out. The hunter made a good thing out of it too. For he got a bounty from the State of fifteen dollars for killing the bear, and he sold the

BEAR FIGHT.

skin to a man for twenty-five dollars, and then he sold the fat — there was a big washtub full of it — and two quarters of the meat for ten dollars more, so that he raked in about fifty dollars out of that bear's hide."

"I should have thought the other fellow would have been mad," observed the Parson.

ERROL DAM (1880).

"He was the sickest man you ever saw," chuckled the driver, "to think he had sold his right to that bear for a quarter."

"I hope we shall get a shot at one before we go home," said Dick.

"Hope you will," echoed the driver. "I should like to be around when you first saw the bear," and he laughed as if the idea suggested something funny to him.

The road along which they travelled was in good condition, and nearly level the greater part of the distance. On both sides were high mountains, that receded a little as they neared Errol, but the Clear Stream flowed merrily along but a short distance from the road, and often made a prominent feature of the landscape, which taken in its entirety the whole party declared charming. About eleven o'clock they came in sight of the Androscoggin and Bragg's Hotel. Just before reaching the covered bridge across the river, they had passed two roads, and the driver, being questioned by Dick about them, had told him that the one on the right followed the river down to Berlin, and that on the left led up to Errol Dam and the steamboat landing. A few minutes later, they had crossed the bridge, and were standing on the hotel piazza, awaiting the older members of the party. They were only fifteen minutes behind, but the baggage wagon did not arrive for an hour.

The landlord, a fat, jolly appearing fellow, stood in the doorway, and welcomed them heartily, and when asked if they could have dinner, remarked with a laugh, " that he guessed he could find a few crumbs for them."

Mr. Van Wyck told the landlord that they should leave all their baggage with him, except a few absolutely necessary articles, which they should take in hand-bags, while they made the tour of the lakes. He also wrote Mr. Marston, at Berlin, to send up a team for them the following Monday, as they would return that way, and after stopping with him a few days, make a trip through the mountains. The boys also arranged to leave their things in Mr. Bragg's care, until they went up the Magalloway on their camping trip.

After dinner they sat out on the piazza, and enjoyed the cool breeze, for the day was hot. The view from the house was quite pretty, taking in a long stretch of the river to the east. Behind the house the river enlarged to a pond known as Bragg's Bay, then narrowed up again, and ran smooth and silent for some miles beyond, until it was again broken up by flashing rapids.

Mr. Bragg notified his guests that they must leave his house by three o'clock to hit the steamer, and at that hour he harnessed a pair of horses to a three-seated wagon, and drove the ladies over to the landing, the gentlemen preferring to walk, as it was only a mile distant over a good road. When the boys reached the landing the steamer was just coming in sight. She was a larger boat than they had expected to see.

THE STEAMER DIAMOND.

"They are running the large steamer," said the landlord; "something must be the matter with the small one."

"Is there business for such a boat as that here?" asked Mr. Arden, turning to the landlord.

"Well, no, there ain't. They use that mostly in the spring for towing logs. It don't pay to run it for passengers."

The steamer swept by them on the opposite side of the river, then made a sharp turn and came in where they stood, bow up stream. There were six passengers on board, — two ladies and four gentlemen.

"That's a pretty good landing for you, Cap'n," laughed Mr. Bragg, as a young man came out of the wheel-house and descended by a ladder to the deck.

"Yes, it will do. Catch this bow-line, will you?" and the captain threw a coil of rope, which settled over the jolly landlord's head like a lasso.

"What shall I do with it?" queried the landlord, as he cleared the coil from his head.

"Make it fast to that stake behind you; or if you prefer," he replied, with an after-thought, "you can stand and hold it."

MAKING A LANDING.

"No, I guess I will hitch it. Where's the small steamer?"

"Down the lake. Any passengers to go?"

"Yes; don't you see the crowd I've brought?"

"I didn't know but what they came over just to see the boat. Two fellows came down with us who are going to Colebrook to-night. Can you put them through?"

"Yes, if Parsons don't want to carry them. He brought these people to my house, and has not started back yet."

"Will he wait till you return?"

"Yes, he agreed to. But what's the matter with the little boat?"

"The shaft is loose. We are going to fix it to-night;" and the captain turned away, and helped the engineer, the two comprising the whole crew, to bring off some trunks, and carry on the baggage for the boys and their friends, which they had cut down to a few light valises and their rods and guns.

The two gentlemen who had left the boat bade the captain good-by, and waved their handkerchiefs to the other passengers, as the steamer with a grim whistle swung out from the bank, and glided up the stream.

CHAPTER VII.

A TOUR THROUGH THE LAKES. — UMBAGOG. — MIDDLE DAM. — LAKE WE-LOKENNBACOOK. — MOLECHUNKAMUNK. — THE UPPER DAM. — MOOSE-LUCMEGUNTIC LAKE. — CUPSUPTIC. —INDIAN ROCK. — OQUOSSOC LAKE. — RANGELEY VILLAGE. — HAINES' LANDING. — ASCENT OF BALD MOUNTAIN. — RETURN TO UPPER DAM.

HEN the steamer was well away from the landing the party broke up and began to scatter about the boat; the older people going into the cabin where it was shady and cool, and the younger ones ascending to the hurricane deck, by a stairway leading from the after-part of the boat. From the upper deck they had a splendid view of the river, and after looking about them a few minutes they passed along to the wheel-house, the doors of which were open. This captain, a pleasant young man, dressed in a neat blue navy uniform, intimated that they might enter if they chose, and the young ladies availed themselves of the invitation, while the boys stood at the doors and kept up a running conversation with their fair friends and the captain.

"Where are we going now, captain?" questioned Miss Arden.

"Over to Sunday Cove."

"And where is that?" chimed in Miss Van Wyck.

"At the extreme upper end of the lake. It is where we connect with the buckboard for the Angler's Retreat and Middle Dam."

"How far is it?" asked Miss Nellie Brown.

"Ten miles from where you took the boat. Six up the river, and four across the lake to the landing."

"What time will you get there?" queried George.

"Half-past four. Then you have five miles to travel before reaching the Angler's Retreat."

"Did you receive a note from me, asking you to have the buckboard meet us at Sunday Cove?"

"I received a note from somebody. It was signed George Howe. Are you the gentleman?"

"Yes; and did you order the buckboard?"

"I did. It will be there probably before we are."

"Will it wait?" asked Maud anxiously.

"Certainly, miss."

"Is not this a large boat for two of you to run?" queried Dick, whose eyes had been roving from one end to the other of the steamer.

"Yes. It needs another man on her. But we seldom run her for passengers. We shall have the little boat on to-morrow, and two men can handle her like a fly. I have run her alone in an emergency."

"How many will she carry?" inquired Ned.

"Twenty comfortably, thirty with a little crowding. The company has another boat the same size on the Richardson Lakes, and when I was engineer on it, we carried forty-five one trip."

"The scenery is beautiful along this river, and how crooked it is," remarked Lucie.

"Yes, it is lovely," returned the captain, "but this river is not half so crooked as the Magalloway. There is one place on that where we have to run south to get north."

"How funny!" observed Grace, and they all laughed. "Do we go on it, captain?"

"Not to-day. We are going directly to the Cove. But we shall pass it. It empties into this river on the left-hand side, two miles below the outlet of the lake."

"You will take the trip up there when we come back," remarked George to the girls.

"Excuse my curiosity, but would you kindly inform me what those letters on your cap signify?" asked Nellie, who for the past ten minutes had been studying the captain's cap.

"They stand for the name of the company who own the steamers," answered the captain with a smile.

"And that is"—

"The Androscoggin Lakes Transportation Company."

"A long name," declared Dick. "I don't wonder they abbreviate it."

"Yes, it's long as the State liquor law," returned the captain.

"Do they own both the steamers on this lake?" inquired the Parson.

"Yes, and the two on the Richardson Lakes; and next winter they are going to build a boat to run on the Upper Magalloway."

"Is this the first boat that ever run here?"

"No. There were two before this. The Andrew Johnson and the Union. The Union was the pioneer steamer, and was nothing but an old scow with a wheel behind, and an upright boiler and engine in her. She would not make over four miles an hour. There is a picture, taken while she was steaming up the Magalloway," and the captain pointed to one side of the wheel-house.

The sketch so interested the Parson that he made a copy of it to take home with him.

"This is the prettiest sail I have ever taken," asserted Grace. "Just look, girls, at those reflections in the water. Aren't they splendid?"

"Just too lovely for anything!" declared Maud, who was apt to gush occasionally.

But the river deserved all the praise showered upon it. The wind had completely died away, leaving the surface of the water perfectly smooth, which reflected every tree and limb, every leaf and fern and blade of grass, that decorated and fringed its borders. It was like

THE OLD UNION: FIRST STEAMER EVER RUN ON ANDROSCOGGIN LAKES.

roaming through Paradise, floating over this mirrored stream, cut out of the densely wooded forests. The trees were of all varieties, in different stages of growth, many overhanging the banks of the river in graceful attitudes, and viewing themselves in the polished surface below them, like a society belle at her glass in self-worship, before attending a ball; some of the trees had long trailing moss hanging from their branches, suggesting the appearance of venerable Druids; others had been partially killed by the freshets of the spring and fall that covered their roots, and now appeared like paralytics, one side green and smiling, the other withering and dead; along the river banks, ofttimes at the very water's edge, wild flowers, ferns, and tufted grasses, also bushes bearing handsome berries of various colors, modestly asserted the charm of their presence, and all united to make up an indescribable spell, the effects of which were not destroyed in a moment.

As the steamer approached a sharp bend in the river, the captain rang the bell, and the boat began to move slower.

"What is that for?" inquired George.

"Shoal and rocky. That point on the left ahead is Quickwater Point. It is the shallowest place in the river, and a rocky bar runs clear across the river there. When the water is low we generally slow down here, so that if we should touch bottom the boat would not be injured."

QUICKWATER POINT.

The dangerous place was soon passed, and the steamer increased her speed again, and puffed and panted more vigorously than ever.

A short distance beyond they passed the mouth of the Magalloway River, and just as they shot by it they were treated to a laughable sight. A rowboat containing four men was drawn up beside the bank, and one of them, who had on long-legged rubber boots, stepped outside of the boat on a rock, the water reaching about to his knees. As the steamer passed he turned to watch it, but his feet slipped off the rock, and in he went all over, to his own discomfiture no doubt, but to the evident enjoyment of his companions, whose faces assumed a broad grin, while the passengers on the steamer laughed in sympathy.

"That fellow has taken a bath," observed George, when he could stop laughing long enough to speak.

"Yes, he was sprawled out like a frog," remarked the captain, and laughingly added, "he will find that is wet water he has fallen into."

"Is he in any danger?" inquired Lucie.

"Not a bit," said Dick. "Don't you see, he has hold of the boat, and they are pulling him in."

"That is the biggest fish they will catch this trip," and the captain threw the wheel to port, as the steamer turned another bend in the river.

The boat had now reached a part of the stream where the water-lilies grew in great abundance, close in to the banks of the river. In fact, the water was carpeted with them on each side for two miles, and the air was full of their fragrance.

A delighted scream broke from the girls as they saw them.

"Oh, what lovely lilies!"

"Aren't they fragrant!"

"Can't we get some?"

"Oh, how beautiful!" and similar exclamations were quickly uttered, and they looked with such wistful eyes at the watery flower-bed, that the captain would have been very ungallant had he not taken the hint.

Giving the steamer a slant towards the starboard bank of the river, he rang the bell to stop; the engineer responded, and the boat ranged up alongside the lilies.

"Get a pail-full of those lilies, York," sang out the captain.

"All right, sir," and the engineer went to the starboard gangway, turned up his shirt-sleeves, and quickly gathered a water-pail full of the beautiful blossoms. The boys, who had gone down to pick a few for themselves, found there was no necessity for it, the engineer had obtained so many; and thanking him kindly, they carried the pail to the wheel-house, and the young ladies made the flowers up into bunches.

The captain rang the bell to "go ahead slow," then for "full speed," and again they were turning and twisting along the river. The young ladies were profuse in their thanks for his kindness in stopping the steamer, and he told them they were welcome.

EAGLE POINT, MOUTH OF SUNDAY COVE.

They had now reached a part of the river banks which for years had been overflowed at high water, killing nearly all the trees, and robbing them of their foliage, and beyond these the lake was seen, stretching off on either hand to the north and south. The dead forests gave a romantic appearance to the scene near them. The trees were of all kinds, sizes, and shapes; some shooting straight into the air, as naked as a vessel's spars when they are first set up; others branching out like huge umbrellas, knotted and gnarled; some merely barren stumps, and others, whose roots were partially uncovered, leaning over at every conceivable angle. Sailing through here in the spring at high water, is like navigating a submerged forest; but now the water had fallen, until it was inside the river banks in all but a few places. As the steamer glided on, the captain showed them a channel called the Richardson Carry, where the stumps had been cut out, and where in high water they could run the boat across, thereby saving a couple of miles on the distance to Sunday Cove. As the steamer approached the lake they scanned the scenery closely, and all thought they had never beheld a prettier view than that off to the south-east, where towered a number of large mountains, Saddleback and Speckled being the most prominent. As the boat ran out into the lake, leaving the marshy outlet behind, they found themselves literally surrounded by mountains, enclosing the lake on every hand. Peaks of all shapes and heights in the foreground, from the round-topped Moose Mountain to the wedge-shaped Dustan, while in the background to the north, the large double peaks of Aziscohos rose above all others in that direction, and in the south the three gigantic peaks of the White Mountains, Washington, Jefferson, and Adams, loomed grandly up, cleaving the blue sky with their white crests.

AZISCOHOS MOUNTAIN FROM LAKE UMBAGOG.

A FISHERMAN'S SPOILS, MIDDLE DAM.

"What a splendid view we have of the White Mountains from here!" remarked Grace.

"Lovely," echoed Lucie.

"We have a finer view of the White Mountains from this lake than from any other in the chain," added the captain.

"How far off do you suppose they are in an air line, Captain?" queried Ned.

"From what I know of the country, I should say about forty miles. You see that sharp-peaked mountain in the north-west," indicating Dustan, "it stands behind the Magalloway River. The sag you see in the land along there is the valley, and our landing is nearly opposite that mountain."

"Mount Dustan does not look to be very far from here," said Dick.

"About eight or ten miles as the crow flies. But the way we go on the steamer, it is double that distance."

The boat was now heading off to the right, and the captain showed them Sunday Cove, and said it was just a mile from Eagle Point at the mouth, to the landing at the end of the cove.

The young people now went below and paid a visit to those in the cabin.

"How do you like it, Mr. Van Wyck?" asked George, addressing his elderly friend, who was comfortably reclining on a settee, and watching the panorama through the open windows.

"Very much. The sail on the river was fine. Talk about the St. John River in Florida, it don't begin to have the beauty of the Androscoggin."

"And the captain says the Magalloway is prettier," chimed in Lucie.

"Then we must certainly visit it when we return. The sail across this lake is delightful too. I should like to see the whole of it."

"Perhaps you can when we return," remarked George.

The steamer now sounded a long blast from her whistle, and they could see they were leaving the main body of the lake rapidly behind.

"We are almost at the landing," observed Ned, "and we shall soon have a chance to earn our supper."

"Five miles is not much of a walk," said Dick.

"It may not be for you, young gentleman," put in Mr. Arden dryly, "but I guess it is all we old fellows care to take."

"I am going to walk part of the way, father," said Miss Van Wyck; "in fact, we girls will have to, for the team will not carry but five besides the driver."

"Then you can take turns at riding."

The boat in a few moments more was at the landing, which consisted of a huge sloping ledge furnished by Nature. This shelved away from the water so sharply that the guard of the steamer lapped over it, and from the forward gangway they were enabled to step directly on shore without need of a gang-plank. A very convenient landing, as Mr. Arden remarked. The team was just coming down a steep pitch, that terminated in a few feet of level ground.

"Come, come, Mr. Brooks, this won't do," said the captain jokingly, as the driver jumped off the team, "you must get along earlier than this."

"I'm here soon as you are."

"We've been here half an hour," said the captain, laughing.

"In a horn you have," retorted the driver, "you haven't got the boat hitched up yet. There's York just tying the stern line now."

"He's only changing it from that rock to a stump."

"Perhaps he is. That's a little too thin. Any trunks?" *sotto voce*.

"No. Nothing but grips."

"Sensible people. Where are they going?"

"I don't know. Up the lake somewhere."

"The baggage is all off, Captain," reported the engineer.

"Well, we must wood up," and the captain turned away, and with the engineer directly busied himself in carrying on wood from a pile near the boat.

The driver now turned his team and buck-board, and began loading the baggage, the smallest pieces being put in boxes under the

CAMPING OUT ON MIDDLE DAM CARRY.

seats, while the larger valises were tied on the hind part of the vehicle with ropes.

"We may as well start along," proposed Mr. Van Wyck to his friends, "and leave the boys to take care of the ladies and the baggage." And the three gentlemen, after inquiring about the road, began climbing the hill before them.

Meanwhile the wagon was loaded. That is to say, the baggage was

OUTLET OF THE POND IN THE RIVER.

put on, and the elder ladies helped to seats. But the girls objected when asked to ride, saying they would much rather walk. Accordingly, when the driver was ready, the young people started ahead, laughing and joking, and talking over the events of the day. There had been no rain in the locality for nearly a month, and the young folks found it very comfortable walking. The road ran through a heavy forest all the way, and it was much warmer than it had been out on the lake. They had several fine views of a river on their way, to the right, and the driver informed them it was the connecting link between the two lakes, and was known as Rapid River.

A little more than half-way to the hotel they stopped for a few moments to rest, at a neat building, known as the Oxford Club Camp, pleasantly located beside the river. Not more than quarter of a mile beyond they passed another small camp, with its name, "Forest Lodge," painted on the side next the road. From the piazza of this little building they had a long view up the river, and the young people pronounced it charming. The Parson declared his intention of making a sketch there when they returned.

Soon after leaving Forest Lodge they caught up with the three gentlemen, and they continued their way together. Mr. Van Wyck asked the girls if they were not tired, and they all declared they were feeling splendid, and enjoying the walk very much. Within a quarter of a mile of the hotel, they passed the camp of a party of fishermen, who they afterwards learned were from Connecticut. The camp was deserted, with the exception of the cook and two guides, the members of the party being out fishing at some of the places near. It was seven o'clock when they reached the Angler's Retreat, they having walked across the carry in a little over two hours. The team came in directly behind them. There were only six guests at the house that night, and they had no difficulty in getting rooms. They were all very hungry, and, after attending to their toilets, descended to the dining-room and had a good supper, to which they did ample justice. After appeasing their hunger, they rested a while on the piazza, and all retired early.

The next morning the boys were up at five o'clock, and going over to the dam, caught half a dozen nice trout for breakfast. Just as they

ANGLER'S RETREAT, MIDDLE DAM, LAKE WELOKENNEBACOOK.

stepped upon the piazza, the girls made their appearance, and were delighted with the fish, one that weighed three pounds being the largest brook trout they had ever seen.

" Who caught the large one?" asked Lucie.

" Fred was the lucky fellow," answered George, and the boys passed along to the kitchen, and asked the cook to fry the fish for their breakfast.

A MIDDLE DAM TROUT.

Returning to the girls, they invited them to inspect the old camp, and take a look at the dam before breakfast. The young ladies were quite willing to accept the invitation, and they started at once, the Parson leading the way.

George, who had become intimate with the contents of the guide-book, gave them considerable information about the old house, and the palmy days of the fishermen, before they were bothered by the appearance of ladies at the lakes, and also gave them some interesting facts about the dam, its cost, the time required to build it, etc. After viewing the dam from each side of the outlet, they returned to the house and found breakfast ready, and the elder people awaiting them. At eight o'clock they embarked on the steamer Welokennebacook, named after the lake they were on. A smaller boat, the Molechunkamunk, lay at the wharf, which the captain informed them was named after the lake above the Narrows. The boat was about to start when they noticed some one running from the Middle Dam, swinging his hat and shouting. A nearer approach showed it to be the Parson, who had been over there making a sketch of the dam, and who had not realized that it was time for the steamer to leave. This dam and the others of the chain have since been rebuilt.

THE OLD MIDDLE DAM.

"You came near being left, young man," said the captain pleasantly, as Fred, almost breathless, jumped on the steamer, while she was backing out from the wharf.

"Yes, but a miss is as good as a mile."

The boat made a half-circle, then the engines were reversed, and the swift little steamer shot ahead, the captain laying his course for the Narrows.

It was a lovely morning, with just breeze enough to ripple the water, and the whole party expressed themselves delighted with the scene around them. From the foot of the Narrows they had a fine view of the White Mountains, but not so complete as that from Umbagog. Speckled and Saddleback Mountains in Grafton Notch also formed a prominent and pleasing feature of the landscape, and between Jackson Point and the Narrows the Parson made a sketch of the lake and mountains. At the foot of the Narrows they saw two loons, and for fifteen minutes the boys bombarded

OLD MIDDLE DAM CAMP.

them, without any result beside wasting cartridges. Occasionally, one of the loons would dive, and when he reappeared, give utterance to a mocking cry, and the girls declared the loons were making fun of the marksmen.

"Are there many loons shot on the lake?" inquired Lucie of the captain.

"I should say not. From what I can judge from observation, I think it takes about one thousand shots for every dead loon. They have a way of diving at the flash of a gun, which makes it difficult to kill them. Yet there are times when one is shot at the first trial, and the funniest loon story I ever read or heard is given in the 'Androscoggin Lakes Illustrated.'"

The strait or sound known as the Narrows, through which the steamer was passing, is two miles long, and from an eighth of a mile to a mile wide. Before the building of the new Middle Dam, a natural wall of rocks that extended along the north shore was always in sight

LAKE WELOKENNEBACOOK FROM ANGLER'S RETREAT.

at a medium or low stage of the water, but the building of the new dam, since the date of this story, has changed the appearance of the two Richardson Lakes very much, and in some places completely blotted out the old landmarks.

Near the head of the Narrows the captain pointed out Metallak Point on the right, with its beautiful sandy beach, telling them it was named for an Indian who once lived on it. As they came out into the upper lake the Parson made a sketch of it. The lake opened handsomely, stretching away toward the north-west for eight miles, the shore line being bow-shaped. Several camps and many high mountains now came into view, and the captain was kept busy, by different members of the party, answering questions about what they saw. The boat was bound for the head of the lake, and this gave the party an opportunity of seeing more than they otherwise would. A handsome summer cottage near where the steamer made a landing, the captain informed them belonged to a wealthy Boston gentleman, and was very appropriately named after the white birches by which it was surrounded, Birch Lodge. It commanded a fine view down the lake, and also of the highest mountain in the lake region, Aziscohos, and its near neighbor, Observatory.

Leaving Birch Lodge the steamer ran down on the opposite side of the lake, giving them a fine view of the range of mountains to the east, known as the Elephant Mountain range.

LAKE MOLECHUNKAMUNK FROM METALLAK POINT.

The steamer had run but a short distance when they noticed a boat containing a lady and gentleman close in by the shore; near them towered an old dead pine, on top of which was a heron's nest, but the bird was not to be seen. Just below here, they passed the mouth of a brook where some parties had gone for fishing, two boats being in sight. Farther down they passed on the left, a barren point, showing marks of fire, on which stood a small, neat cottage, belonging to another visiting sportsman. A short distance below they reached the stream, through which flowed the waters of the upper lakes. Gliding swiftly by this they soon came in sight of Camp Bellevue, a cluster of log and frame buildings, belonging to a party of Philadelphia gentlemen, who, with their families, spend a large part of the summer in this beautiful spot. While the boat was passing this camp, the captain rang to "slow down," and a minute later to "stop," and the steamer glided gently alongside the wharf at the Upper Dam landing. From this point the party obtained two very fine views, one up, and the other down, the lake.

VIEW DOWN LAKE MOLECHUNKAMUNK FROM BIRCH LODGE.

The captain told them the Oquossoc, on which they were to take passage for Indian Rock, was not in, and they waited on the steamer while the Parson made some sketches. Just as he put up his book and pencil, the other boat whistled, and they walked across the road to the Upper Dam, about an eighth of a mile distant. They found the steamboat fastened to a little pier above the dam, and asked the captain what time it left for Indian Rock. He answered about half-past three, but that he would leave in a few minutes for Bemis Stream. As the party did not care to make so long a wait at the Upper Dam, the boys coaxed the captain to take them to Indian Rock; and this after a little argument he consented to do, and he informed George he would start in half an hour. Mr. Van Wyck told him they would take a look at the dam and buildings, and if they were not at the boat when he was ready to leave, to whistle for them, and they would come at once.

The half-hour was pleasantly occupied in an inspection of the dam and hotel, and reading up on the subject from their guide-books. The Parson, who became more enthusiastic over the country with each day of his sojourn, sketched away as if working on a wager, catching a view down the river from the middle of the dam, with a fisherman in the foreground, on one of the piers, making a very pretty picture. In one of the camps he found a photograph of the large trout taken at the dam the year before by two Boston gentlemen, and made a copy of it. The boys fell into conversation with a fellow who was fishing near the dam, and he gave them a great deal of information about the trout fishing, also told them of the lumber operations conducted in the vast territory around them, intimating that if they wished to see one of the most interesting sights of the region, they should be there during the month of June, and watch the bateaux and the logs run through the sluice of the dam. A very interesting account of this exciting business is given in Farrar's "Androscoggin Lakes Illustrated."

THE HERON'S NEST.

A whistle from the little steamer now warned them it was time to leave, and hastening to the boat they embarked. The steamer quickly brought them in sight of the lake proper, about a mile from the landing. As the boat passed out of Trout Cove they had Brandy Point on their left, the two largest islands in the lake, known as Student's and Toothaker's, in front of them, and Bemis Bay and stream off to the right. Across the lake they could see Bald Mountain, a rugged, round-topped peak, descending to the water's edge,

BROOK FISHING, LAKE MOLECHUNKAMUNK.

and at its base Camp Allerton nestled among the trees. To the left of Camp Allerton, Richardson's Hotel at Haines's Landing stood out with prominence, and near it were two smaller camps owned by private parties. Far in the north were the Deer and Kennebago Mountains, the former sloping gradually down to Cupsuptic Lake.

The day was lovely, the sky so clear they could see a long distance, and the sail was very enjoyable. When they passed through Cupsuptic Narrows, the captain pointed out the camp of Hon. William P. Frye, charmingly located upon Eagle Point. Here the well-known and talented senator retires for a few weeks each season, shaking off for the nonce the harassing cares of public business, and devoting the time to rest from his labors, and to angling for the wary trout, and returns to Congress a new man, and abundantly able to wrestle with the Tariff and Civil Service Reform. Dame Rumor says that the senator is an expert angler, and as he has been a devotee at the shrine of the trout for many years, we have no doubt she is correct. His wife often accompanies him on these fishing excursions, and any one who has been fortunate enough to have accepted their hospitality when this charming and estimable lady was present to do the honors of the camp, will be sure to treasure it as one of the brightest hours in their lives.

AZISCOHOS MOUNTAIN FROM UPPER DAM LANDING.

Swinging away from Eagle Point, the steamer turned up the narrow river forming the outlet of Kennebago and Oquossoc Lakes, and was soon at the wharf in front of the Indian Rock Camps. Here is the junction of the two streams flowing from the lakes mentioned above; Indian Rock, from which the locality derives its name, is a flat ledge on the right bank of the river, opposite the steamboat landing, and is neither romantic nor suggestive. The buildings of the Oquossoc Angling Association are on the left-hand bank of the river, prettily situated on high ground, a few rods from the water. Toward these the party directed their steps, and finding the superintendent, were invited to look the buildings over, which they did.

George made some inquiries about dinner, and learned that only the members of the club and their friends were entertained there. The superintendent informed them that they could procure dinner at the hotel near the foot of Oquossoc Lake, about two miles distant, and directed them how to reach it. The path led from the opposite side of the river, and was sufficiently distinct for any one to follow it. After thanking the gentleman for his information, the party returned to the river and saw that the steamboat had gone. Accordingly, the boys had the fun of ferrying their friends across in a scow, and although the girls enjoyed it, the elder ladies did not seem to think much of the arrangement. The Parson, busy as ever, succeeded in getting a sketch of the junction of the rivers, also a general view of the camps.

UPPER DAM CAMPS.

Leaving Indian Rock behind them, they struck into a path which might have been better, and might have been worse, running through the woods. The wind did not get into the forest much, and they found it decidedly hot. After an hour's slow walking they reached the little wharf at the foot of Oquossoc Lake. Here they came upon a camping party, who had just landed from a new boat, and who were starting with their things for Haines Landing, a mile and a half

FRYE'S CAMP, EAGLE POINT, LAKE CUPSUPTIC.

distant, on the shore of Mooselucmeguntic Lake. They made a comical appearance as they staggered along under their burdens, accompanied by a small black and tan dog, who, from his incessant barking, seemed to thoroughly enjoy the occasion.

Dick asked one of the camping party how they could reach the hotel. He told them, if they blew a blast upon a horn hanging near by, a boat would come from the hotel for them. Thereupon the boys began exercising their lungs with the horn, and the whole party became merry over it, as the girls tried to sound it, but with ill success. After a while the boat came, but could only carry five, and the three gentlemen with Mrs. Van Wyck and Mrs. Arden went in it. When the boatman returned he brought another boat with him, and the balance of the party were enabled to go at the same time, avoiding another twenty minutes' wait. They passed a pretty little cottage on their left on their way to the hotel; it stood on a point jutting out into the lake, and the grounds about it had been neatly cleared up. As they reached the wharf in front of the hotel, they saw the steamer a short distance away just coming in. They went up to the Mountain View House and registered their names, then returned to the piazza to see if there was any one among the steamer's passengers whom they knew. But the arrivals were all strangers to them.

THE MEETING OF THE WATERS.

It was now half-past twelve, and they were getting hungry; just as George was starting to stir the landlord up on the dinner question, the bell rang, and they gladly responded to its invitation. After dinner they embarked on the steamer that left for Greenvale, at the head of the lake.

When the writer first visited Rangeley, or Oquossoc Lake, to give it its proper name, the only camp at the outlet was a small story-and-a-half building, kept by old Uncle George Soule (as every one called him), one of the best guides in the country. It had only accommodations for a dozen people, and everything around the house was in a very primitive state. Below is a picture of the old camp, engraved form a photograph made on my first trip. After the steamer was

CAMP HENRY.

placed on Oquossoc Lake, the travel increased, and the accommodations of the camp became inadequate to the demands of sportsmen. It was then that Mr. Henry Kimball bought out Uncle George's interest in the camp and landing, and built the commodious hotel now known as the Mountain View House, capable of accommodating about seventy-five guests. A carriage road runs from the house to the village of Rangeley, seven miles distant.

The course of the steamer carried them along the northern shore of the lake, giving them a fine view of the surrounding mountains. Unlike the other lakes in the chain, Oquossoc has a great many farms upon its borders, more than half its shores being cleared land, and therefore has not the wild appearance of the others, which are entirely surrounded by forests. The boat did not stop at the village of Rangeley on its way up the lake, but ran straight to Greenvale, the landing at the upper end. It stopped here an hour, giving our party time to go on shore and inspect the Greenvale House and its sur-

RANGELEY OUTLET.

roundings. The hotel is small but comfortable, and is the headquarters of a great many fishermen in the months of June and September. The younger people in the party also visited a cascade near by, with which they were greatly pleased, and gave a glowing description of its beauties to the old people when they returned.

When the passengers and baggage brought by the stage from Phillips had been loaded, the whistle was sounded, and the boys and their friends hurried down to the steamer. Going out of the river the steamboat grounded on a bar at its mouth, and for half an hour various unsuccessful attempts were made to get her afloat; but finally perseverance triumphed, and the boat was headed for Rangeley "City," a nickname for the village. The distance was three miles, and in half an hour from the time they left the bar they were landed at the little pier in Rangeley.

They found a team from the Rangeley Lake House; and delivering their baggage to the driver, the whole party walked up to the hotel, that stood but a short distance from the wharf. Here they were to stay until the next morning. After they had been shown rooms, they hired a couple of teams and drove to a high hill a mile or so from the hotel, commanding a fine prospect of the lake and a large part of the surrounding country. The best view they obtained from

RANGELEY DAM, AT FOOT OF OQUOSSOC LAKE.

a field a few rods from the road; and the Parson, who had brought his sketch-book along, made a very creditable attempt in transferring the landscape before them to its pages. From this point they also had a fine view of Ram Island, the largest island in the lake. An attempt was made a few years ago to build a large hotel on this island, but the projectors of the enterprise finally abandoned it from want of faith in its financial success. After an hour spent on the hill in a pleasant manner, they returned to the hotel.

A party of half a dozen gentlemen and two ladies had just come out from Kennebago Lake, and were going to stop at the house over night. After supper the boys and their friends entered into conversation with the party from Kennebago, and heard the story of their experiences in the wilderness. The party had camped out, having carried tents with them. One of the gentlemen said that fish, small ones, had been very plenty, and flies and midges plentier, and gave them a graphic and humorous account of one night's experience, when

LAKE POINT COTTAGE.

they were kept awake all night by these pests. He advised the boys, if they had any thought of going to Kennebago, not to visit it before September, if they wished to have any peace, and showed them a sketch he had made of the night attack of the midges. This pleased the Parson so much that he begged leave to copy it, and the gentleman kindly allowed him to do so. Later in the evening the whole party amused themselves with singing, and when they broke up to retire for the night, they all felt like old friends. It does not take long to make acquaintances in the backwoods, and the most of the tourists who visit the lakes are cultivated and travelled people, with whom it is a pleasure to meet and converse.

An early breakfast was served to our party, who left on the boat at half-past six. They had been well pleased with their hotel accommodations, and promised the landlord to visit him again some day. They reached the landing at the outlet at half-past seven, and found a team by which they sent their valises and bags across to Richardson's, while they walked, the distance being a mile and a half. They followed the same road they had travelled the day before for a short distance, and then reached a sign-board pointing to a road on the left,

RANGELEY LAKE AND RAM ISLAND.

and directing to the Moose-look-me-gun-tic House at Haines' Landing, on the shore of the Great Lake, as this, the largest of the chain, is sometimes called.

The carry was none too good, and the ladies found a great deal of fault with it ; but as all things have an end, so, too, did this carry, and after a slow walk of three-quarters of an hour, they were rewarded with a sight of the lake, and a few moments after were at the camp. Two other people, a lady and gentleman, had crossed the carry with them, and were going down to the Upper Dam on the steamer which was lying at the wharf in front of the camp. The steamer left immediately after the two passengers had embarked, and George told the captain that his party would go down with him the next morning.

Mr. Richardson, the proprietor of the hotel at Haines' Landing, gave them a warm welcome, and made them feel at home. He

CAMP KENNEBAGO, INDIAN ROCK.

showed them to pleasant front rooms overlooking the lake, with which the ladies were greatly pleased. The hall in the second story opened out on an upper piazza, making a delightful place for the party to sit and chat. During the forenoon the three elder gentlemen, accompanied by guides, went out on the lake for deep-water fishing, and returned at noon with five trout weighing from one to three-and-a-half pounds. The young people lounged about the hotel during the forenoon, and George, who was seeking information from Mr.

Richardson, learned that by rowing down to the Allerton place, a mile or two below, they could make the ascent of Bald Mountain from that point very easily.

George then made a proposition to his young friends to spend the afternoon in making an ascent of the mountain, which they eagerly accepted, and invited Mr. Richardson to accompany them, and after a little persuasion he agreed to make one of the party. At dinner the talk of the young people was about the mountain trip, and the girls'

Mooselucmeguntic House, Haines' Landing.

parents became interested in the matter; and Mr. Van Wyck, learning from Richardson that the ascent was not very fatiguing, concluded, after talking with the other two gentlemen, that the whole party would go.

Immediately after dinner three boats were made ready, and the party embarked, Mr. Richardson rowing one boat, George and Dick the second, and Ned and the Parson the third. There was only a slight ripple on the water, the lake being quite smooth, and the ladies, old and young, enjoyed the ride down to Bugle Cove very much. The party landed just below the immense ledge on which the camp stands, and clambering up the rough path, reached the piazza of the house, where they sat down for a few moments. The camp was closed, the owner not visiting it that season. The view from Allerton Lodge is one of the finest about Mooselucmeguntic, and second only to that from Haines' Landing. It commands a large part of the lake, with a fine chain of mountains for a background. While the party were chatting on the piazza, the parson whipped out his sketch-book, and quickly made a copy of the

ALLERTON LODGE, BUGLE COVE.

landscape before them. The sketch finished, Mr. Richardson led the way to a path behind the camp; and the real business of the trip commenced. Although steep, the path was not difficult; and whenever they reached a windfall, or obstructions of a kindred nature, their host, who had brought an axe with him expressly for that purpose, would remove the obstacles, thus making the climb easier for the ladies. The distance to the summit from where the first view is obtained is about a mile; but, owing to the frequent stops to clear the path, an hour was taken in the ascent. The path was originally cut out by Jerry Ellis, a Rangeley guide, who for several years had charge of Allerton Lodge, and who also cut out four places on different parts of the mountain from which the surrounding country could be overlooked.

Through the first of these vistas could be seen the lower end of Lake Mooseluemeguntic, including the long sweep of Bema Bay, with Student and Toothaker Islands, — spots of emerald amid the watery waste. Beyond the southern shore of the lake, across the narrow border of forest, a portion of the Richardson Lakes shimmered in the sunlight; beyond, another strip of green, and then like a silver

LAKE MOOSELUCMEGUNTIC.

ribbon, fluttering in the wind, appeared the narrow and crooked Umbagog, most beautiful of all these lakes ; at the foot of Umbagog the little hamlet of Lakeside, with its excellent hotel nestling at the foot of Hampshire Hill, and in the farthest distance the grand chain of the White Mountain peaks closing the view in that direction.

From this point the party followed Mr. Ellis' trail across the mountain-top, bearing to the east, and reached the second opening. This brought in sight the whole of Bema Bay, with Bemis Stream cutting into the forest from the end. The cluster of log cabins a few rods from the lake look like brown spots, and are almost lost in the forest. A turn to the left discloses a part of Oquossoc Lake, including South Cove and South Bay Island; the farms along its shores detract from the romance and wildness of the view, but make the picture more suggestive of civilization. The Saddleback Range in the direction of Phillips, and the twin peaks of Mount Bigelow toward Kingfield, are the prominent heights from this point.

Another short walk and the party reached the third vista through the mountain forest, and beheld spread out before them nearly the whole of Oquossoc Lake, with the village of Rangeley on its northern shore, and the farms adjacent. The East and West Kennebago Mountains, thickly wooded, form the background of this picture, while almost under foot are the outlet of the lake and the Mountain View House, the hotel a mere speck on the landscape. Turning westward, a few minutes' walk brought the party to the last of the little clearings. From here you have the finest picture of the four, as the view includes the whole of the northern wilderness stretching away to Canada, whose mountains cleaving the blue sky for many

VIEW AT BEMIS STREAM.

miles impose an impenetrable barrier in that direction. The upper part of the lake, with its cluster of islands, Cupsuptic Narrows, Haines' Landing with Richardson's Camp, Frye's Camp on its rocky bluff, Eagle Point just above, the whole of Cupsuptic Lake, Birch Island, Deer Mountains, the clearing at Indian Rock, with Camp Kennebago, West Kennebago Mountain, and several of the Boundary peaks, form the line between American and British possessions. The symmetrical, round-topped peak of Observatory Mountain, and the giant peaks of Aziscohos, the monarch of the hills in this region, are also brought within range from this point of observation. From here a walk of twenty minutes brought the party to the foot of the mountain; and, after a short rest, they again embarked in the rowboats, and returned to Richardson's, reaching the hotel at six o'clock, all delighted with their excursion. Supper, for which they all felt a craving after their romantic scramble, a fine sunset view from the piazza, and several songs in the evening, completed a most satisfactory day.

CAMP AZISCOHOS, MOLECHUNKAMUNK LAKE.

The next morning at half-past eight they bade Mr. Richardson farewell, and went on board the steamer. They had been much pleased with their stay at Haines' Landing, and expressed their regret to their pleasant and obliging landlord at having to leave him so soon. The team from the other lake now arrived; and the driver informing the captain there were no passengers to come, the lines were hauled in, and the boat steamed toward the Upper Dam.

CLEFT ROCK, BEMIS STREAM.

CHAPTER VIII.

UPPER DAM TO SOUTH ARM. — BUCKBOARD RIDE. — DEVIL'S OVEN. — — BLACK BROOK NOTCH, DEVIL'S DEN. — HERMIT FALLS. — SILVER RIPPLE CASCADE. — A NIGHT IN ANDOVER. — A JOLLY RIDE. — A PICNIC DINNER. — SIGHTS BY THE WAY. — THE LAKESIDE HOTEL. — CAMBRIDGE. — LAKE UMBAGOG. — STEAMER PARMACHENEE.

"DO you think we can catch any trout at Upper Dam, Captain, before the Welokennebacook arrives?" inquired Dick, as the steamer came in sight of the dam.

"No, you will not have time; the other boat is probably there now, and they will leave at once after we get in."

"We have been just an hour and a quarter coming down," remarked George, as the steamer was made fast to the pier.

"Pretty fair run," said the Parson.

The party exchanged greetings with the captain, who had been very pleasant to them, and then walked to the other boat. Arriving at the wharf they learned from Captain Emerson that the engineer, who had gone over to the camp for the mail, had not returned, and they had a wait of fifteen minutes, the Parson improving the time by making a sketch of the cluster of buildings comprising Camp Bellevue, which were in full sight. The engineer arrived before the Parson's sketch was completed, but it was so nearly done that he was able to finish it afterward.

As the steamer left the wharf the captain informed George that he had to run down to Camp Whitney to take on a party who was going out from there. The boat accordingly followed the shore of the lake, and soon passed a neat and attractive camp, which Ned learned from the captain was Camp Aziscohos, belonging to a party of Boston gentlemen. A half mile from Whitney's the whistle was twice sounded, to announce the steamer's coming; and when they were within a few rods

CAMP BELLEVUE, MOLECHUNKAMUNK LAKE.

of the landing, a row-boat came out bringing two gentlemen, who were going home. The boys and their friends were much pleased with the appearance of Camp Whitney; and finding the two gentlemen who had left it pleasant and sociable, they asked a great many questions about the place. One of the gentlemen, in reply to a question from George, told him the house was christened Camp Whitney, after its owner, J. P. Whitney of Boston, a wealthy gentleman, largely interested in

FISHING AT MILL BROOK.

mines and railroads, who passed a large portion of each summer there, and who occasionally braved the inclemency of a northern winter by a visit to the camp in December, for the shooting. The boys were much interested in what they heard; and the Parson, learning the captain had some photographs of the place on board, bought two different views, and united them in a sketch.

The two gentlemen from Camp Whitney gave the boys a graphic account of a day's fishing they had enjoyed on Metallak Brook, and informed them that it was one of the best trout streams emptying into the lakes, besides being very picturesque. They pointed out the mouth of the stream, as the steamer shot by it.

METALLAK BROOK.

"Which way do you go out?" inquired the Parson.

"By way of Andover," answered the elder of the two gentlemen, and then he gave our friends such a glowing account of the ride through the woods on a buckboard, and the beauty of the scenery around Andover, that the whole party were induced to go out there, as the captain informed them they could easily hire teams to carry them the next day from Andover to Cambridge, where the steamer stopped. They could spend the night at the Lakeside Hotel, and the next morning could take the boat and make their trip up the Magalloway.

WOODING UP, LAKE WELOKENNEBACOOK.

As this route would give more variety to the trip, the younger members of the party expressed themselves in favor of it at once; and as the young ladies' parents were not very particular which way they returned, the Andover excursion was decided on, providing they found teams enough at the Arm to take the whole party out. The captain informed Mr. Van Wyck that there was a telegraph office at the South Arm, and that if there were not teams enough at the wharf they could telegraph for one, and get it there in a couple of hours. This decided them fully.

The steamer received three passengers at the Middle Dam Landing on her way down, which made the team question more doubtful. But one of the gentlemen from Camp Whitney told the boys he had no doubt there would be teams enough for all, and added that there was a special team coming in for himself and friend, and it could carry three of the other party if necessary.

On their way down the lake, the steamer ran into the shore a few moments to wood up; and the Parson, ever ready with his book and pencil, skipped on shore and made another sketch, telling his friends that he was bound to do their whole trip on paper or perish in the attempt.

After leaving the woodpile, the captain asked the passengers how many wished dinner at the Arm, then he could telegraph the cook by whistles. The whole party expressed a desire to get dinner there if they could; and when within a mile of the wharf, the captain gave his landing-signal, and then whistled for the dinners.

"I suppose they will be all ready for us when we get there," remarked Dick to the captain.

"Yes, you can sit down to the table the moment you get to the house."

"Do they set a good table?" asked George.

"Good enough for me. I get my dinner there," and the captain proceeded to give them an idea of the bill of fare.

The boat soon after stopped at the hotel-landing. The captain notified the passengers that the teams had not arrived, and that they would have plenty of time for dinner, and also advised them to leave all their baggage on the steamer, and he would carry it down to the team-landing, and take care of it.

"Don't the teams come to the house?" asked George.

"No, they stop a few rods below. The people at the house will send you down in row-boats, or you can walk. There is a nice path through the woods."

Accepting the captain's advice, they left their things on the boat and went up to the house. They found it new and clean, and well furnished, and sat down to dinner at once, it being all ready. They were delighted with the meal, and surprised at the moderate charge, it being only fifty cents. After dinner, when paying the bill, George asked the young man who had charge of the house, whom the hotel belonged to, and he was informed that it belonged to the company who ran the steamers. The building was very pleasantly located on a side hill, near the water, and commanded a charming view of the lake.

LAKEVIEW COTTAGE, LAKE WELOKENNEBACOOK.

The people concluded that they had better walk to the teams, one of the gentlemen saying that he needed a little exercise after that dinner; and following a pleasant woodland path for a few moments they reached the landing, where they found six buckboards, one being the special team ordered by the gentlemen from Whitney's Camp. The teams had brought in twenty-five people, thirteen of whom were going to the Upper Dam to work for the Union Water Power Company; the others, eight gentlemen and four ladies, had started on a tour through the lakes. As there were six teams, each of which would seat five passengers comfortably, and only

I. STEAMER AND BUCKBOARD AT SOUTH ARM, LAKE WELOKENNEBACOOK.
II. BLACK BROOK AND BLUE MOUNTAIN.
III. DEVIL'S OVEN, BLACK BROOK NOTCH.

nineteen to go out, there was no trouble about the buckboards. The boys found their things safe at the landing, the captain having piled them all up together. While the drivers were loading their teams, the Parson made a sketch of the steamer at the wharf, and some of the buckboards. These teams had a canvas cover over the top, but open at the sides, making them very comfortable on a hot or rainy day.

NATURAL ARCH, LAKE ROAD.

In about half an hour the baggage had been loaded on the teams, and the passengers sought their places. Grace, Lucie, George, and Dick rode together, and their team had the start. They were followed by Mr. and Mrs. Arden and the Van Wycks. Next came the two Miss Browns with the Parson and Ned. Mr. and Mrs. Brown had a team to themselves, as did also the three who had taken the steamer at the Middle Dam, and the two gentlemen from Camp Whitney. As the teams started, the young folks waved their handkerchiefs in adieu to the captain, who tooted the whistle as a farewell.

The road wound through a thick forest, and a few moments' ride had taken them beyond sight of the lake. There were trees of nearly every variety peculiar to New England forests along their way, and raspberry and blueberry bushes were noticed from time to time growing in thick patches. The road was in unusually good condition, free from mud, and the teams went along at a pace that raised the spirits of the whole party, and the young people declared that buckboard riding was jolly. There were no long hills on the road at first; but once in a while they would go down a short pitch, and the drivers would send their horses along then at a pace that made the dust fly.

On one part of the road they passed under a natural arch, formed by two large yellow birches, whose thick foliage uniting overhead made a grateful shade. For several miles the forest was so dense that nothing could be seen; but as they neared Black Brook Notch, through or over the tops of the trees they obtained occasional glimpses of the mountains that walled it in, and the driver called their attention to a large opening in an overhanging ledge at the top of the mountain, on the left side of the road, which was known as the Devil's Oven, although when or how his Satanic Majesty did cooking there is rather a mythical question. When they reached the Notch they were charmed by its romantic surroundings. On one side was Blue Mountain, scarred and furrowed by slides which had been tumbling down for years; on the other, the thickly wooded bluffs of Mount Sawyer, rising step upon step, until they ended in a barren peak. Singing along the bottom of the valley at the foot of those dizzy heights, ran the sparkling waters of Black Brook, a fine trout stream, and across which a rude dam had been built, to assist lumbermen in running logs out of the brook in the spring. The buckboards were stopped here about fifteen minutes, and then began the climb over Cedar Hill, the only rise in the road of any account for nine miles. From the top of this eminence they obtained a fine view of the Notch in each direction. From this point, less than an hour's drive took them to a place where the Parson found ample work for his pencil, and mourned because he did not have more time to devote to sketching.

THE DEVIL'S DEN, LAKE ROAD.

This was a spot known by the unromantic name of Smith's Mill, from the fact that a member of that numerous family had once owned a mill on the stream in that locality. They first visited an immense chasm in the rock, hollowed out by the unceasing friction of the water, and rejoicing in the peculiar name of the Devil's Den. The horrible gulf was spanned by a couple of square timbers, relics of the old mill; this bridge, not particularly safe at any time, showed evident signs of speedy dissolution. Dick and Ned crossed on it, but were well rated by George for doing so, as there was no necessity for it, there being a path around the upper end of the dam, that could be travelled with perfect safety. The stream which had formerly flowed through this dangerous chasm had either been turned or had sought for itself a new channel some rods beyond; and thither the party went, to admire a beautiful cascade that rippled down over the rocky ledges forming the bottom of the brook, guarded on each side by perpendicular walls. This beautiful piece of water scenery was happily called Silver Ripple Cascade. It was indeed a lovely spot, and tempted the whole party to linger until the drivers announced that if they wished to reach the hotels at the regular supper hour they must be moving in that direction.

Three miles beyond this lovely place, a turn to the right brought them out on the main road, and a few rods farther on they crossed Black Brook over a wooden bridge, below which some very nice trout are caught. From the bridge for a mile or more the road ran mostly through the woods, but as they approached Andover the cleared spots increased in numbers and acreage. They passed one section covered with tall poplars; on this land in former years there had been a luxuriant growth of pine, still attested by the immense stumps from four to eight feet in diameter, scattered over the ground, and that were now fast rotting away. Less than a mile from the hotel they caught their first glimpse of Andover, scattered along the foot of the mountains in the Ellis River Valley, the only compact settlement being at the " Corner," so-called. A little nearer the " Corner " the teams stopped a moment on high ground, and the party had an extensive view of the village bathed in the golden rays of the declining sun. With the bright and sparkling river in the foreground, and the dark green mountains beyond, it made a charming picture, and brought forth many

ANDOVER HOUSE, ANDOVER, ME.

complimentary remarks. From the high land where they had halted, the road descended to the river, and the horses trotted down the hill as if they could smell the oats that were to furnish their supper. As they left the Byron road, they made another sharp turn to the right, then along under a canopy of stately elms, crossing the covered wooden bridge over the Ellis, and up a broad but dusty road to the " Corner."

Here they found the Andover House, a good, solid, old-fashioned, New England hotel, its open doors suggestive of the hearty welcome they received a moment later. But here came a hitch. The hotel was nearly full; and while the landlord could feed the whole party, he had not sleeping accommodations for all. Accordingly, the elder people with the young ladies stopped in the hotel, and Mr. Thomas engaged rooms at a private house near for the boys and the three gentlemen who had come from Middle Dam. The two gentlemen from the Whitney Camp also procured accommodations at a private boarding-house.

After supper the boys went over to their lodgings for a few moments, and when they returned Mr. Van Wyck informed them he had made arrangements with Mr. Thomas, the landlord, to furnish three buckboards to take them to Umbagog Lake the next day; and as the ladies wished to stop at Cataract Brook, to look at some falls and cascades, he wished to start by eight o'clock. He added that he would send one of the teams to the house for their luggage about eight o'clock, and they must have it ready then.

The boys promised to have their things ready, and then went into the parlor and joined the young ladies, and passed the evening in singing. At ten o'clock the party broke up, and the boys found Mr. Thomas, and questioned him in regard to the road they were to ride over the next day. He gave them considerable information, and also told them they ought to climb to the summit of Bald Mountain, as they would be directly under it when visiting the cascades.

"We should like to do it first-rate," answered George, "but it would detain us too long."

The next morning when they went out they set their valises on the piazza, asking the owner of the house to put them on the buckboard when it came, then walked over to the Andover House, and ate their breakfast. Afterward they came out, and found two teams at the door and another just starting out of the yard. The driver asked them if their baggage was ready.

MAIN STREET, ANDOVER, MAINE.

"Yes," replied George, "it sets out on the piazza," and the team rattled off after it.

Stepping into the parlor they found the ladies about ready, and asked Mr. Van Wyck how they should ride.

"We will see when the ladies are ready. Did you have any dinners put up, George?"

"No, sir. I thought we should reach the Lakeside Hotel by noon."

"So did I. But the girls have been studying Farrar's guide-book, and find there are a number of pretty places to be seen at different points along the road if we take the time for it; and Lucie and Grace suggested a lunch, giving us till supper-time to reach Lakeside, and we old fellows," with a glance at Arden and Brown, "have agreed to it, and I have ordered dinner put up for the whole party."

"Very kind in you, sir," returned George.

The ladies now announced that they were ready, and all the

A BIT OF ANDOVER CORNER.

party stepped out, Mr. Van Wyck directing the loading of the teams. Mr. and Mrs. Arden, Mr. Brown, Lucie, and George were placed on the first buckboard; Mr. and Mrs. Van Wyck, Mrs. Brown, Dick, and Grace took possession of the second; and the Parson and Ned, with Nellie and Maud, brought up the rear. They bade Mr. and Mrs. Thomas good-by as the teams drove off, promising to come and see them again some time, and make a longer stay.

They found the road to the "Cataracts," as the driver called the falls, in first-rate condition. It left the "corner" opposite the Andover House, advancing in a generally western direction. Old Bald Pate looked smilingly down on them from a distance, and seemed to beckon them onward. To the right the river ran sparkling through the

LOWER FALL, CATARACT BROOK.

meadows, and on their left the stores and houses stretched down the highway toward the Grand Trunk Railway, the outlet for that little corner of the world. Everything was fresh and green with the glory of the morning, it being clear and fair; but in old Sol's rays there was a suggestion of uncomfortable warmth during the middle of the day. They were in sight of the Ellis River most of the way, and part of the distance was through little patches of woods that furnished an agreeable shade. As they left Andover behind, the valley up which they rode grew narrower, and the mountains higher, while one huge mass of dark ledge in the distance seemed to bar the way at that point. Five miles from the hotel, the horses were turned to the left, and leaving the road, entered a clearing, formerly a farm, but now growing up fast to bushes. A few rods from the road they stopped their horses, and informed the party they could go no farther with the buckboards.

"Here we go, then!" cried Dick, jumping off the buckboard, and assisting Grace to alight. His example was followed by the others; and under the direction of the youngest driver, they began climbing the path leading to the falls. The first they halted at was the "Lower Fall." It was about twenty feet in height, with an inclination to the semi-circular in shape, as the dark rock over which it fell had been worn away at the back. The amount of water going over was sufficient to make quite a roar; and in the sunlight it assumed prismatic colors, clothing itself with gorgeous raiment, that formed a brilliant contrast to the dark and grim-looking ledges by which it was surrounded.

"A very pretty fall, and charmingly embowered among these woods," remarked Mr. Van Wyck, as the party, turning away, sought the path again, and continued their climb up the mountain-side.

A quarter of a mile above they reached the lower pitch of the "Upper Fall," and were surprised at its height and beauty. This is the highest fall on the stream, and the perpendicular drop in two pitches is not far from seventy-five feet. As will be seen in the engraving, the entire bed of the stream, where the water takes its first leap, is a solid ledge; at the bottom of this the water gathers in a round basin, worn from the solid ledge, of

UPPER FALL, CATARACT BROOK.

unfathomable depth according to local tradition. A charming place for wood-nymphs to take their morning bath. The water and frost have played sad havoc with the granite walls of the stream at this place, and immense bowlders have been detached from the upper part of the cliff, and fret their lives away in the stream at the second fall. This work of destruction is constantly going on, and there must be more or less change in the appearance of the place with each successive year.

The deep-toned cataract is surrounded on both sides by thick woods, and the spot has a conscious but indescribable charm that will cause people to linger long after they have seen all of interest. It would furnish a fitting abode for a sylvan goddess, and you can almost imagine some Diana appearing and greeting you with a smile of welcome.

> "That spirit moves
> In the green valley, where the silver brook
> From its full basin pours the white cascade;
> And babbling low amid the tangled woods,
> Slips down through moss-grown stones
> With endless laughter."

After viewing the falls from the foot of the cataract, the party clambered over the rough sides of the amphitheatre to the top, from whence they could obtain an equally satisfactory, but very different, view.

"What a beautiful stream this is, and what a lovely place!" observed George to Lucie, as they stood together on an overhanging bluff at the top of the fall.

"Charming. And I am so glad that we came out to Andover. I never enjoyed a trip so much in my life as this one, and all the girls say the same. I hope we shall come up this way somewhere another summer."

"So do I," returned her cavalier; and afterward, *sotto-voce*, "if I can come too."

"Come along," cried Ned at this moment, "we are going up the stream farther."

Leaving the double fall, they made their way half a mile up the mountain-path, which ran in close proximity to the stream. The bare and scarred summit of old "Bald Pate" now frowned down upon them, as if questioning their right to invade his domain; but little they cared for his temper, which came to them in the shape of a dark shadow from a cloud that just then swept across his brow.

They stopped at one of the most beautiful places to be found on this charming stream, where the mountain torrent poured over the whitest of granite rock, worn smooth as glass from the action of the water, forming a series of delightful water-slides, known as the "Sylvan Cascades." Here the sunlight streamed in, causing the water to sparkle like diamonds, and furnishing a strong comparison to the darkness of the "Flume" above. There are basins worn in the solid rock here, that for beauty of shape and finish would put to shame many works of art. One can sit for hours feasting the eye on the exquisite beauty of the place, the ear enchanted by the gentle murmur of the rippling waters.

THE FLUME.

If one is inclined to solitude, no more beautiful spot could be found in which to indulge in seclusiveness, for here you are entirely surrounded by nature. The musical stream, the granite rocks, the dark forests lit up a little by the delicate birch and silver-maple on either hand; below, the smiling valley to which the torrent hastens; above, the frowning peaks of mountains, and over all, the clear blue sky, — majestic canopy of earth.

> "Pleasant it was, when woods were green,
> And winds were soft and low,
> To lie amid some sylvan scene,
> Where, the long, drooping boughs between,
> Shadows dark and sunlight sheen
> Alternate come and go."

Half an hour was devoted to the cascades, and the party continued up the stream a short distance, until they reached the "Flume."

"This is commencing to be warm work," declared Mr. Van Wyck, mopping his face with a silk handkerchief; "is there anything more to see in this direction, driver?"

"No, sir; unless," mischievously, "you wish to climb the mountain."

"We will leave the mountain until another year. I guess it will keep."

"The scenery grows wilder and prettier," cried Grace, as they reached the lower end of the "Flume," and gazed at the long, narrow tunnel before them.

At this point on the stream, for several hundred feet on both sides of the brook, the rocky walls rise to a height of from twenty to sixty feet, the purling water flowing swiftly along the bottom. A tree has been felled across the chasm, affording an insecure bridge by which to cross. It is much safer and wiser, however, if you are going from one side to the other, to cross on the stones in the bed of the brook at the lower end. The width of the flume is from ten to twenty feet. A thick growth of fir and pine has obtained a foothold on each side of the cliff, shutting out the sun, except perhaps for a short time at noon, when it is directly overhead. The gloomy darkness adds to the weird and solemn appearance of the place, and you gaze with feelings of awe along the cavernous sides of the frightful looking ravine before you, —

> "Through the narrow rift
> Of the vast rocks, against whose rugged feet
> Beats the mad torrent with perpetual roar,
> Where noonday is as twilight, and the winds
> Come burdened with the everlasting moan
> Of forests and of far-off waterfalls."

After inspecting the "Flume" from above and below, the party returned to the buckboards, and once more taking their seats, were a moment later rattling along the road.

Across the intervale on the right, one of the drivers pointed out a mountain, on which, according to local belief, was a lead-mine, although no one was able to find it. The story ran, that many years ago the Indians in that part of the country used to sell lead which came from this mountain. And that later two white hunters, in crossing the mountain, had accidentally stumbled upon the out-croppings of lead, and had cut some off the ledges. While engaged in doing it, they heard voices, and for fear of being discovered, joined the other party, who were also hunters, and craftily drew them away from the vicinity of the lead-mine. To avoid all suspicion, they continued on to the village with the party they had met, without blazing any path. Afterward they spent weeks in trying to find the place again, but never succeeded, and it still remains undiscovered.

"I don't think much of lead-mines," said Ned; "but if you know of any lost gold-mines about here, we will try and look them up."

The driver confessed that he did not, and touched up his horses, that were just then disposed to lag.

Two miles from the opening where they had stopped to visit Cataract Brook, they reached the path leading to Dunn's Notch, a romantic pass in the mountains. The young ladies wished to visit the Notch, but Mr. Van Wyck thought it too hot for them to do any more climbing just then, but consented to the boys' going; and the young fellows struck across the meadows to the left, while the party kept on. It was nearly one o'clock when the panting horses began climbing the first long hill between them and the lake. Near the top they found a sparkling little brook on the right of the road, and leaving their seats, threw themselves down in the shade of the trees, and had the drivers bring the luncheon. They had just commenced eating when the boys made their appearance, looking hot and tired, and the Parson showed them a sketch of the Notch he had made from below, and told them that he did not go to the top, as they found it would use up too much time. The sketch was admired by all, and Mr. Van Wyck said they were wise not to attempt climbing to the top of the Notch.

An hour was passed in dinner at the spot where they had halted; and a merry time they had, the girls declaring it was equal to a picnic. The drivers also improved the opportunity to feed and water the horses. A little after two o'clock the party started again; but as the next five or six miles were nearly all hills, the horses were driven slowly, and occasionally some of the party would walk for a change.

At East B Hill they waited nearly half an hour to enjoy the view from that sightly locality, which commanded part of Lake Welokennebacook, nearly the whole of Umbagog Lake, the Dixville Peaks, and Mount Washington. With their glasses they could distinguish the hotel on the top of the mountain, and the steamers on the lakes. From here, a few minutes' ride brought them to the top of another hill, where they stopped a short time to get a more extended view of Umbagog Lake and the mountains surrounding. It was a beautiful picture; the lake, long and crooked, stretched away for miles, accompanied on all sides by thickly wooded mountains, on the most of which the forest growth reached the summit; a few bare peaks towered above the others, and looked down with dignified contempt on their more lowly neighbors; two or three small farms, at the lower end of the lake, alone prevented the country from being a howling wilderness. A mile beyond they passed a post-office, and the road leading down to the mill, and, continuing on straight along the main road to

DUNN'S NOTCH FROM BELOW AND ABOVE.

Colebrook, shortly reached a pretty new hotel, eligibly located on a plateau on the left of the road, but a short distance from the lake. At the door of the Lakeside the buckboards stopped, and the party were warmly welcomed by the landlord. After their long ride they were glad to rest for a while in the large, flag-bottomed seats on the wide piazza, and rest their eyes on the charming landscape in front of them before proceeding to their rooms. Later on they inspected

AT LUNCHEON.

the interior of the hotel, and were all given pleasant, well-furnished rooms. About half-past five George descried the steamer coming down the lake; and the young people went down to meet the boat.

"There are six passengers," remarked Lucie, as the boat drew near the wharf.

"There's Captain Farwell," observed Grace; "wave your handkerchiefs, girls." And a moment later four dainty bits of white floated out on the air, the gallant captain replying to their welcome by swinging his hat.

"Throw us your bow-line!" yelled Dick as the boat glided into the wharf. The engineer gave it a toss; Dick caught it, and put two half-hitches around a post with a celerity that showed him to be expert at handling ropes. Then he caught the stern-line, and made that fast with equal readiness; and the boat was secured.

The passengers came on shore, and walked up to the house, the captain telling them the team would be down shortly and get their luggage.

VIEW FROM LAKESIDE HOTEL, LOOKING NORTH-WEST.

"How are you, Captain?" said George, as they shook hands; "we are going up Magalloway with you to-morrow."

"I am glad of that. Where is the rest of your party?"

"At the house. The older people were quite tired after the ride."

"How did you enjoy it?"

"First-rate, all of us. We had a splendid time. It is one of the prettiest rides I ever had in my life."

"So this is your small steamer, Captain?" said Grace.

"Yes. How do you like it?"

"Very much; it's a little darling: much better than the large boat."

"Who were your passengers, Captain?" inquired Ned.

"Some New York people. I did not learn their names. They came down from the Middle Dam, and are going out to Bethel to-morrow morning. Did anybody come on the stage to-night?"

VIEW ON ROAD, LAKESIDE FARM.

"I don't know," answered George; "I don't think it had arrived when we left the house."

"There it is now!" cried Maud with a little quiver of excitement; "let us return to the house, and see who has come."

The captain accompanied the young people, and they reached the piazza just as four gentlemen alighted from the stage. Later the captain told George they were going to the Middle Dam.

After supper, while the old people formed the acquaintance of the other guests, the boys and girls went out rowing on the lake. It was a splendid moonlight evening, the water like a sheet of silver; and the young people enjoyed the sail as only young folks can, and returned about nine o'clock. They were all loath to come in; but the girls were afraid their parents would not like it if they stopped

ON THE PIAZZA.

out later, and the boys knew better than to get them into trouble. They went up to the house, but stopped on the piazza a while before going in.

"Where do we go next, George?" asked Mr. Van Wyck as they all sat around enjoying the moonlight and the beauty of the evening.

"Up the Magalloway to the Berlin Mills House to-morrow; stop there over night, and Sunday make the ascent of Aziscohos; then return to the hotel, stop over night, and Monday come down' the river to Errol Dam, where Mr. Marston will meet you at night."

"I don't like the idea of Sunday excursions. Couldn't we go up the mountain Saturday or Monday?"

"There would not be time, sir, if any of the ladies are going with us."

"And we are all going, father," put in Lucie, as if it were an assured fact.

"Yes, yes, I dare say you are all wishing to go. You girls are becoming regular romps up here. But I'll decide the matter when we get up there. And now I think you had all better retire. I am going to myself. Come, Mrs. Van Wyck, let us set these young people a good example;" and, as the old folks started, the whole party broke up and retired to their rooms.

CHAPTER IX.

FROM CAMBRIDGE TO SUNDAY COVE. — ERROL DAM. — THE MAGALLOWAY
RIVER. — POINTS OF INTEREST.

 VERYBODY was up early the next morning, and, after breakfast, bundled their traps together, and they were taken down to the steamer by the team, the passengers following on foot. Several of the ladies and gentlemen who were spending their summer at Lakeside went down to the landing to see them off. The four gentlemen who had arrived from Bethel the night before also took passage on the boat. When all were on board the lines were thrown in, and amidst a flutter of handkerchiefs from those on the steamer, replied to by those on shore, the saucy little craft steamed up the lake.

As they left the landing swiftly behind, the captain called his passengers' attention to a point opposite, which he called B Point, and told them that the year before, one morning while the steamer was passing the point, he saw two deer standing on it. He stopped the steamer, pulled the whistle two or three times, and halloed at them, but they showed no fright, and kept on browsing. He started to make a landing, the deer watching him curiously a few moments, and then they walked leisurely off into the woods.

"Why did you not shoot them?" asked one of the gentlemen.

"For the best reason in the world: I had no rifle. And even if I had, I would not have dared to fire, for some of these countrymen round here would have complained about me if I had killed one; and it would have cost me fifty dollars."

"They keep a nice house where you stop, Captain?"

"Yes, sir. That is the best-kept hotel, and the best-looking one, in this part of the country."

"Do the Transportation Company own it?"

"Yes, sir."

"We had a nice dinner at the South Arm," remarked George.

"Yes," replied the captain, "I suppose you did. The Company own that house also."

The attention of the passengers was now attracted by the beauties of the lake; and they plied the captain with so many questions that it was fairly a burden to him to answer them.

The course of the steamer was past B Point on the right hand, or starboard side, and the Big Island on the left, or port side. From the head of the island the steamer was slanted toward the east, leaving the last house (Heywood's) on the port, and Bear Island on the starboard; thence through the Narrows, past Loon Island and Metallak Island. On the latter was a party who had left the hotel early in the morning, and had rowed up to the narrows for fishing, and who were now getting their breakfast at a fire they had kindled on the beach. The steamer passed so near the island that those on board were able to converse for a few moments with the amateur camping-party.

"There is a splendid sweep of water beyond that island," observed Mr. Van Wyck.

"Yes," replied the captain; "that is known as Tyler Cove. There is a beautiful sand-beach at the head of it. There used to be a farm in there years ago known as the 'Tyler Place,' and the cove adopted the same name. There are several very large and pretty coves around this lake."

The sound of a fowling-piece ahead now attracted their attention; and they noticed a man in a boat pick up two ducks, while a few more flew off in the distance.

"Rather early for ducks, I think," said one of the gentlemen who was bound to the upper lakes.

"Yes, those must be old ones; the young ones do not fly much before September; and the captain gave his wheel half a turn to

BREAKFAST ON METALLAK ISLAND.

starboard to bring them a little nearer the boat, the occupant of which, having picked up his game, was now pulling straight for the eastern shore.

"He is going to land somewhere," remarked the Parson.

"Yes," answered the captain, "he is heading for B Brook Point. I don't care to follow him in there: it is rocky off that point, but we can go near enough to get a fair look at him."

"Do you know where all the rocks in the lake are, Captain?" asked Dick.

"All the worst ones."

"I suppose you bring up on one once in a while."

"No, sir," laughed the captain, "we 'bring up' before we get to them, and give them a wide berth. I don't care to try and turn rocks over with this boat: she is not strong enough."

"The man has reached the shore," said Grace. "I suppose he is going to cook his breakfast."

"I don't see what he is doing in there," remarked the captain. Most of the campers pitch their tents over to Moll's Rock: I can't imagine where the fun comes in camping alone."

"Oh, he has a dog with him!" cried Nellie.

"Well, I had rather have a dog with me than some men I have seen," added George dryly.

"Where is Moll's Rock, Captain, that you spoke of a moment ago?"

"Over on the west side of the lake;" and the captain pointed out a spot where a large ledge swept shelvingly into the water. "There is plenty of firewood there, and a good spring of water. I don't believe that fellow will stay long where he has landed."

"In what direction is the outlet, Captain," inquired Mr. Brown, who had been sweeping the shores of the lake with his glass.

"Over in that dead wood, sir;" and the captain nodded in the direction indicated, then added with a laugh, "but it would puzzle you to find it."

"What a quantity of mountains there are in this country, Captain!" remarked Mr. Van Wyck. "We are literally surrounded with them."

"Yes, sir: every piece of land here that isn't a hill is a mountain."

"Have they all names?"

"Not that I know of, sir, but a great many of them have. That wedge-shaped one in the north-west you saw the other day is Mount

Dustan; that large double-peaked one ahead is Mount Aziscohos. The round-topped one off there in the north-east is Moose Mountain. That high one abeam of us is Blue Mountain, over in Black Brook Notch. Those two large ones in the south-east are Saddleback and Speckled, and they form the walls of Grafton Notch. These gentlemen," nodding to the four strangers, "came between those mountains yesterday on their way from Bethel to the lake."

THE LONELY CAMPER.

"Yes, and a charming drive it was," put in one of them.

"Very pretty," replied the captain; and then, turning to Mr. Van Wyck, continued, "You see, from this lake Saddle Back shows two peaks; but over in Andover you can only see the highest, the white granite one, and for that reason the Andover people call it Bald Pate."

"Yes, we passed quite near it in riding over to Lakeside."

"Exactly. Those peaks directly south of us loom up behind

the hotel, and are known as the Hampshire Hills. The Company intend some time to cut out a path from the hotel to the top of the nearest one, and build an observatory on it."

"That would be splendid!" cried Lucie.

"Charming!" echoed Grace.

"It would command a fine view of the lake and the surrounding country," assented the captain; and then continuing to Mr. Van Wyck, "Those high peaks just coming in sight are the White Mountains; they lie south-west of us, and you will obtain a much better view of them in the next fifteen minutes. Those nearest mountains west of us are in Errol and Dummer; and there are about a hundred other peaks about us that I have never learned the names of, allowing they have any."

"Have you ever been on the summit of Aziscohos, Captain?"

"Yes, sir."

"Would it pay for an old fellow like me to climb it?"

"Yes, sir: it would pay if you didn't have but one leg. You can get the finest view from the top of that mountain that there is to be had in this country, and, besides, it is not a hard trip. You can ride to within two miles of the summit, and there is a good path the rest of the way."

"I suppose I had better not take my wife with me," with a sly glance at her. "Don't you think ladies are a nusiance?"

"No, sir," declared the captain with a blush. "I always take my wife with me wherever I go. She enjoys it, and so do I."

"But your wife is not so old as mine."

"I don't think your wife is an old-looking lady by any means."

"Thank you, Captain," broke in Mrs. Van Wyck laughingly, "for your exertions in my behalf; and I can assure you that Mr. Van Wyck will not get rid of me so easily. If he ascends the mountain, so shall I."

Amid the general laughter that followed this speech, Mr. Van Wyck assured his wife that she might make one of the mountain party.

The steamer had now reached the entrance of Sunday Cove; and the captain gave one long whistle as a signal to the team that the boat would land passengers.

As they swept around Eagle Point a large flock of young ducks, accompanied by their mother, took fright, and paddled for shore as swiftly as their little feet would carry them.

PINE POINT, UMBAGOG LAKE.

"Oh, the little dears! Just see them swim! Can't they fly, Captain?" cried Lucie.

"No, they are not old enough."

"Why, Dick, see them bob their heads under!" said Grace to her enthusiastic admirer, who was making a mental calculation of the distance they were away, and wondering if he could have hit them if they had been large enough to eat.

"Yes, they are regular divers."

"Aren't they cunning?"

"Yes; and see how the old one keeps behind and looks after them."

"Is the team here every morning, Captain?" asked one of the gentlemen, who was to leave the steamer.

"Yes, sir, it has to be. We carry the United States mail, and they meet us regularly."

As they approached the landing they noticed two canoes anchored beyond the wharf, a little way from shore. This excited the captain's curiosity, as he declared there were no canoes there the night before; and he wondered where they could have sprung from.

The team was waiting; and, as the boat glided in to the wharf, the usual amount of chaff was strewn to the winds by the captain and the driver.

"What makes you so late this morning, Captain? Out to a dance last night?"

"Late?" queried the captain with a contemptuous sniff: "we are ahead of time. I suppose you and your horses stopped down here last night; if you hadn't you could never have been here at this time in the morning."

"Tell that to the marines, you sea-monster!" returned the driver; "don't I have to wait here for you about four mornings out of a week?"

"I should think you did. This is the first morning you have been on time this week, and to-day is Saturday. And I'll bet five dollars you came off before breakfast this morning."

"You ask the cook if I did. Back water! you'll smash the wharf."

"Don't you fret! I'm running this boat. Catch that bow-line, and don't give us so much cheap talk;" and amid a recurring fire of hits and counter hits between the driver and the captain, the boat was secured to the wharf.

While the captain and engineer were unloading their freight and the gentlemen's baggage, the passengers strolled on shore to stretch their limbs. Three ladies and two gentlemen now appeared on the brow of the hill, who had ridden on the buckboard all the way but the last mile, and that they had walked.

Half an hour was passed in transferring passengers, baggage, freight, and mails; and then the driver and the captain had their

STEAMER AND BUCKBOARD AT SUNDAY COVE.

last shot at each other. The passengers exchanged farewells, and the little steamer, with a whistle that awoke the echoes of the forest, glided swiftly out toward the lake.

"Did you find out whom the canoes belonged to, Captain?" inquired George, who had overheard him quizzing the driver.

"Yes: they belong to some fellows who are going up Magalloway. They sacked them across the carry yesterday afternoon, and have gone back for their tent and the rest of their things."

" Do you mean that they brought them down themselves? Why, they must be awful heavy!"

" They will weigh about seventy-five pounds each. They take them on their shoulders, and travel with them like a lobster in his shell."

" I should rather pay to have the team haul them down if they were mine."

" So would I. But some people will work themselves to death to save a dollar."

The newcomers soon became acquainted with the other passengers, and they exchanged experiences about their different trips through the lake region, where they were going, and the strangers informed Mr. Van Wyck they were from Boston.

" Then we are near neighbors six hours removed," returned Mr. Van Wyck with a laugh. " We come from New York. We are bound up the Magalloway, shall ascend Aziscohos, and see whatever else there is worth seeing up the river. Would your party not like to join us?"

" Thank you. We should be very happy to, for we intend visiting the mountain later; but we are to meet some friends at Dixville Notch to-morrow, and therefore will have to go directly there."

" Which way are you going out when you return home, Mr. Simpson?"

" Through Grafton Notch to Bethel."

" Then you will have to stop at the foot of the lake over night, and there you will find the best hotel in this part of the country, I'll warrant."

" That will be pleasant, for some we found above the Middle Dam were very poor."

" How did you come in?"

" By Farmington and Phillips."

"I don't know anything about that route."

"It is a nice way of approach to the lake system, and a great many people come in that way. I should advise you to try it some time."

"I will. For although this is my first visit to the Androscoggin Lakes, it is by no means my last."

At this moment George, who had been intently gazing out on the lake, jumped up excitedly, rushed to the forward part of the boat, and climbed up on deck, where, steadying himself by the flagpole, he looked through his glass at some object in the water, off on the starboard bow.

CANOES AT SUNDAY COVE.

As everybody turned to see what had started him so suddenly, he cried out, "A deer! a deer! don't you see it? It is swimming for the shore."

There was a flurry of excitement at this announcement, and all who had glasses levelled them in the direction George indicated.

"Chase him, captain!" cried Dick; "we can run him down."

"I don't think we can. It's a large buck, and they swim very fast, and he is a mile away from us now."

"Head the boat towards him, and I will try a shot," said one of the Boston party, who opened his gun-case and brought forth a rifle.

The captain swung the boat towards the deer, and the gentleman went forward where George stood, and loaded his rifle.

"I can't run over that way very far," remarked the captain, "because it is shoal. And if we should run aground going at full speed, loaded as deep as we are now, it would take us all day to get afloat again, and that would not be very pleasant."

"True enough," observed Mr. Arden. "I would not take any risks, Captain."

The gentleman now tried a shot at the deer, but did not come within twenty yards of him. He said he would fire again when the boat was a little nearer, for the steamer was now fast overhauling the deer.

A DEER CHASE ON UMBAGOG LAKE.

"Give it to him now," urged the parson, who, like the others, had become interested in the chase.

The gentleman brought his rifle to his shoulder; but just as he pulled the trigger the captain put the wheel hard a port, bringing the deer abeam, and causing the rifle bullet to bury itself in the water, at least a quarter of a mile from the deer.

"What did you do that for?" called back the gentleman rather sharply; "you spoiled my shot."

"Better spoil your shot than keep you here all day and perhaps half the night," laughed the captain. " The bottom is getting too near us; we should have been fast in the mud a minute later. See how roily the water is. The keel touched bottom when I made the turn."

" All right; I forgive you," said the gentleman, as he came aft and put up his rifle. " But I should have liked to capture that fellow."

" He is wading to the shore now," observed Grace.

" Yes," added Dick; "and there he goes into the woods. That is the last we shall see of him."

When the steamer was back on her regular course, the captain pointed out the Inlet, where the Rapid River swiftly joined the lake, after its impetuous five-mile flight, and nearer to them a pretty headland called Pine Point. Opposite, on the starboard side, was Moose Point, its name commemorative of the time where, years before, whole families of moose had taken to the shallow water near it to feed on the succulent lily pads, or to escape from the irritating attacks of black flies and midges.

" Are you going to the foot of the lake now, captain? " asked one of the gentlemen, who had joined them at Sunday Cove.

" No, sir. But we have to run down to a point about opposite of Moll's Rock before we can get into the Androscoggin River."

" Where is Moll's Rock?"

" Off on the starboard bow, where you see that tent on the shore."

The attention of the Boston people was now called to the view of the White Mountains by Mr. Arden, and the passengers exchanged ideas on the scenery and surroundings. Under the skilful guidance of the captain, assisted by sundry stakes driven into the bottom to mark the deepest water, the steamer crossed the bar, and entered the river to follow its crooked and sinuous channel. The ladies who had taken the steamer at Sunday Cove soon noticed the beautiful water lilies, and made so many remarks about them, that the captain would have been hard-hearted indeed if he had not taken their hints, and stopped for a few moments, while his fair passengers surfeited their desires for the sweet-scented water flowers. The ladies remarking that they had not seen any lilies on the lakes above, the captain assured them that Umbagog Lake was the only one in the chain where these beautiful blossoms were at all plenty.

The engineer then took pick-pole and pushed the steamer away from the pads,

CAMPING OUT ON MOLL'S ROCK.

and after reversing the wheel four or five turns to get the stems off the shaft, the boat was started, and, when clear from the stems and pads, continued at full speed down river. Just below the mouth of the Magalloway they saw a very large bald eagle perched on top of an old tree that projected over the river. The gentleman who had fired at the deer took out his rifle and blazed away at old Baldy, and struck the under part of the limb on which he was sitting. The bird uttered a hoarse and defiant screech, and spreading his huge wings sailed away over the forest.

After this they passed several flocks of ducks, the antics of the little ones causing them no inconsiderable amusement. Lucie said they looked like little puff-balls, and that she should like to have one. At the head of the Big Meadow they saw a blue heron stalking solemnly along the bank, and the gentleman tried his rifle again, but with ill-success, as the bird gave itself a shake, and flew lazily away down the river.

A SHOT AT A BALD EAGLE.

At this point the steamer whistled to let Bragg know there were passengers for him, and the noise frightened two or three muskrats who were sitting on the river bank, and they jumped into the river and swam away. At the foot of the meadows they passed a large party of campers on shore, who looked as rough as a band of gypsies. They had two teams, and three skinny-looking horses, and near two tents a fire was burning. The campers stopped whatever they were doing, and stared with open-mouthed astonishment at the steamer and its passengers, as the boat shot swiftly past them.

In answer to an inquiry from one of the ladies, the captain informed his passengers that the campers were from some place back in the country, and had come to the river for fish and berries, the latter growing plentifully along the banks.

"They don't catch any trout here," said Ned.

"No. It is pickerel they are after. They salt them down in butter-firkins, and carry them home. I have seen fifty people at a time strung

CAMPING AT FOOT OF BIG MEADOW.

along the river in different places during August and September, some of whom had come a hundred and fifty miles from their homes, and rode all the way behind just such old plugs as you saw at that camp."

"What a taste!" cried George in disgust. "Salted pickerel!"

"That would be as bad as sauerkraut for me," added Ned.

"Or Limburger cheese," put in the parson.

As the steamer ran alongside the wharf, Bragg drove up in a Concord wagon with a pair of horses. He brought nothing but the mail. He exchanged greetings with the Van Wyck party, and the captain notified him that he had five passengers who wished to go to Dixville Notch.

The Boston party bade their fellow-voyagers good-morning, and expressed the hope of meeting them again, and going on shore climbed into the wagon. Their baggage was landed; and the steamer pointing her prow up river, sent a parting whistle after her late passengers, which, much to the jolly landlord's delight, set his horses to dancing, and was soon out of sight.

"Now for the Magalloway and Aziscohos!" cried Dick with enthusiasm, when they could no longer see the landing.

"Yes; and won't it be fun!" chimed in Grace.

"I will show you some fun now," added the captain, who had overheard the remark.

The steamer was then nearly up to the campers, and the captain slanted the boat in a little, then ran close along the shore. As they passed the camp, the captain pulled the whistle twice, and the horses, which were only tethered by halters, at the unusual noises so near them, pricked up their ears, and exhibiting more life than you would have supposed they possessed, broke their fastenings, and kicking their heels into the air, started off on the road in different directions, much to the amusement of the steamer's passengers, but to the evident disgust of the campers who started in pursuit of them.

Half an hour brought them to the Magalloway, than which there is no more beautiful or crooked river in the world. Turning to port, the steamer entered it, startling a flock of ducks from their feeding. The principal characteristics of the stream were similar to the Androscoggin. There were the same beautifully wooded banks, with many overhanging trees. Numerous old firs were covered with trailing moss. But the turns in the Magalloway were sharper, and twice as numerous; and the additional attraction of mountains was here presented, there being one or more constantly in view.

As they steamed up the river the captain pointed out to them the place where, a few years ago, a boat containing two persons was overturned, one of whom lost his life. It was in the spring, when the stream, swollen to twice its natural size by the fast-melting snows of winter, sent down a dangerously swift current, and the water about the temperature of ice. A physician, accompanied by a man to row him, started from the foot of the lake in a small boat to visit a patient up the Magalloway. They reached their destination safely; but on their return, the boat when only a short distance from the mouth of the river struck a snag that ran out from the bank under water, and was instantly capsized. The doctor was a good swimmer, while his companion could not swim a stroke. But in spite of the fact he was drowned, while the oarsman escaped. The doctor was loaded down with thick clothing and a large overcoat, which probably injured his chances of safety. The oarsman managed to hang to the boat when it overturned, and floated down the river with it, until it lodged against the bank, where he made his way to the shore. He was so cold and exhausted from his exposure that it was some time before he recovered sufficiently to walk, and then he started through the woods, and, after a hard tramp reached Errol and related his sad story. A party of men was formed to look for the doctor, and two weeks later his lifeless body was found floating down the river.

A half mile above, as the steamer turned a sharp bend, they came upon three men in a boat fishing. They were rough, uncouth-looking fellows; and one of them tipped up a flask and took a drink as the steamer passed them, while the others waved their hats.

"I should think those fellows were in danger of getting capsized if they drank too much whiskey," remarked George, as they left the boat behind, "and what a fearful-looking craft that was."

"Yes, a regular old tub," answered the captain. "Isn't safe to cross the river in. But you can't get one of those fellows drunk; they are steeped in liquor all the time. As old Bill Burnham used to say, 'They can't hold enough to make them drunk.'"

As the boat progressed up the river the passengers became more and more enthusiastic over the beauties of the wonderland through which they were travelling.

"There is Pulpit Rock," remarked the captain, pointing to a large bowlder on the right bank of the river. "It is a favorite spot for camping-parties, there being a good spring of water near it. And right there," indicating a spot nearly in the middle of the river, "and about three feet under water, is the ugliest rock ever planted for a steamboat to land on. That is why I hug the port side of the river."

A DRY CROWD.

They passed many low places along their route that were submerged by the high waters of spring, where the trees had been killed. Many of these were knotted and knarled, of fantastic shape, with long moss trailing down from their broken limbs, and swinging in the wind, presenting in the twilight a startling and weird appearance.

Occasionally they looked back to see a long vista of shimmering water, nearly over-arched with trees, ending in the dark green forests as they came together at a bend in the river.

A mile above Pulpit Rock, after turning one of the numerous curves in the river, they came to another long bend, and here, as the captain informed them, he "jumped the river bank;" or, in other words, he passed through a narrow, artificial cut on the left bank of the river, called the "cut off," thus saving about a quarter of a mile. Beyond here the river made a sweep toward the road, which came into sight at a point called Bear Brook, spanned by a tumble-down looking wooden bridge, whose abutments were formed of loose logs piled one on top of another at right angles to the road, and these were kept in proper position on the banks of the stream by perpendicular logs, the lower ends being driven into the mud, and the upper mortised into the cross-timbers. The construction was novel, and I should judge original.

At the mouth of Bottle Brook stood a rude log cabin, noted as being the first house seen in ascending the river, and also as once having been the residence of an old Indian squaw, who had a young white husband, a fellow probably with more stomach than brains. It being rocky off the mouth of the brook, the navigation at this point is considered a little hazardous, and the steamer was slowed down while making the turn in the river opposite the log cabin.

ON THE MAGALLOWAY.

Some twenty minutes or more brought them to another house, a small story and a half frame building, on the left bank of the river, which the captain called "Chases." It stood at the base of a neck of land which ran a long distance into the river, making the sharpest turn they had yet encountered. This, the captain informed them, was "Sharp Shins." Half a mile beyond and they had reached the

"Lower Landing," and the steamer was stopped a few moments to discharge some freight, and the mail-bag was delivered to a boy who was in waiting to carry it to the post-office.

From this point to the hotel owned by the Berlin Mills Company, where they were to stop, the captain informed them, was by road only a mile and three-quarters, while by the steamer's course on the river the distance was six miles.

The farther they ascended the river, the stronger grew the current; and it took them an hour to make the Upper Landing, directly opposite the hotel. At one place along the course they sailed two miles, and only made a few rods advance on their route, the captain showing them the narrow strip of land dividing the two parts of the river. As they ran into the landing, they passed a huge bowlder in the middle of the stream, against which the current dashed, only to be thrown back and divided, uniting again below the rock.

"I should think navigation was dangerous up here, Captain" said Mr. Van Wyck, "for I can see quite a number of rocks in the river."

"It is unless you have plenty of water. We can't run up here but a few days longer. There is a set of rips half a mile below here that the steamer will soon drag on."

CHAPTER X.

THE BERLIN MILLS HOUSE. — GUNNING AND FISHING. — ASCENT OF AZIS-
COHOS. — FROM BROWN FARM TO ERROL. — DEPARTURE OF THE GIRLS.

AS the boat shot into the landing, it was met by a motley crowd of natives, and it looked as if the whole town had turned out to greet them. There was no wharf; but the steamer was laid broadside to the bank, and a plank being passed on board, all landed without difficulty. Mr. Lowe, the landlord of the hotel, a wide-awake, pleasant-looking fellow, greeted them, and asked them to leave their grips at the landing, and he would take them to the house.

"Any passengers to go down, Mr. Lowe?"

"Yes, Cap; there are five. I did not know you were coming up here, and I sent them down to the 'lower landing.'"

"All right. We will pick them up on our way down. Shove her off, Eugene."

"Can't you stop and have some dinner, Cap?"

"I guess not, it is so late. Besides, we have our dinner on the boat, and can eat it going down."

"Come up for us on Monday," called out Mr. Van Wyck, as the steamer turned her bow down river.

"All right, sir. I'll be here at one o'clock," and the captain waved his cap to the ladies, who were swinging their handkerchiefs.

The road was close to the top of the river bank, and the hotel just opposite. The whole party walked over to it, passing through the crowd of gaping rustics, and found a group upon the piazza inspecting a string of fish that one of the gentlemen and his guide had taken that morning up the Diamond. The party halted a moment to inspect the trout, and then passed into the house.

Mr. Lowe shortly made his appearance with their luggage and showed them to rooms, and then departed to see about their dinner,

A CAMPING-PARTY AT HOME.

returning after his guests had come down-stairs with the welcome announcement that dinner would be ready in half an hour.

"Thank the Lord for that!" exclaimed Dick fervently aside to Grace. "I am about starved."

"So am I. I believe I could eat pickles and slate-pencils if there were nothing else forthcoming."

While waiting for dinner, the party strolled out on the piazza and scanned the surroundings. They found the house faced west, and stood almost in front of Mount Dustan, they had so often noticed from the lake. Above it, higher up the river, were the Diamond Peaks, and Half Moon Mountains. The settled part of the valley extended some three miles below them and about six above, terminating at Aziscohos Falls. A covered bridge spanned the river a short distance above them, and the country road to Errol crossed it. The landscape views, both up and down the river, were fine, and presented many choice bits for an artist's pencil; and the parson, despite the pangs of hunger, was hastily transferring to his book an outline sketch of Dustan. Before he could finish it, the ringing of a bell announced dinner, and all found their way to the dining-room. Having taken breakfast at seven o'clock, while it was now two, they were all really hungry, and enjoyed the bountiful repast spread before them.

Dinner over, and there was a scattering.

George and Dick, with Grace and Lucie, started off for a stroll toward Sturdivant Pond, the boys taking their guns with them, as Mr. Lowe had spoken encouragingly of their finding partridges in the vicinity, besides telling them about a deer shot in the pond while swimming across the summer before, and this tempting bait had determined the boys to carry their fire-arms. Nellie and Maud, with Ned and the parson, hired a boat belonging to the hotel, and rowed up the river. The old people, feeling rather disinclined for any more exercise that day, passed the afternoon at the hotel as best suited their fancies.

It was six o'clock when the boating-party returned, bringing some twenty trout. The parson had not taken his rod, but had made a sketch of the falls on the Diamond, and another of a party who were camping on the Magalloway. He reported the water rather low in the river in some places, and they had been obliged to push the boat along with their oars instead of rowing. "And I tell you what," he added with enthusiasm, "I never saw such a country as this; the farther you get into it the prettier it is." Of the fish, the girls had taken eight and Ned the other twelve; and the latter declared that if the whole party had been provided with rods and lines, they might have caught all they could carry.

"Where did you catch your trout, Ned?" asked George, after

CAMPING ON THE MAGALLOWAY RIVER.

the fisherman had returned from the kitchen, where he had left his finny prize.

"At the Falls. There was a dam there."

"I would like to know where you can go in this country without finding a dam? Half of the natives carry them in their mouths," put in George quickly.

"Now, don't give us any more of that," replied his friend, "or I shall leave you, because it makes me weak."

"Well, fire away then," said George, the smile fading out of his face.

"We had the best luck near the dam," resumed Ned. "We did not go up the Diamond with the boat. We passed it, and landed a short distance above on the west side of the Magalloway at a sort of ferry. Then followed a path that led through a man's wood-shed, struck a pasture, crossed that, and entered a road which ran up the right-hand side of the river, and followed that till we reached the Falls."

"Much of a walk?"

"No; and a very pleasant one. What luck did you have?"

"We brought back thirteen partridges."

"You don't mean it!

"Honest Injun! Ask the girls."

"Yes, we did," added Lucie.

"I'll tell you how it was," continued George. "We went out back of the barn, and started up over the hill. We soon reached some small spruces, with hard wood intermixed, and we worked our way through that towards the pond. When we were well into the forest, we flushed a flock of partridges that must have contained fifteen or twenty. In fact, I should think they were holding a convention. I saw them first, and let drive both barrels. Dick, who had the parson's gun, followed, and we bagged seven at the first fire. The others flew, but after skirmishing around awhile we found two of them and shot those. Then we continued on to the pond. After we found it we followed around the shore towards its head, until the girls began to feel tired, then resting awhile, we made a circuit route back toward the house, and on our return ran across some more birds which I think were a part of the first lot we saw, and we knocked over four of those. They are fat as butter, although of course not full grown; and I tell you, my boy, they will make good eating."

"How long have you been back to the house?"

"Came in about half an hour ahead of you."

"There is the supper-bell," said Grace, and the conversation was brought suddenly to a close.

During the evening their plans were completed for the ascent of

SHOOTING PARTRIDGES.

the mountain, and the entire party retired to rest quite early, so as to be strong for the next day's jaunt. The young people were very anxious in regard to the weather for the next day; but Mr. Van Wyck told them it would not make a bit of difference, no matter how much they worried, and they had better dismiss the subject from their mind and go to bed. His advice was accepted.

In the night there were heavy showers; but certainly one could not wish for a more pleasant morning than greeted George and Lucie, who were the first to make their appearance. The rain had laid the dust and cooled the air, which for the past three days had been rather oppressive, and the pearly raindrops on the grass and flowers and trees gave them a perfume and freshness that had been wanting for some time. The sun was shining brightly, and it was altogether lovely.

"Certainly we have many things to thank God for," remarked Lucie, as she and George sauntered up and down the piazza.

"We have, indeed. And although we appreciate them, and feel thankful for favors received in our own careless way, still we are not half thankful enough."

"You are ahead of us," said Grace, appearing at this moment; "where are the others?"

"Not down yet," replied Lucie; "but here come the boys."

"Capital morning, this," remarked Dick, saluting them: "couldn't have a better day for our purpose. I see it rained last night."

"Yes," returned Grace; "and how fresh and beautiful everything looks! I should like to be at home this morning and go to church."

"Well," suggested George, "we can worship to-day as the old Scotch covenanters used to — from the tops of the mountains."

Just then the elder people made their appearance, and the sound of the bell gave token that breakfast was ready.

After the morning meal, an hour slipped by while they were making preparation; but at nine o'clock, when the wagons were brought to the door, they were ready. The young people took possession of the first one, with Mr. Lowe for driver, and the old folks, with the hired man for driver, in the other. As they started off the "stay-at-homes," who were assembled on the piazza, wished them a good time and a clear day.

They followed the road to the upper settlement, and, as the wagons were without covered tops, had an uninterrupted view of the lovely valley up which they were driving. The singular shaped Diamond Peaks and Half-Moon Mountain on their left, with Aziscohos on their right, were the principal mountain features, although there were numerous other smaller peaks. Some of the houses by which they passed bore evident marks of age, and one or two in the valley, it is said, can claim a hundred years. Curious faces, both old and young, peered at them with astonishment from the windows of the houses along their route; and when the party met pedestrians, as they sometimes did, the natives would stare at the strangers while they were passing, and then watch them out of sight.

THE DIAMOND PEAKS.

The appearance of these well-dressed and pleasant-looking tourists, was a break in the monotony of their narrow existence, and would furnish them food for talk and gossip for many days to come. So far from the busy world were the lives of these people passed, that things of the most trivial character to a city person became of the highest importance to them, and were remembered for days and months afterwards.

Those living along the valley are generally well-to-do country people; and one old fellow, whom report says can neither read nor write, who has lived there for many years, it is said has amassed eight or ten thousand dollars, a fortune in that country. This money was acquired by the most rigid economy and by denying themselves of every luxury and many of the actual necessaries of every-day life. In his earlier years, his wife and himself would sit at home evenings, she knitting socks and mittens, and he making axe-handles by what light the fire afforded, not using candles on account of the expense.

But even in this out-of-the-way corner of the world, the spirit of speculation is rampant. It takes the shape of a desire to do a "little loggin';" and when once indulged in, unless quickly nipped, generally proves the ruin of the farmer. For in this business he nearly always loses, while the large operators and the wealthy lumbering companies make the money. One of these farmers will take a contract to "put in" from half a million to a million feet. It is needless to say that all the fat of the contract is on the lumber company's side. They furnish the supplies (provisions), at a large profit, advance the farmer a little money, charge him roundly for stumpage, and hold a lien on all the logs he cuts, until they are made whole. The result generally is that the small operator comes out in the spring in debt to the lumber company. So he must log the next winter to pay that, which leaves him deeper in debt, and unless he has the nerve to shut down on the business with what experience he has already bought, he generally loses all he has. And the number of this class of unfortunates in this back country is by no means small, if the writer can believe what he has been told.

Window glass seems to be either a scarce or very expensive article in the valley, judging by the number of old hats, bonnets, newspapers, and every conceivable substitute, appearing in the windows of some of the houses. Bare-footed urchins, and girls in the same condition, some of whom must have been fourteen or fifteen years of age, met them as they rode along, and gazed at them with wondering eyes and open mouths. Berry-pickers were numerous; and from time to time several men and boys were seen, with fish-poles across their shoulders, heading for the river.

The country road at last ended by a gate crossing it. Mr. Lowe, who was ahead, jumped down and opened it, and George drove through. Then the landlord resumed his place, leaving the gate open for the other driver to close. The road now ran through a pasture, and reached another gate, and still another before ending at "Clark's," where they stopped, this being the end of their route with horses.

When the second team arrived Mr. Lowe directed the driver to put up the horses in Clark's barn, and then follow them with the lunch, part of which the landlord carried with him; he also took a light axe to cut out any troublesome windfalls.

When the ladies were ready to start Mr. Lowe led the way. They crossed a field, then passed through a gate and followed a rough tote road that led to the head of the falls. After a few minutes' walk Mr. Lowe left the cart road, striking into a path from the right-hand side of the road, leading up into the woods. After following the path for a quarter of a mile, their guide told them the rest of the way was perfectly plain, and they would find no difficulty in following the trail, and that he would go on ahead to remove any obstructions that might be troublesome to the ladies. With that he left them, and they saw no more of him until they reached the summit.

The ascent at first was very gradual, but the farther they went the steeper grew the way. But the footing nearly the entire distance was excellent, and there was very little danger, with ordinary care, of sprains or falls. As they penetrated deeper into the woods, the heat increased, but very little wind getting to them, and they were compelled to stop frequently and rest, and wipe the moisture from their faces. They crossed several sparkling streams that came tumbling down the mountain side, and at these places drinking cups were in demand. As they climbed slowly upwards they occasionally came to rough spots where the ladies were glad to avail themselves of a helping hand from some of the gentlemen. The last half-mile, through stunted firs, spruces, and cedars, was a great deal like work, but the path continued good.

THE GUIDE ON THE SUMMIT.

Finally they cleared the woods, and beheld Mr. Lowe, standing on the highest ledge of the northern peak, awaiting them. He swung his hat to them as they appeared, and the young people cheered and waved their handkerchiefs. After coming out on the flattened summit of the mountain, it was yet quite a climb to the peak where the landlord stood. But in fifteen minutes they had all gained it and sat down to rest.

The weather still continued to smile on them, and it was as clear a day as they could wish. The rain of the night before had taken all of the haze out of the air, and the most distant peak cut the turquoise blue of the sky like a cameo. A light breeze from the south-west swept across the mountain, and fanned their flushed and fevered faces with its delicious coolness.

The peak on which they now reclined appeared to be about five hundred feet above the southern one. While the one upon which they rested was entirely bare, the opposite one had a few bushes and stunted trees that kept up a desperate struggle with the forces of nature for a bare subsistence. The distance between the two peaks was about a mile, over a rough pathway of loose rocks. All around them were huge bowlders, torn from the massive head of the old mountain by the lightning and frosts. There were many seams and fissures, running down to a depth of twenty or thirty feet, and undoubtedly the work of destruction is steadily progressing.

While the party were enjoying the view, the other driver appeared with the balance of the lunch, and, assisting Mr. Lowe, they soon had a fire going, fed by dry roots and mosses, and over this a kettle of tea was hung to steep. This ready, the luncheon was opened, and all were invited to partake, the two drivers waiting on the party to the best of their ability. Bread and butter, cold meats, cheese, doughnuts, and tea comprised the meal, which was partaken of amid laughter and jests on all sides.

The ladies were not used to such strong tea as Mr. Lowe brewed, and missed their accustomed milk. But the entire meal was a novelty to them, and after the appetites they had awakened from their unusual exertions, they were little disposed to be fastidious. The party ate from their hands, no dishes having been brought, with the exception of half a dozen tin dippers for the tea, and those were passed from one to the other as occasion required. As Mr. Lowe said, "It was about all he and the driver wanted to sack the grub up, without lugging dishes."

When all had finished eating, an hour was devoted to sight-seeing and another to rambling to the farther peak and back.

From the top of Mount Aziscohos you gaze upon a forest wilderness, bounded only by the blue sky in which it is lost. A grand

DINNER ON AZISCOHOS.

upheaval of mountain peaks and ranges, many of which are wooded to their summits. Circle upon circle of billowy ridges, their tops green or gray, extending from beneath you to the utmost limit of your sight. This is the first impression of the view as it bursts upon your bewildered gaze. Afterward you have time to notice that between nearly all of these mountains are ponds, lakes, or rivers. Indeed, I doubt if there is a mountain in New England from whose summit you can distinctly see and count so many other mountains and so many pieces of water as from this one. I have climbed more than the average number of mountains allotted to most men, and I have never found its equal in this respect. I could not name half of the mountains and pieces of water seen from the summit of old Aziscohos, and I doubt if it has ever been visited by any one who could.

Some of the principal ranges and peaks seen and known are, the Half-Moon, Dustan, Moose, Blue, Sawyer, Deer, Kennebago, Saddleback, the Bigelow Peaks, Swan, Bald Pate, Speckled Mountain, Mount Katahdin, the higher peaks of the White Mountains, Mount Chocorua and the Boundary Mountains. The entire chain of the Androscoggin Lakes, the Richardson Ponds, Beaver Ponds, Sturdivant Ponds, the Androscoggin, Magalloway, Kennebago, and Rangeley Rivers are but a few of the bodies of water. The occasional small clearings are but white islands amid the vast green ocean, and do not detract from the wildness of the view one particle.

In our opinion a small house will be built on the summit of Aziscohos at no distant day for the accommodation of tourists, for that the mountain is destined some time to become famous in the eye of those who love the beauties of nature is beyond cavil or doubt.

Under a cairn of stones, on the highest peak, a tin box is kept for the receptacle of cards and communications that visitors may choose to make, and over those already in the box the party paused half an hour, and then added their own "last will and testament," as Dick expressed it.

In the summer of 1882 the U. S. Signal Coast Survey established a station on Aziscohos, and erected a beacon on the highest peak for some scientific purpose. It has since been blown down by a hurricane.

Before going down the mountain, the party grouped on the barren ledge at the request of Mr. Van Wyck, and with uncovered heads sang those glorious hymns, " Nearer, my God, to Thee," " Let Your Lower Lights be Burning," and " America," after which he made a short and appropriate prayer, thanking God for the mercies vouchsafed to them, and for the pleasures they had by his help enjoyed while on their trip. Surely no more hearty service, or no more fitting tribute, ascended to the Almighty that day than went up from one of his own pulpits, on that barren mountain in the middle of a Maine wilderness, five thousand feet above the sea.

Before returning to the team they stopped and chatted a few minutes with two young fellows who were camping below on the river, and who had come up on the mountain that forenoon, and who intended to stay on the summit over night, to get the sunset and sunrise from the highest elevation in that section of the country. Where the scrub spruce ended and the barren rock alone remained, they had extemporized a rude shelter for one night, which they had christened " Bleak House ; " and a very bleak house the ladies thought it was.

On their way down, Mr. Lowe pointed out both bear and moose tracks, that were fresh, and told them the animals had been there within a day or two. When they had made half the distance, the drivers left the party, for the purpose of harnessing the horses and getting all ready for a start. This they accomplished; for when the party reached Clark's, they had only to step into the wagons, and the horses trotted gayly homewards, arriving at the hotel in an hour.

Afterward refreshed by sundry ablutions and an excellent supper, they gathered in the parlor, where was a very good organ, and passed the evening in singing.

The next forenoon was passed quietly at the house by the older people, while the younger ones went up the river boating, but returned to the hotel in season for dinner. About quarter of one they heard the steamboat whistle, and immediately put on their things and went over to the landing. The steamer was in sight, and a few moments later had reached the river bank and was tied up. There were three ladies and gentlemen on board who were to stop at Magalloway, and after they had landed the ladies of the Van Wyck party were helped on board,

BLEAK HOUSE, MOUNT AZISCOHOS.

and the gentlemen followed. In the mean time, the captain and engineer were tumbling seven or eight Saratoga trunks out on the landing. As the last one went on the pile, the captain gave a sigh of relief, and, pushing the steamer's bow around, she steamed down.

"These people seem to have plenty of baggage," remarked Mr. Van Wyck to the captain, who was mopping his face with his handkerchief after his recent exertion.

"I should think they did. Six people — eight Saratoga trunks.

Now, ain't that a pretty sight," pointing to the pile of baggage on shore that was being surveyed by Mr. Lowe with a great deal of disgust, " to bring up into such a country as this. And there were two of those trunks that would weigh from three hundred and fifty to four hundred pounds, if they would weigh an ounce. Then they had valises and bags, bundles in shawl-straps, and I don't know what else. And the man who paid the fares growled like a western tornado because I charged him two dollars extra on the baggage."

" They must be a mean crowd," said George, " not to be willing to pay two dollars extra on such a pile of stuff as that. They have enough baggage there for a theatrical company. It will take Lowe and his man all the afternoon to get it to the house and up to their rooms."

" Yes, and perhaps that is a job he'll like," returned the captain with a grin. " But what kind of a time did you have? It was a lovely day yesterday."

" Charming!" and George gave the captain an interesting account of their excursion.

The steamer made a quick run down river, and reached Errol Dam at three o'clock. The Van Wyck party bade the captain good-by, and the boys promised to be at the landing the next forenoon to go up river with him.

Mr. Bragg was not there when the steamer arrived; and the captain was just on the point of leaving when the jolly landlord and one of his sons drove up in two vehicles with eight passengers, who were going down to Cambridge to stay a few days.

" You're behind time," cried the captain, as the horses drove up in front of the boat.

" No, I'm not — I'm behind a pair of horses," chuckled the landlord, and then he jumped down and helped his passengers to alight.

There were five gentlemen and three ladies in the party from the hotel, and they with their baggage were quickly transferred to the steamer, and she started up river, giving several loud whistles as a farewell.

The Van Wyck party now filled the seats in the wagons, and were quickly driven to the hotel.

About five o'clock Mr. Marston made his appearance with a large carriage drawn by six horses, capable of carrying the whole party, and the boys realized that they were soon to part with their pleasant friends.

VIEW ON THE MAGALLOWAY, JUST ABOVE THE BRIDGE.

But they passed a jolly evening, — sang, and danced, and played games, even the older members of the party entering with zest into the sport, and, somewhat fatigued, they retired to rest at ten o'clock.

Mr. Marston wished to start by eight o'clock, and Tuesday morning all were up in good season, and at seven o'clock they sat down to breakfast.

In the time they had been together the party had become well acquainted, the younger members especially forming a strong attachment for each other, and the idea of separation caused them to be a little serious at the breakfast table. But the thought of the pleasant correspondence that would follow their separation soothed their feelings somewhat; and it was with hopeful, if not very cheerful, faces that the young people exchanged their farewells. The older people had observed nothing in the conduct of the boys to find fault with, while on the other hand, they had noticed a great deal to commend, and therefore gave the young gentlemen a hearty invitation to visit them at their homes when an opportunity offered, an invitation which the youngsters

THE DEPARTURE OF THE GIRLS.

assured them they should avail themselves of at the earliest possible moment after their return home in the fall.

The carriage was now brought to the door, the young fellows helped their friends in, the baggage was loaded on, and a moment later, amid the cheers of the boys, and an old shoe thrown by the landlord for luck, the wagon rattled over the covered bridge across the Androscoggin, on its way to Berlin.

CHAPTER XI.

RETURN TO LOWE'S. — CAMPING OUT. — CAMP COOKING. — A LITTLE DIFFI-
CULTY. — A TRIP TO DIAMOND PONDS.

"POOR Dick, I pity you," said the Parson, as the boys sat down on the piazza, after the wagon had disappeared from sight.

"Do you?" indignantly. "You had better transfer some of it to yourself, you can hardly keep from crying now," and Dick, with mock sympathy, offered the Parson his pocket handkerchief.

"Quit your fooling now, and attend to business," remarked George. "When we get up to Lowe's again, we had better pack up all our best clothes, and everything else we don't need in the woods, and send down to Cambridge by Captain Farwell, and they will be there when we return."

"A good idea," acknowledged Dick.

"We must arrange with Mr. Lowe this afternoon about stores and boats, and get everything in readiness for an early start somewhere to-morrow morning. I think it would be a good idea to go over to the Diamond Ponds and spend a few days. They are only about twelve miles distant from the Brown Farm, and there is a good road all the way. What do you say, fellows?"

"Anything for sport," cried Dick.

"I go in for it," agreed Ned, "the more we see of this country the better."

"I am with you," chimed in the Parson.

"Suppose we get our things down now, and then stroll over toward the dam," suggested George. "Mr. Bragg can bring them over when he comes with the mail."

"All right," said Dick. "But we have not settled our bill yet. Here, Parson, hunt Bragg up and pay the bill, and we will get your duds down with ours."

The Parson, who was the treasurer of the party, paid the bill, while his friends brought down their baggage, and then the boys crossed the bridge over the river. Just as they were turning toward the dam, Dick suggested a visit to the one store which Errol boasted, to see if they could make any purchases. They went to the door, but it was locked; and after banging away on it for a while, an old lady made her appearance on the inside and let them in. They found some amusement in looking over the stock, it was so different from that in the stores where they lived, there being almost everything in the room that one could think of. While they were looking around, a barefooted urchin came in with a hen's egg, which he exchanged for peanuts, and a woman brought in a pair of mittens of her own manufacture, which she swapped for sugar. The boys bought a few needles, pins, a spool of thread and another of silk, some buttons, and a paper of court-plaster. Then Dick suggested that the treasurer be allowed to treat from the general fund, and the others agreeing, the Parson bought two pounds of candy and four quarts of peanuts.

These paid for, George noticed some hooks and lines, and invested in half a dozen ordinary lines, and a dozen fish-hooks.

"I don't know how it is," he remarked, "but some of these country boys, with an old alder pole, and a common line and hook, with a bunch of worms on the end of it, take more trout than we do with our fancy rigging, and I am going to try their way of fishing some day."

THE WAY COUNTRY BOYS FISH.

"I can tell you the reason," laughed Dick.

"What is it?"

"They know where the trout are."

Just as they were leaving the store, a man came in with a minkskin, and wanted to trade it for molasses.

"What next, I wonder?" observed George. "I would like to know if these people ever take any money. The old lady had three customers while we were there, and didn't get a cent out of them."

"I'll bet she hasn't seen so much money before in a week as we paid her," asserted the Parson.

"I guess they do mostly a barter business," added Ned. "Storekeepers down here have to take anything they can get."

It was only ten o'clock when they reached the landing, and as the steamer would not be due for half an hour, Dick proposed they sit down on the bank and sample the candy and peanuts. No one objecting, they threw themselves on the grass and the Parson opened the treat, and helping himself, told the others to do likewise.

While sitting there, they heard the noise of wheels on the little bridge between them and the dam, and soon a single buckboard, rather the worse for wear, containing two old and "roughlooking Pilgrims," as Dick expressed it, passed them. It was drawn by a horse who had evidently seen his best days, and who, as Dick dryly remarked, "might have been fifty years or he might have been less; but the latter was doubtful."

"Mornin'," said the man nearest them, as the buckboard rolled by.

"Good-morning," replied George. "Are you going fishing?" Two bamboo poles as large round at the butts as a silver dollar, and twenty or thirty feet long, suggested the question.

"Yes. Goin' pickerelin'."

"Good luck to you," cried Dick.

"Thank ye, young man," and the old team rattled and jolted along just fast enough to keep the poor horse enveloped in a cloud of dust, what wind there was being with them.

"What do you think of those for fishing-rods," inquired Dick of no one in particular, as the men passed out of hearing.

"If you are speaking to me," returned George, "I should as soon think of using that pine on the river bank," and he pointed to a tree below them, about two feet in diameter and seventy-five feet high, and he smiled at his own conceit.

Just then the steamer whistled, and the Parson wrapped up the candy and peanuts.

THE PICKEREL PARTY.

"There are passengers on board," remarked George, "they are whistling for the team."

Soon the little steamer appeared in sight, and they could see that she was crowded.

"She's a saucy looking craft," exclaimed Dick, as the steamer swept toward them.

"Yes, she is, and a fast traveller too," said George. "See what a clean wake she leaves behind."

The boat was close in on the opposite bank of the river, and as she

reached the lower end of the wharf the captain threw the wheel hard-a-starboard, and rang for the engineer to slow down. Minding her helm instantly, the beautiful little boat made a complete circle, and swung in alongside the wharf, bow up the river, without even scarring her paint.

"A neat landing, Captain; good-morning, how are you?" and George shook hands with the captain, and took the stern line and made it fast, while Dick caught the bow line.

"I am nicely," returned the captain. "Going up this morning?"

"Yes, sir; we are."

"Where's Bragg?"

"Has not come yet. He will be over in a moment with our things."

"There he comes now," shouted Dick, as they heard a rattling on the bridge.

Six ladies now left the steamer, and went up to the road, and their baggage was carried up to them.

"I guess your clock was slow this morning," said the captain as Bragg made his appearance.

"It's fast enough for you, any time," chuckled the landlord. "I don't like to get over here and wait an hour for the boat."

"Why, you old heathen, you know you are never here when we get here, that is, hardly ever." And then the captain thought what he had said, and his face turned white, and he looked about in affright.

"All right, Captain. That was probably a slip. We won't hang you this time, but beware of the next offence. That remark has caused the death of several men in Boston," and George smiled, while the gentlemen on the boat who had heard the conversation roared with laughter.

"Where are all these women going?" inquired Bragg in an aside of the captain.

"To Dixville Notch. They are teachers off on a vacation. Look out you don't fall in love with one of them."

"No men with them?"

"No; it is a goose party."

"Where are those men on the boat going?"

"Up to Magalloway and back: they are making the round trip. But I must be off. Come, Bragg, show your gallantry. Don't you see the ladies are waiting for you to help them into the wagon?" and the captain chucked the landlord under the ribs, and stepped on board the steamer.

As they sailed up the river, the boys scraped acquaintance with the gentlemen on board, and found them very pleasant companions. Nothing of unusual occurrence took place on their run up river, except that the captain ran into Flint's landing, and stopped there. He told the boys that as the water in the river was stead-

STEAMER PARMACHENEE AT FLINT'S LANDING.

ily falling, he did not dare go to the upper landing. He whistled just above Bottle Brook for the team to come down, and again at Sharp Shins, and when the steamer reached the landing Mr. Lowe was there with his three-seated wagon, and a pair of horses.

"Can we get dinner about here anywhere, captain?" inquired one of the passengers as they all left the boat.

"Yes, sir; this gentleman will drive you straight up to the hotel. I will wait until you return, but be quick as you can, please."

Mr. Lowe and the captain loaded the boys' baggage on the wagon, and George advised the captain that they should send some things down to the landing the next day, and they wanted them taken down to the Lakeside Hotel at Cambridge, for safe keeping until they put in an appearance there.

"How long before you will be down?"

"Probably six weeks. Possibly eight."

"You are going to have a pretty good time. The flies and mosquitoes are gone now, and you can be comfortable."

"I wish you were going with us, Captain."

"So do I; but I have my bread and butter to earn, you know."

"All ready, boys," called Mr. Lowe.

"Come on, George; good-by, Captain," and Dick climbed to a seat, followed by his friends.

Between the lower landing and the hotel were quite a number of houses the boys had not seen before, and some of these possessed peculiarities which caused the party to laugh. They passed one nice set of buildings when near the hotel, which upon inquiry they learned belonged to a Mr. Sturdivant, the wealthiest man in that section. A year or two before he had lost all his buildings by fire, and had now built them up again. Although there was not a fire-engine within forty or fifty miles of him, he had carried no insurance, and his property was a total loss.

During the afternoon and evening the boys busied themselves in overhauling and sorting out, and packing up their things. All that they did not need they placed in their trunks and valises for transportation to Cambridge, and the rest they packed in leather knapsacks, which they were to carry on their backs by means of straps, when they travelled in the woods. Their guns, rods, and axes, and some cooking utensils, would have to be carried in their hands when they left the water. They had no tent, having determined after a spirited argument on the subject to trust the weather, and exercise their ingenuity in building camps.

The next morning after breakfast, Mr. Lowe took them up to Bennett's Landing in a boat, and leaving them on shore wished them "good luck."

"When do you think you'll come back," he asked as he pushed off from the shore, and dipped his oars in the water.

"In about a week, if the bears don't eat us up," replied George with a laugh.

George helped the others shoulder their packs, and then swung up his own. They had to carry their guns and their rods on their shoulders, and the two axes, the four boys took turns in bearing. Their packs weighed about fifty pounds each, and they found this about all the load they could carry, and as the sun grew higher and hotter, the sweat poured down their faces in streams, and George counselled a rest, wisely observing that it was no use to get played out the first day.

ON THE TRAMP.

It was about eleven o'clock when they halted; and George sent Dick out to see if he could raise any partridges, and the Parson to the river for a mess of trout, while he and Ned built a fire, made coffee, and prepared for dinner.

"Now, Ned, get some wood and start a fire along side of that large rock to your left, and I will manufacture a table and seat."

Ned, grasping one of the axes, began hunting for fire-wood, while George with the other felled some small forked maples. He cut four of these the proper length, and drove them into the ground two feet apart one way, and six feet the other. Then he cut two small sticks a couple of inches in diameter, two feet and six inches long, and placed them in the forks of the table-legs. After which he cut about ten small maples, there being plenty in the vicinity. These last he made a little over six feet long, flattening them on one side with the axe, and then laid them on the cross-pieces. A couple of alder withes, one bound around each end of the table, made the whole thing complete and ready for the dishes. The same arrangement along one side of the table, only lower, and with an extra pair of legs and cross-piece in the middle to resist the spring of the poles, furnished the seat.

CAMP FURNITURE.

"You would make a good wood butcher," said Ned, as he came up sweltering under a huge armful of wood. "I'll be hanged if you haven't displayed a good deal of ingenuity in the construction of that table and bench. Ever make one before?"

"No; but let us get a blaze going," and helping Ned they soon had a nice fire under way.

"Now, Ned, if you are not too tired, I wish you would go over to that clump of alders, and cut down eight or ten of the largest, and bring them here, and cut them up into pieces eight or ten inches long. Alder makes the best coals for cooking you ever saw in your life. I shall have to draw on the river for a pail of water, before we can start the coffee;" and George took from his knapsack something that looked like a nest of tin plates, but which on a shake by him changed to the form of a ten-quart tin pail.

"That is the boss tin pail, George: where did you find it?"

"Had it made to order. When we first talked of coming up here in the woods, I thought the thing over a great deal, and wondered what we would do for a pail, thinking it would be an unhandy article to lug around the woods. Then an idea struck me, and I acted upon it. I had seen a drinking-cup like this made of German silver, only without any bail. I bought one, carried it to a tinman I knew, told him what I wanted, and this pail is the result. It's a mighty handy thing, and I have half a mind to patent it. You see, when it is folded you can carry it in your blankets, valise, or knapsack, without any trouble in packing, and it is always ready to use."

"George, you have a big head!" and Ned patted him softly on his shoulder. "I should get that pail patented when you get home, and if you make a fortune I'll divide with you and take half."

"You're very kind. But suppose you tackle the alders, while I go for the water."

About half-past twelve Dick returned with a couple of partridges, and shortly afterward, Fred came in with fifteen small trout. George had the dishes, tin plates, and dippers, with common knives, forks, and spoons, on the table, and his coffee from the fire was sending forth a royal essence.

"I wish I had carried a gun with me," said the Parson. "Kingfishers were plenty where I was fishing; I saw five or six."

"Why do you wish to kill them?" asked George.

"Oh, for the fun of it. Then, they are a pretty bird to set up."

"If you can give no better reason than that, I am glad you had nothing to shoot with. There is no fun in shooting just for the pleasure of killing; and you could not keep the bird till we could get a chance to send it out, if you had shot it."

"That's so, George. And I am glad I had neither gun nor rifle with me, as I might have been tempted to use it."

"I declare that coffee smells good!" exclaimed Dick. "Phew! I tell you I took quite a tramp," and he mopped the perspiration from his forehead.

THE KINGFISHERS.

"Where did you find your partridges?" inquired George.

"About a mile away on a branch logging road."

"See any more?"

"Two, but they flew. How are you going to cook these? I'm as hungry as a bear."

"I don't know. Let me think. Is there any clay or mud down to the river where you were fishing, Fred?"

"Yes, there was a clay bank near where I caught the last trout. I will go and show you."

"Come on, then. But did you dress your fish?"

"Yes. I knew we couldn't eat them until they were cleaned."

"Parson, you'll make a good backwoodsman in time: go ahead, and show us the clay," and George took the two partridges and followed his friend.

When they reached the clay bank, George split open the birds and took out their entrails, cut off their heads and feet, then washed and laid them on a clean, smooth stone. Then taking some of the clay he kneaded it in water, until he made a soft paste and with this he covered the birds until they resembled two large balls of mud more than anything else in the world. The Parson watched him with wonder depicted on his countenance, and at last broke out:—

"George, old fellow, what are you doing? You have spoiled those partridges."

"Don't you believe it. Let's go up to camp. I hope Ned put some of those alder limbs on the fire. I told him to do it before we left."

Ned had obeyed instructions, and they found a splendid bed of alder coals, and into these George unceremoniously plunged his "mud balls" as the Parson called them, and with a stick covered them completely with the coals. Then he cut up a few slices of pork, and placed in the frying-pan, and told Ned to hold it over the fire. While he rolled the trout in meal, he sent the Parson to the river with four good-sized potatoes to wash, and told him to place them under the coals on his return.

When the pork had tried out, George laid the trout in the frying-pan, and in fifteen minutes, after being once turned, they were fried to a beautiful brown. They were then salted a little, and put on the back part of the fire to keep warm until the potatoes and partridges were cooked. In about fifteen minutes longer, George raked open the coals, and found the potatoes nicely baked, and told Ned to wipe them on an old towel they had brought along to use about their cooking. Then with a stick he poked out the partridges. The clay had become as hard as a rock, and had all cracked open; and with a knife George freed the birds from their earthern covering, the clay taking off all the feathers and skin, as it fell away. When they were entirely cleaned, he put them on a plate, and put a little butter, salt, pepper, and flour, on each, and they sent forth a smell that actually caused the saliva to run out of the corners of the Parson's mouth.

DINNER BY THE ROADSIDE.

"George, you are a brick!" exclaimed Ned. "Where did you learn that trick?"

"Learned it here, just now."

"But where did you see it tried? I never heard of such a thing."

"Nowhere. I read of it, and thought I would try it. Now let's have our dinner. The hard-tack are in your knapsack, Dick; get out some."

The coffee, trout, potatoes, and hard-tack were now placed on the table. A can of condensed milk was produced, and opened, a piece of butter was put on a plate, and the boys gathered around the appetizing viands.

George poured the coffee, and Dick helped them to the solids, and they were soon appeasing their hunger.

"I didn't know George was a prize cook, did you, Ned?" said Dick, as he filled his mouth with partridge.

"No. But if this dinner is a sample of what he can do, I think he had better apply to Young's for a position as *Chef* when he returns home. These partridges just lay over any I ever ate before in my life."

"And these trout are cooked the nicest of any I have eaten since we left home," chimed in the Parson.

"And this is an A No. 1 cup of coffee," added Dick, who was smacking his chops over his favorite beverage.

"Come, come, fellows, a truce to compliments," commanded George, blushing. "I am not used to being soaped. I am willing to do the best I can for you cooking, but don't make any more talk about it."

"How modest," said Ned. "I told him once before, and now I repeat it, he has a big head."

"Yes," put in the Parson, with a chuckle at the joke, "wears a number twenty-two hat."

"Oh, confound you! let up, or I won't cook the supper."

"Silence! for heaven's sake, then," said Dick with mock solemnity, "only think what a calamity that would be."

The meal went on with more or less chaffing between the friends, and was only finished when every vestige of the partridges, fish, and potatoes had disappeared, while each one of the party had managed to surround three hard-bread in addition to the other things they had eaten.

"Come, boys," called Dick, jumping up, "don't be swine because your fathers were."

"You call any one a hog," said George dryly, as he arose, "after what you have eaten! You are small, but oh my! I'll leave it to

Ned and the Parson, if you have not eaten more than any fellow in the crowd."

"Yes! Yes!" asserted the two, as George appealed to them.

"I don't think George ought to touch the dishes," remarked Ned, "after getting us up a dinner fit for a king. I'll wash them, if you'll wipe them, Dick."

"I'm your man."

A dish-cloth, towel, and a piece of soap were now produced from one of the knapsacks, and in fifteen minutes Ned and Dick had the dishes all ready to pack. The fire was put out with water brought from the river, and the table and bench were left just as they were, to use on their return.

It was half-past two when everything was ready for a start, and shouldering their packs, and taking the other articles, they started on again. They travelled as quickly as the heat would permit until five o'clock, only stopping once, when Dick, who was in advance, flushed a flock of partridges, from which they shot three.

"Here is a good place to camp, boys," remarked George, as he dropped the butt of his rifle to the ground. "There is plenty of fire-wood, and the river is handy for water and fish. As it is going to be a warm, pleasant night we don't need much of a camp. We must be half way to the ponds, sure."

"Let us stop here, then," said Dick, dropping his pack, for truth to tell, he was well tired out.

"So say we all of us," added Ned, and down came his pack, the Parson following suit.

"Now for our camp," observed George. "Ned, you can assist me, while Dick and the Parson get up some fire-wood."

"I can get all the wood we shall want," returned Dick. "You will have to use one of the axes and then the Parson can try for a mess of trout. He did well this noon."

"All right," replied George. "Anything to facilitate matters;" and Dick seized one of the axes, and pluckily tackled a dry spruce, a windfall, while Fred took his rod, and started for the river.

"Now, let me see," said George, "we have four rubber blankets and four woollen ones. We can use two of the rubber ones on top of our camp, and put the other two under us to sleep on. A few boughs stuck up at the sides will answer for shelter in that direction, it is going to be such a pleasant night. I want a couple of crotched maples or white birches first, Ned, about eight feet long, and " (looking around him) " here we have the very thing," pointing to a clump of maples a short distance away.

Ned went for them, and soon had the saplings down, cut to the right length, and one end of each sharpened. Telling Ned to cut a straight pole about seven feet long, George brought the other two, and selecting a level place near the road, after hard work managed to drive each of the forked sticks a foot into the ground. Ned now came up with the straight one, and this was placed on top the other two in the crotches. Then they cut seven more about eight feet long; and these George placed one end on the ground, and the other end on top of the horizontal pole and the framework of the camp was finished. On these poles he spread two of the rubber blankets, covering them with boughs, and laid a couple of heavy spruce limbs to keep them in place. If there had been promise of any wind he would have tied them securely to the framework as they had plenty of twine. A few small firs and spruces were now cut and stood up at the ends, and some

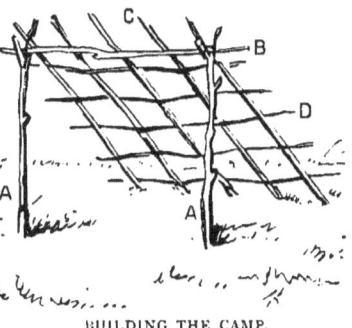

BUILDING THE CAMP.

fine spruce boughs, there being no cedar in the vicinity, were obtained and spread on the ground inside the camp. On these were placed two of the rubber blankets, and three of the woollen ones. The other being rolled up oblong, and placed at the back of the camp for a pillow, and their beds were ready. They then turned to, and made preparations for supper. While Ned built a fire, George peeled and sliced some potatoes, tried out some pork, and fried them, and as he was removing them, the Parson came up with two dozen nice trout all cleaned, which George also cooked. These, with potatoes, hard-bread, and coffee, furnished their supper.

CAMP COMPLETE.

George said they had better save the partridges shot that afternoon for breakfast, and then he would fricassee them.

"Fricasseed partridges!" exclaimed Dick. "Yum, Yum. Didn't I tell you we had a jewel of a cook?"

After the dishes were washed up and plenty of wood brought in, they sat around the fire and told stories and sang until about nine o'clock.

"Shall we keep guard to-night, the same as we did the night we were in the woods over in the Notch?" asked Dick of George.

"The dickens, no. What is there here to hurt us? No, we will all turn in, and have a good night's rest."

"I say, Dick," called Ned, "you might lay awake to-night, to see if you snore, if you wish to."

"Go to grass!" laughed Dick: "you need not be making game of me."

"I am not going to grass, but I am going to my balsamic couch, and I advise the rest of you to follow;" and George began to prepare for bed.

"What shall we do with the fire, George?" inquired Ned.

"Let it burn. It will be all right; and now," laughed George, "don't any of you fellows get frightened to death, if you happen to hear an owl in the night."

Following George's example they turned in, and in a few moments were sound asleep, and it was seven o'clock the next morning before either of the lads awoke.

THE FIRST NIGHT'S LODGING.

CHAPTER XII.

A LITTLE DIFFICULTY. — THE START NORTHWARD. — BOATING ON MAGALLO-
WAY. — CAMPING OUT. — A VISIT FROM A MOOSE.

FRED aroused first, and in a few moments they were up and dressed. George, with the help of the others, had the breakfast ready at eight o'clock; and when they had dried their blankets, which had gathered a little moisture during the night, they started on, and reached the ponds about four o'clock in the afternoon.

They found a deserted log cabin at one end, and here they made their headquarters, cruising around more or less every day but two, when it rained, for ten days, and then returned to Magalloway, reaching the hotel Saturday night, after an absence of nearly two weeks.

On their way back, they met some loggers trying to get up the river in two boats, but the water was so low they had to drag or pole them about all the way. A half mile below the boats, in the road, they ran across two rough-looking men, probably belonging to the same party, whom they judged to be a Canadian and an Irishman by their speech. On their approach the men hailed them, and inquired how far above the boats were.

Dick told the man, and was passing along, when the largest one snatched his rifle, remarking that it was a nice-looking rifle and he guessed he would keep it himself.

The other tried for the Parson's gun, but Fred was too quick for

him, and ran for Ned and George, who were ahead, and had not noticed this little *contretemps*.

"You give me that rifle," cried Dick savagely, who made a grab for it, only to be caught by the smaller man, the Canadian, and sent spinning across the side of the road, where he tripped over a rock and fell to the ground.

Just as Dick went down, George and Ned turned, and found Fred running, nearly up with them, and saw Dick roll over. George grasped the situation by instinct, and, ridding himself of his knapsack, he brought his rifle to a line with the Irishman's head, and took deliberate aim. His face was as white as a sheet, and his eyes fairly blazed.

The Irishman and his companion were laughing at Dick, who was now scrambling to his feet, when George called to him, —

"Drop that rifle, and make yourself scarce. I'll give you just two minutes to do it in."

The Irishman looked at George, and then glancing down at the rifle he held, and seeing it was loaded, attempted to raise it.

"If you raise that rifle," warned George, "you are a dead man. I never miss my aim. This rifle is cocked, my finger is on the trigger. If that rifle is not out of your hands by the time I count five, your interesting friend will have a chance to bury you. One! two! three!" —

"*Sacre!*" cried the Canadian. "He is *ver* resolute — he means what he says. Let's be off, Mike."

"Four" — and the Irishman stood the rifle against a tree.

"Now be off with you," said George.

"I was only fooling. Trying to frighten him a little," returned the Irishman, as the men went on.

George came over to where Dick stood, and watched the men

until they were out of sight. Then he helped Dick shoulder his knapsack.

"Did he hurt you any, Dick?" George asked, as they started on.

"Not a bit. I should not have fallen down, but I tripped over a rock."

"It's lucky for them they did not," asserted George as he picked up his knapsack, and the party started for the house.

They ferried over the river at Bennett's and then walked down the road to the hotel, and were glad enough when they reached it.

Mr. Lowe was at home and was pleased to see them. The boys told him of their adventure with the two men, and the landlord informed them that the men had probably been drinking, and said that he should have been glad if George had winged him.

ACROSS THE CARRY.

The next day being Sunday, the boys passed it quietly at the house, but immediately after breakfast Monday morning, they started in the wagon with Mr. Lowe, who was going to carry them up to Clark's. He told them he had hauled up two boats since they had been gone, and fixed them up nicely, and he would go over to the head of the falls with them, and see them started. After the landlord had put up his horses at the farmhouse, the boys shouldered their packs, and Mr. Lowe led the way up the same road they had taken when they ascended the mountain. But this time they did not branch off on the path, but followed the carry road, meeting two guides on the way, and after a walk of a little less than an hour, they reached the head of the falls, and found the boats above the dam, all right. Mr. Lowe helped to launch and load them, and telling the boys to leave the boats with John Danforth if they did not come back that way, bade them good-by, and wished them good luck.

"A mighty nice set of young fellows," murmured Mr. Lowe to himself, as he turned away from the river. "I hope they won't meet with any accident."

George and Dick went in one boat, and Ned and the Parson in the other, and they were as nearly equally loaded as possible.

"I will take the lead," said George, who was at the oars, while Dick paddled, "and you can follow me. It is going to be a hot day, and we will take it easy. We are not obliged to hurry and jump as if our lives depended on it. And we can keep the boats near enough together to converse without trouble."

In the other boat Ned plied the oars, and the Parson the paddle.

"Don't you think, George," suggested the Parson, "that it would be a good idea that Dick and I should have our guns by us in case we see any ducks?"

"Yes, it would. It is the fifth of September to-day, and ducks must be large enough to eat by this time, and we certainly ought to run across them on this river, or some of the adjacent ponds. But, by the way, you have both the shot guns in your boat. You know Dick and I both have rifles. You had better let Dick have Ned's gun. Load it with duck shot, and give him a half dozen extra shells;" and George ceased rowing, and the two boats drifted together, and the gun and ammunition were passed over to Dick.

The boats now went on, George leading, the boys keeping a

sharp lookout for game. The river was dark and apparently still, where they now were, and the banks were heavily wooded. They passed Beaver Brook without stopping, although Fred Flint, who kept the camp near the head of the falls, had told them they would find trout at its mouth. As they advanced into the heart of the wilderness, the river grew more crooked, and the scenery wilder, and more beautiful. Aziscohos Mountain played about them like a will o' the wisp, — now on one side, and then on the other; this moment directly in front of them, and the next behind their backs. The water was a translucent mirror; and the green pines, firs, and spruces, the white birches, the gray trunks of the maples along the banks, the blue sky over head, and the old mountain as it occasionally came into line, all were reproduced in the stream with the utmost minuteness of detail.

A few maple leaves, prematurely ripened, added their gorgeousness to the more sombre tints of green. A round-topped mountain on the left of the river, known as Parker Hill, played them as many tricks as Aziscohos.

In turning a bend of the river about a mile below Parker Hill Pond Eddy, they came suddenly upon a flock of a dozen or more black ducks. Dick's gun was at his shoulder in a moment, and he gave them one barrel while they sat on the water, and the other as they rose. It had been a long shot, but, fearful of frightening them, he had taken the chances, and blazed away at sight. Three ducks rewarded his efforts. As the flock arose they wheeled and started down the river directly over the boys' heads, and that gave the Parson a chance, which he eagerly availed himself of. Letting them have both barrels, right and left, he knocked over five, which fell with a splash into the water. " Good boys!" shouted George, " pick them up before they float off. Although this is apparently dead water, there is a strong current underneath;" and he rowed over to where the ducks had been discovered, and Dick pulled them in, while Ned and the Parson floated around for those the latter had shot.

"Eight black ducks," remarked Ned; "a pretty good haul. I never found them so tame before."

"It is after eleven," George observed, with a glance at his watch. "I think we had better stop when we get to Parker Hill Pond Eddy, and have dinner."

"How far is that from where we started?" inquired Ned.

"About four miles."

"We shall not get very far to-day at that rate," suggested Dick.

"What does it matter whether we are a day or a week in going up the river? We have plenty of time and ought to take it easy and enjoy ourselves."

A LUCKY SHOT.—DUCKS.

"But one naturally likes to get ahead."

"You can walk, Dick," put in the Parson, "if you are in a hurry."

"No, thank you, old Sober-sides, the water is too wet."

"I think if we get to the Narrows to-night, we shall have accomplished enough for one day," George said, as he pulled on up the river.

"That is only ten miles from the falls," replied Dick.

"True," acknowledged George. "And would you swallow the wilderness at one mouthful? Gobble it as a boy would a lump of sugar? For my part, I prefer to take it a little at a time, and extract the honey at my leisure. I am in no mood to drive at a Tam O'Shanter gait through this charming country. Hurry, worry, and tumult are the curse of our nation. We are away from the world. Why should we bring any of the unpleasant habits of the world into this Paradise? Let us be content to take what the day brings forth for us, and not grasp it by the throat and try to choke out a little more from its fruitful store."

"The philosopher has spoken," said Dick, with a little irony in his tone. "Let all obey."

"Isn't the philosophy sound?"

"Yes, there was considerable sound to it," assented Dick. "If you had kept your mouth shut, though, there wouldn't have been so much."

The boys laughed at this sally, and for a while conversation ceased. Occasionally a blue heron, frightened by the dip of their oars, while trying to gorge himself with frogs along the bank of the river, would utter a startled cry and fly lazily away, only to return when silence again reigned. On them the boys wasted no ammunition, for they did not believe they were good to eat. I have heard of people eating them. I would as soon eat a turkey buzzard. They saw several bald and gray eagles, but the kings of the air were wary, and did not venture within gun-shot.

It was not quite noon when they reached the eddy, and George thought they had better not attempt to cook the ducks until supper-time, it would take so long. Accordingly, while he and Ned made preparations for dinner, Dick and the Parson caught what trout they thought necessary for the consumption of four hungry voyagers.

Fried trout, boiled potatoes, hard-tack, and coffee, made up the meal, and good appetites were not lacking. Dinner over, and the dishes

A FANCY SKETCH. — DEER.

washed, the boats were loaded, and then the boys lay around for half an hour, and talked over their plans for the future. The Parson took but little part in the conversation, but seated on a sunny rock, with his back against a fallen tree, and his beloved sketch-book in his hand, he amused himself with making a fancy sketch.

At two o'clock the boys stepped into their boats, and pulled on up the river. A mile from where they had eaten dinner, they passed Bog Brook, flowing into the river from the left; and a mile beyond

THE NARROWS, LOOKING DOWN RIVER.

this, another stream, known as Otter Brook, which emptied in from the right. No otters were seen in its vicinity, but they caught a glimpse of three muskrats. From time to time a snag, or a tree that had fallen across the river, gave them more or less trouble, but this was all the excitement the afternoon produced until they reached the Narrows.

Here the bed of the river narrowed to a third of its usual width, and poured down between two high ledges, a smooth but very powerful current. Although there were good camping-grounds both above and below the Narrows, George thought they had better land above. Accordingly they had quite a lively time in getting up through; but after hard work, and two or three unsuccessful attempts, they accomplished it, and at four o'clock ran their boats up on the right bank of the river, a short distance beyond the head of the Narrows. Some gentlemen from Boston were camped here, whom Lowe had told them of, and had spoken highly of them to the boys. George found three of the gentlemen near the tents, and introduced himself and his friends to them, and told Mr. Vanderpool, the leader of the party, that himself and friends would camp near them if the gentlemen had no objections.

"Delighted to have you for neighbors," replied Mr. Vanderpool, "what time we stay, but we go up river to-morrow."

"So do we," said George, as the boys went back to their boats.

"You'll give us some biscuit for supper to-night, won't you, old chap?" queried the Parson, as he began to joint his rod.

"Nary a biscuit," replied George, with a twinkle in his eyes that belied his words: "they'll make you dyspeptic, and get your stomach out of order."

"Oh, confound your dyspepsia! I'm tired of chewing hard-tack."

"Soak it in coffee," suggested the *chef* with a smile.

"Now, look here, George," desperately, "if you don't give us some biscuit, I won't catch any more fish."

"Ha! rebellion!" cried George with mock consternation. "Know, then, my would-be dyspeptic, that if you don't catch the fish, I shall resign my office."

"Don't say that," laughed the Parson. "I will catch the fish, or at least I will try. I should starve if I had to do my own cooking. Or if I ate it, I should have dyspepsia sure."

"Run along, now," replied George patronizingly. "Be a good

little man, and catch a lot of trout, and I will see what I can do for you later;" and he turned to his cooking, while the Parson went down to the foot of the quick water to cast a fly.

After boiling the ducks an hour, George took the kettle off, and emptied out the water, made some stuffing from crackers and sewed the birds up neatly, then placed them in a pan with a little water, and set

CAMP AT THE NARROWS, MAGALLOWAY RIVER.

the pan on a tin baker, which he placed near the fire. The pan was turned from time to time, to present both sides to the heat; and when the ducks were thoroughly roasted, he made some gravy in the same pan. He cooked four of the ducks, reserving the others for breakfast. Ned and Dick now came in with two quarts of raspberries, and George told them to look after the fire, and keep the ducks hot.

Just then the Parson was heard in the distance, and George told

Ned to cut some slices of pork and place in the frying-pan, and put it on the fire. Shortly after Fred came in with his fish all cleaned, and they were rolled in meal and placed in the frying-pan. He had caught seven trout, weighing about half a pound apiece.

FISHING ON MAGALLOWAY RIVER.

"Didn't have very good luck fishing," said Ned.

"The fish bit well enough, but the minges bit a great deal better. Great Scott! weren't they thick down there! I did not have any fly preparation with me, and I became tired of trying to do two things at once. It took about all my time to fight minges, and I did not have much left to fish in."

"I have not seen any here," remarked Dick.

"No, there is a little breeze on this knoll ; down at the river it was perfectly still. Besides, your smoke keeps them off here."

"Now, Ned, look out for those fish, and don't let them burn, and I will make some biscuit." And George took a basin, and sifted into it a quart of flour, and two heaping teaspoonfuls of Royal Baking Powder. Then he rubbed into the flour a piece of butter the size of an egg, and mixed it up with water.

"I wish I had milk to mix this flour with, the biscuit would be so much better."

"I'll risk them, George," replied the Parson. "If we run across any cows lying around loose here in the woods, we'll milk them."

"Will we?" questioned George. "Did you ever milk a cow, Fred?"

CAMP NEAR LINCOLN BROOK RIPS, MAGALLOWAY RIVER.

"No."

"I would give five dollars to see you make your first attempt;" and George laughed till the tears ran down his cheeks, and the fever proving catching, his companions laughed in chorus.

The boys had brought a small sieve and cake board, but no rolling-pin, and in lieu of the latter, George used an empty bottle to roll out his dough with, and the cover of a small round tin box served as a cake cutter. In a few moments the biscuits were in the baker before the fire; and while George watched them, his friends set the table, which, with the seat, had been constructed like those described in the former chapter.

The biscuits were soon done, as brown as berries on top, and proved to be as light as cork. The roast ducks, fried trout, and mashed potato, flanked on either side by the biscuits and the ripe, red raspberries, were placed on the table; and the boys, with their appetites strengthened by the afternoon's work, ate as only healthy men and boys can eat, when in the woods. Some of the remarks made at their table would be very amusing had we space in which to give them; but suffice it to say, that amid the endless round of repartee that enlivened their meal, some very good jokes bubbled to the surface, and wit and humor were the order of the moment.

The night passed peaceably and without alarm; and after breakfast Tuesday morning, George proposed that they should take a cruise off to the eastward of the camp, explore the country a little, and see if they could run across a deer. Ned and Dick signified their willingness to go, but the Parson thought he would rather stick to the camp and make some sketches along the river, there being one a short distance above the Narrows that he wished particularly to get. George did not object to this; and taking a luncheon, — for they did not intend to return until four or five o'clock, — a drinking-cup, a pocket compass, and some matches, they started into the woods.

"Pick some raspberries for supper, will you, Fred?" shouted Dick.
"I will if I agree to," laughed the Parson.

After his friends had gone, the Parson took the blankets and spread them out in the sun to air and dry, and then taking his pencils and sketch-book, went up the river to obtain his coveted sketch. Securing a shady place on the bank, he went diligently to work. After an

A HUNTING PARTY ON THE MAGALLOWAY.

hour's steady labor, he had the picture finished, but it did not suit him. It lacked life. "I know what I will do," said he to himself, "I will put in a boat at the foot of that little fall with a couple of fishermen in it. That will give some character to the thing." This he proceeded to do, and the result was satisfactory. Then he went back to the camp and looked after the blankets ; and it being then about eleven o'clock, he fished an "Androscoggin Lakes Illustrated" from his knapsack, and read until dinner-time.

"I shall have to take a cold lunch, the same as the rest of the fellows," he remarked, as he threw down his book. "Hang it, I wish I could cook equal to George! I wonder where he learned. It must come natural to him. What a sardine he is! He can do most everything. Well, here goes;" and starting to his feet, he rummaged around a while, and found some cold duck, biscuit, and potatoes. He began by nibbling discontentedly, but ended by making a hearty meal. Thus was the eternal fitness of things reversed, and for a time matter triumphed over mind. When he had appeased his appetite he went out to the berry patch, and for half an hour amused himself with plucking the delicious fruit, and filling all the little nooks and cavities, where the more solid food had left space vacant. But at last with a sigh he was forced to cry "Peccavi!" and returned to camp.

"I don't think I should like to be a Robinson Crusoe," he said, as a dim sense of loneliness dawned upon him. "I'll stroll down the river bank and make a sketch of the Narrows. I would go down in the boat if it were not such a beastly pull getting back. I don't believe I could get up alone anyway; so I guess I will walk."

Taking his book he went below the Narrows; but after trying two or three sketches, none of which was satisfactory, he returned to camp. He folded up the blankets now and brought them in. "I think I must have eaten too much dinner," he said. "I am awful sleepy, and it's confounded hot. I'm blest if I don't have a snooze;" and half opening one of the blankets, he lay down at the front of the camp, with one hand resting on his gun.

He was soon fast asleep, and snoring with a freedom born of an innate knowledge that there was no one about to disturb; he had slept about an hour, when he awoke with a start, feeling something cold and soft on his face. As he opened his eyes, his blood seemed to chill in his veins, and his heart almost ceased to beat. Each hair of his head he fancied he could feel stick out "like quills upon the fretful porcupine." He trembled like a leaf, but at last his fears found vent, and with a yell that would have frightened a Comanche Indian, as used as they are to howling, he bounded to his feet, bringing his gun with him.

This was the cause of his excitement. A solitary moose had strayed up to the camp, and attracted by curiosity had approached the Parson to see what manner of creature he was. The touch of his cold nose had awaked Fred, with the result as given above.

A QUEER VISITOR.

As the alarmed boy howled and sprang to his feet, he frightened the moose, if anything, worse than the animal had frightened him, and the old bull backed three or four paces away snorting with terror. This gave the Parson a chance, and making for the woods a few rods distant, he went for a tree, up which he climbed, with the moose, who had recovered from his fright, close behind him. Dropping his gun while shinning the tree, he was at the mercy of the moose. The animal, however, was very well behaved, and after smelling of the gun and casting a glance or two of inquiry at Fred, browsed around the tree awhile, and then, hearing some noise that frightened him, he started off at a shambling gait, waded the river, which was shallow a short distance above the camp, and disappeared in the woods on the other side.

As the animal became lost to view the Parson slowly descended the tree, and picking up his gun found it uninjured.

"Well, by jingo!" he exclaimed as he walked to camp, "if this does not knock spots out of anything we have seen yet. A real, live moose. And if I had not been so frightened that I did not know whether I was on my head or heels, I might have had a shot at him. I wish the boys had been here, he would not have escaped so easily. But deliver me from having any more such visitors when I am alone. I guess I will go out and pick those berries now, that Dick wanted, and I will take my gun along too. If the moose in this country have no better manners than to walk into a fellow's camp, and kiss him while he is sleeping, one might as well be prepared for them;" and the Parson changed the shells in his gun, which were loaded with bird shot, for two loaded with buck shot, and put a couple of extra ones in his pocket. Then taking a basin he started for the berries.

After picking about three quarts, he carried them to camp, and taking his rod and gun went down the river fishing. At five o'clock he returned with thirteen trout, and, much to his relief, found his friends awaiting him.

"How goes it, Parson?" inquired George.

"If you had been here, you would have found out."

"So I suppose. What have you been doing?"

"Various things. Did you see any game?"

"Bagged three partridges, and that is all the game we have seen the whole blessed day."

"And we have walked about fourteen hundred miles," added Dick.

"But we saw lots of deer tracks," chimed in Ned.

"Deer tracks? That for your deer tracks!" and the Parson snapped his fingers contemptuously. "Look here," grabbing George by the arm and leading him along, "what do you call that, and that, and this?" pointing to the tracks left by the moose.

"You don't mean,"—began George excitedly.

"Yes, I do, too. There has been a moose, larger than the side of a house, right here in this camp this afternoon." And the Parson gazed around him in triumph.

"You don't mean it?" cried Dick incredulously.

"You can't put that sell on us," asserted Ned, "it's too thin."

"There is no sell about it. I tell you it is the truth. I can swear to it on a stack of Bibles as high as Bunker Hill Monument."

"Give us the facts," said George, who saw by his companion's face that he was in earnest, and telling the truth. And without any more circumlocution, the Parson told his story. Then the boys walked over to the tree, where Fred had gone to roost.

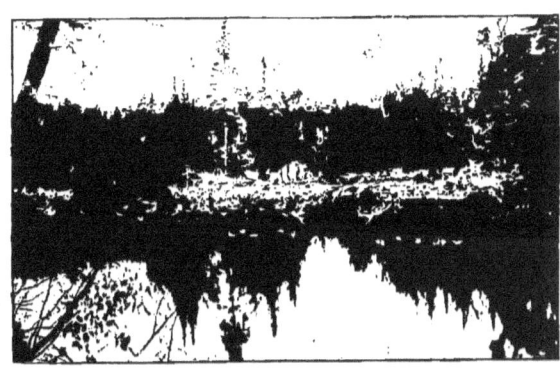

CAMP AT MOUTH OF LINCOLN BROOK ON MAGALLOWAY RIVER.

From here they followed the tracks to the bank of the river and saw where Jumbo had entered the water.

"We must get on that fellow's track to-morrow," remarked George enthusiastically. "We have two rifles, and with those and our two double barrels loaded with buck shot it will be strange if we can't give Mr. Moose his quietus. But now let's have supper, for I feel hungry after that tramp."

"So do I, and I, and I," echoed the others.

The boys were so excited that it took them longer than usual to prepare their meal, and all supper-time the moose furnished the only subject of conversation. When the dishes had been washed and cleared away, fresh fuel was thrown on the fire, and until ten o'clock they sat excitedly discussing the probabilities of their finding the moose on the morrow. Finally George told them they would be good for nothing the next day if they did not get some sleep that night. And reluctantly they followed his example and turned in.

CHAPTER XIII.

AN UNSUCCESSFUL MOOSE-HUNT. — A MOVE UP RIVER. — RAINY DAYS. — A NIGHT ALARM. — DIFFICULT NAVIGATION. — THE FORKS. — " WHICH ROAD SHALL WE TAKE?" — PARMACHENEE.

HALF-PAST seven Thursday morning found them ready for the start, and taking one of the boats they paddled across the river. They found where the huge animal had left the water, and began tracking him. It would have been slow work for those accustomed to it, but for novices like our young friends it was both slow and perplexing, and they frequently lost the trail, and spent half an hour in finding it. But they stuck to it with the pertinacity of blood-hounds, and about noon found where the moose had lain down. This encouraged them somewhat, thinking he might be in their immediate neighborhood, and after silently eating their lunch they resumed the trail. But as the moose had done a good deal of straggling about in the vicinity, another valuable hour was lost here.

At three o'clock they were following the trail, but had seen or heard nothing of the moose, and George announced his intention of returning to camp.

"I hate to give the old fellow up — am sorry as any of you," he remarked, as he noticed the disappointed look in his companions' faces, " but here we are five or six miles from camp, and the afternoon half gone, and I think it safer and better for all of us to turn back. If an hour's more travel would bring us up with the moose, I should say go on, but we may follow his trail a week and then not find him."

His companions acknowledged that George's advice was good, and as he was their chosen leader, they made the best of their discomfiture, and turned back with him. And it was not long before they all felt glad they had taken his advice. For they found that they could not travel a great deal faster returning than they had in going, and it was nearly dark when they reached camp. They managed the best way they could to cook their supper in the semi-darkness, and ate by the light of their lantern and fire.

TRAILING A MOOSE.

Friday morning after breakfast they broke camp, and proceeded up river. During the forenoon, they passed two or three shallow places where the boats dragged, and they had to get out and wade to lighten them. When they reached the Lower Metallak Pond they stopped about an hour, and paid it a visit. They found a lot of black duck in it, and secured five. Deer-tracks were numerous in the vicinity, many of which were fresh, but they saw no deer. As Dick

LOWER METALLAK POND, FROM MAGALLOWAY RIVER.

facetiously put it, " the deer had made tracks," and the boys realized the full significance of the saying.

Below the foot of the Meadows they spent a couple of hours in dining and resting, at a hunter's camp by the side of the river, and about half-past three reached the Upper Metallak Pond, where they concluded to pass the night.

Shortly after taking to their boats in the afternoon, it began to cloud up, and looked more and more like rain as the day waned. This determined George to camp early, and he paid more attention to the camp than any they had yet built, doing his best to make it tight. He also made it larger than usual, to give room for all their provisions, or other articles that would be liable to be injured by the rain. When this was done they had supper, and after the meal was over, and the things cleared up, Ned proposed that they should take a look around the pond and see if they could spot any deer.

All were in favor of this, and with their rifles and guns loaded with duck-shot, they started forth on a mission that proved very unfruitful. For although they stayed several hours, and thought they heard deer, they did not see any, and none of them fired a shot. They reached camp about midnight, and tired and sleepy, retired to rest. When they awoke in the morning, it was raining, — a cold, cheerless drizzle.

LOWER METALLAK POND, LOOKING TOWARDS THE RIVER.

They had a few trout left over from the catch of the night before, and these George cooked for breakfast. As a good fire seemed a great deal like a friend on such a day, they built a large one near the camp, and kept it snapping all the time. This made the inside of their camp dry and comfortable.

"Who has nerve enough to go over to the pond with me and see if we can get some ducks?" queried Ned, about ten o'clock, as the boys lay on their blankets comfortably in camp.

"I have," answered Dick. "I am tired of doing nothing, and had rather get wet than stay cooped up here."

"You mean you had rather get a duck-in," grimly remarked the Parson.

"You deserve hanging for that," replied George, as he laughed in concert with the others.

The two hunters donned their rubber coats and boots, and sallied forth, while George amused himself with a book and the Parson in sketching anything and everything in sight of him. It was not quite twelve o'clock when the Parson said that he heard footsteps. George laid aside his book and listened, and soon heard voices, and

HUNTER'S CAMP, MAGALLOWAY RIVER.

Dick and Ned presently appeared, the water pouring from them.

"Come in out of the wet, it appears to be raining outside," was George's greeting as the boys stepped up to the camp.

"Don't care if I do," said Dick, as they pulled off their rubber coats displaying nine fat ducks.

The Parson's eyes opened. "You had good luck after all; we

did not hear you fire a shot, and supposed you would come back empty-handed."

"We are not the boys to return empty-handed," asserted Ned.

"Four of those are wood-duck — the best eating duck there are according to what I have read," observed George.

"You can cook those for me, George," suggested the Parson.

THE LUCKY HUNTERS.

"Don't be so fresh; put a little wood on the fire," and George turned his attention to the ducks.

"The other five are black, I suppose?" interrogated Dick.

"Yes. There will be enough for dinner, and breakfast to-morrow morning, and the Parson can catch trout for supper," and George threw a humorous glance at that individual who was replenishing the fire.

"Fish won't bite in the rain," asserted Fred.

"Try them and see. Perhaps it will hold up a little during the afternoon."

The boys now assisted George about getting the dinner, and five black ducks were roasted, the others being retained for breakfast. Boiled potatoes, coffee, and hard-tack completed the bill of fare. They had to take their plates on their laps in the camp, as it rained so hard there was no eating out of doors. During the afternoon it slacked up about an hour. George and the Parson took advantage of it to catch some trout for supper, getting fifteen between them. The rain returned with renewed vigor while they were fishing, and they hurried to camp without waiting to clean their fish. Here the Parson put on his rubber coat, and then took the trout to the river and dressed them. After he came back, the boys told stories and sang until supper-time. This meal was provided under some difficulties ; for as the night drew on, it rained a great deal harder than it had earlier in the day. But perseverance will overcome any difficulty, and the boys finally triumphed in the fact that they had cooked their supper and eaten it.

The morning of Sunday greeted them with no change in the weather, and they stuck as close to camp as their duties would allow. They retired early, the rain still falling, and along in the night they were awakened by a tremendous crash, fairly shaking the ground under them. They started up in turn, and looked from one to the other, with wonder and fear depicted on their faces. They found to their surprise that the character of the storm had changed. The air was filled with a blaze of light, as flash after flash of lightning illumined the dark forests, and their ears were almost deafened by the continued peals of thunder that sounded like salvos of artillery.

A WET TIME.

"This is a fearful storm, fellows, but we are in the hands of God. I think the noise that awakened us was some large tree knocked over by the lightning, and we have reason to be thankful that it did not fall on our camp," and George lay back on his blanket again, but with every nerve wide awake.

The roar of the thunder continued, and the boys instinctively hugged up to each other. Sometimes it seemed directly over their heads, and then would roll away in the distance. The lightning not only flashed with a brilliancy unusual, but it often assumed the form of chain lighting, and darted through the air like fiery serpents. The darkness after the lightning's glare was something horrible. The boys fancied they could almost feel it; and through all this din and uproar the rain poured in torrents, seeming at times to literally come down in sheets.

"Isn't this a frightful night, George," ventured Dick, after they had been quiet for some time.

"Yes it is. I wish it were morning."

For two hours, as near as George could judge, they were kept awake by the terrors of the storm. But after that time the tempest gradually slackened, and finally died away. Then the boys fell into an uneasy slumber, from which they awoke about six o'clock, and to their joy they found it had stopped raining.

They turned out, and after dressing looked about the camp. A large pine that had stood a little above the camp had been shivered by a bolt of lightning, thrown to the ground, and lay close behind their camp, parallel with their heads. Had it fallen two feet nearer they must every one have been instantly killed. They all saw their narrow escape, and realized it the more, from the fact that by all mathematical rules the tree should have fallen upon them, and it was with some unknown but strong impulse, and white faces, that they shook each other by the hand.

A LOGGING-CREW AT HOME.

"Boys," said George, "you are all friends of mine and good fellows, and I feel as if we all have been very near death. And although I never before uttered a prayer in public, I am going to do it now," and the blood mounted to his face, for he felt a good deal embarrassed.

The boys uncovered their heads, and George sent up to the throne of mercy a heart-felt petition, thanking God who had saved them from

LUMBER CAMP NEAR UPPER METALLAK POND.

such a frightful death away from all their friends. As he thought of his father and mother, his voice trembled, and the tears came into his eyes, for he was as tender-hearted as a child, although by no means a coward. After George had finished his prayer breakfast was prepared and eaten; but it was a quiet meal, and it was with a feeling of relief that the boys placed their camp kit in their boats, and made ready to leave a spot that had come so near proving a grave to them.

Before starting away, however, they visited a logging-camp near them, and found the whole crew, who had come up the river a few days before, at home, and had a very pleasant call. George obtained some

A GRAY MORNING.

valuable information from the boss about the country up river, and the Parson made some sketches that pleased both himself and the men. He was an adept at drawing faces, and put every man in the crew in his picture. After half an hour's chat they returned to their dismantled camp ready to proceed.

It was ten o'clock when they pushed off from the landing; the mists were rising from the river and forests, ascending in fantastic shapes that were whirled and blown about by the wind. Half an hour later the sun broke through the vapor that had enveloped them, and they caught sight of the first blue sky they had seen for nearly three days.

"VERY THIN WATER."

"Welcome, old Sol," cried Dick, as a sunbeam struck fairly upon him, enshrouding him in a halo of golden light. "I never was so glad to see the sun before in my life."

"It would be a gloomy world without it," remarked George, "but I think we shall have colder weather after this storm. We may not notice it in the middle of the day but we shall nights and mornings."

As they made progress up the river they found the water "very thin" as Dick put it, in places, and were obliged to wade in the stream and haul their boats by the painters. It frequently took all of them to get one boat over a bad place, and then return for the other, so that at noon they had only reached the head of the Meadows, and here they stopped for dinner.

About two o'clock they started again, and at four had reached the foot of the "big rips." They found the water very low at this point, and were obliged to partially unload their boats, and carry some of their stuff around the rapids, before they were able to get the boats into dead water. But they worked like beavers, and at half-past five had

CAMP LANDING, LITTLE MAGALLOWAY.

reached the Forks, where the Little Magalloway enters the main stream from the left. They landed at the carry road, hauled up their boats and held a "pow-wow" as the Parson termed it.

"Now," began George, "according to 'Farrar's Guide Book,' we are half a mile from Spoff Flint's camp, about four miles from the lake by the carry road, and about five by the river. If we get to the lake by the river we shall have to pole and drag, and perhaps tug the boats about all the way. If we go by the carry road, it will be a solid lug of everything we have, boats, provisions, and all, unless we can get our things hauled over. They used to keep a horse on this carry; suppose we go up to Flint's Camp, and see if the animal is here now, and then we can decide which road we shall take."

CAMP ON THE LITTLE MAGALLOWAY.

"Go ahead," said Dick, "and we will follow. It must be an awful job getting a horse up here where there are no roads."

"They lead him through the woods, probably," remarked Ned, "but I should not want the job."

"Nor I either," returned George.

As they were about starting, Ned happened to look up the Little Magalloway, and a few rods beyond saw some of the party, whom they

RUNNING THE RAPIDS.

had camped beside down river, in a boat and canoe at what appeared to be a landing, and immediately hailed them.

"That must be some of the Boston party," declared George.

"Of course," returned Ned, "and they are coming down here."

In fact, while he was speaking the sportsmen had begun paddling toward them, and in a few seconds the bows of their light craft ran on the bank where the boys were standing.

"How are you, boys," said the eldest, "have you just come up?"

"Yes sir," replied George.

"Well, we have had quite a rain," remarked Mr. Vanderpool, "but I guess we will have good weather now."

"I hope so, sir," said George. "That was an awful storm."

"Yes it was. Do you camp here, or are you going to the lake?"

"We are going to the lake, sir."

"We have a nice camp up here. Come over and see it: we will take you right along and bring you back here."

"Is there room for all of us in your boats?" asked the Parson.

"Plenty. Jump in."

The boys, nothing loath, accepted the invitation, and paid a visit to their friends' camp, where they passed a pleasant half-hour. Then the gentlemen had their guides ferry the boys back to where their boats were.

"Now," said George, "we have had a pleasant call, but have lost over half an hour in making it, and we must move quickly."

Leaving everything in their boats they walked up to the camp, which stood on the left side of the road hard by the borders of Sunday Pond, a trout preserve for the house. Three men were down to the pond fishing, and a gentleman stood in the doorway. He welcomed them cordially, asked them where they came from, who they were, and so forth. Introduced himself as Mr. Daniels of New York, and told them the proprietor had gone up the lake, but would return soon.

A REST ON PARMACHENEE CARRY.

"Do you know whether there is a horse here now?" asked George.

"Yes, I do. There is no horse here this year, and the guides sack everything across the carry on their backs."

"Then it will be easier for us," said George, turning to his companions, "to stick to the river. It's a pretty good tug to carry three boats over this road, and we should have to make two trips, as we could not carry but one at a time."

"That's so," added Dick, "and two more trips to get our luggage over."

"Have you any guides with you?" queried the gentleman.

"No, sir," answered George, "we paddle our own canoe."

"So do we," returned Mr. Daniels. "I expected to find Spoff Flint up here, who has been with us two or three times, but he is off with another party, and we concluded to go it alone. Those gentlemen down to the pond are my friends, and we are stopping here for the present. We are going over to the lake next week."

"Do you think," asked George, "that they could accommodate us here to-night?"

"Yes, and a dozen more. We are the only party stopping here at present."

"What do you say, boys, to taking supper, lodging, and breakfast here. It will be a change, and you must be sick of my cooking by this time."

"No, sir, we are not: you know better, George!" exclaimed his three friends vehemently.

"Good cook, is he, boys?" and Mr. Daniels laughed at their earnestness.

"He's the boss," said Ned.

"All the other cooks are out when he is at home," added Dick.

"Quit your fooling, now, fellows, and speak soberly. What do you think of stopping here to night?"

"I'm in favor of it, for one," returned the Parson. "Besides, it is getting a little late for us to build a camp to-night."

"So am I," added Dick.

"I row in the same boat," chimed in Ned.

"Come on, then," and George started for the boats. "We will bring up our rods and guns, and cover the rest of the stuff up so the dew will not wet it."

Returning to the river, they unloaded the boats, and made two compact piles of their things, covering them with rubber blankets, and then turned one of the boats bottom up over each pile. They laid the oars and paddles snug to the boats, and then went back to the camp.

On their way back they came suddenly upon a sportsman and his guide, who had stopped for a rest while crossing the camp. They recognized him as belonging to the Boston party camping on the Little Magalloway, and chatted a few moments with him. He had evidently been to one of the back ponds for deer, but did not say whether he shot one.

He invited the boys to pay his camp a visit, and George told him they had already been there, and then the parties separated, and the boys continued on to Sunday Pond.

The man who had charge had come in; and he gave them a warm welcome, and told them he had plenty of room for them. He informed them that supper would be ready in about fifteen minutes, and the boys left their guns and rods in the house and went down to the pond where the gentlemen were fishing. Mr. Daniels was there and introduced them to his friends, and the boys had quite a pleasant chat with them. The gentlemen had already taken quite a number of trout, and declared that the pond was full of them. George noticed one that would weigh two pounds lying on the bank, and called the attention of his friends to it. While they were examining the fish a horn was blown as a signal for supper, and all went up to the camp.

After supper, the evening being cool, a fire was lit in the open Franklin, and gathered around its cheerful blaze, the two parties of sportsmen met as old friends, and passed a very pleasant evening, songs, stories, and reminiscences of forest life being the order of the night. During the evening one of the gentlemen read the following story about a deer hunt, from a periodical he had brought with him.

"Bill and I were camping one fall on the upper Richardson Lake. It was rather late in the season, and the deer that a few weeks previously had been in the habit of coming to the edges of the streams and lakes to nip the lily-pads and wade about in the shallow water were seldom seen. Occasionally an old buck would come out at evening and take a stroll along the sandy margin of the lake, adding for the moment a touch of wilder beauty to the dark forest background, and after standing proudly at some rocky point and surveying the scene would disappear again into the woods.

A CALL TO SUPPER.

"A small bay half way up the lake seemed to be a favorite place for the deer, as innumerable tracks were always to be seen in the sand along the shore, and one afternoon when we were almost out of venison in camp I suggested to Bill that it would be the proper thing for us to make a trip in the evening to this place.

"The wood for the camp-fire was cut and piled at a convenient distance from the mouldering back-log all 'ready for a glorious blaze on our return; and just before sundown I took my place in the bow of our little boat with the Ballard across my knees, while Bill took the stern with the paddle.

"Long shadows were reaching out from the big pines and hemlocks on the west shore, the valleys were already in darkness, and the long red rays of the fast setting sun streaming through the tree-tops illumined the rest of the forest with a hazy evening light. Great tree-trunks lay half sunken in the dark clear water, their arms reaching grimly out, and quiet reigned over all, the paddle in Bill's skilled hand making not the slightest sound.

"As we silently glided along, a loon far up the lake caught sight of us, and his wild querulous call ringing through the forest was answered by echo and sent wavering from cliff to cliff. Again and again the weird cry echoed and re-echoed from the mountain sides and was sent from shore to shore, and an eagle soaring high overhead answered with its screams. The reverberations ceased, and the stillness was broken only by the song of a white-throated sparrow within the short range of his little voice. A mink came swimming alongside of us, his bright mischievous eyes trying to make out what we were. Suddenly an otter's head appeared above the water, and soon another, and another, and in the most amusing way they bobbed up and down and spit at us in their spiteful way. For two or three minutes the otters swam along ahead of us, diving and appearing again, and finally they disappeared all at once, probably going to pursue their calling of catching the big trout which abounded in the lake.

"Gradually we neared the little bay, and as we rounded the rocky point Bill stopped paddling. The boat glided slowly along with its own motion as we carefully scanned every fallen hemlock for a sight of red hair, and in a moment I heard a low whisper, 'See that buck on the right!' at the same instant catching sight of a pair of horns behind a stump that stood quite a way out in the water, and not more than ten rods from us. The old fellow had evidently been watching us just a little longer than we had been watching him, and had taken good pains to keep his eyes over the stump and mighty little of the rest of his body in sight. I felt the tremor of the boat again as Bill cautiously plied the paddle, and we tried to move to a position where I could see enough to shoot at, but the buck knew what we were up to and kept backing around until he could go no farther, when with five or six long bounds, with flag raised, he made for a windfall and stopped behind it for a minute, snorting and stamping, before taking his final leap into the underbrush. He stood tail toward me, with his head turned and looking over his shoulder, supposing that he was well protected by the branches, but there was where he made a miscalculation, for at least a square foot of the seat of his pants was in sight. Quickly I levelled the rifle, and as the echoes rang through the forest the buck made one grand leap and stumbled as he struck the ground, rolling clear over with feet kicking wildly in the air. In an instant he was up again and had disappeared. A few quick strokes with the paddle toward shore and Bill jumped out and started in the direction that the deer had taken, stopping long enough to motion to me that he found blood.

"For several minutes I waited in suspense. It was fast growing darker, and the minutes were getting twice as long as in a stopped watch, when I heard Bill call from a point along the shore above me. The paddle was no longer needed, so I pulled out the oars and getting them into the locks rowed as rapidly as possible toward Bill. He had tracked the buck to the water's edge, and was just saying that we would find him mortally wounded along the shore somewhere, when, with a great snapping of branches and splashing of water the old fellow sprang out of a windfall into the lake and started to swim for a little island near by. Bill jumped into the bow, and I pulled the oars with a vengeance, but guided by the hoarse breathing of the panting deer as he swam.

Rapidly we neared him, and just as Bill called out ' Right oar, quick ! ' the boat gave a lurch and I knew that he had the game by the tail. At that moment the handles of the oars came against my abdomen with a jerk, and pressed so hard that I couldn't catch a breath for the life of me. ' Hold on, Bill ! ' I gasped. ' For H-e-a-v-e-n-'s s-a-k-e hold up ! ' The oars kept pressing so hard that I could not get out another word, until Bill, roaring with laughter, reached around and threw one of them out of the rowlock. In my excitement I had forgotten that Bill was not the motive power at the bow, and that the fast swimming buck was the cause of bringing into practice a very simple problem in levers.

" We only had a few yards more to go before shallow water would be reached, and picking up the rifle, I intended to stop our locomotive, but the boat was unsteady and I fired the bullet somewhere into the Androscoggin wilderness. Another bullet went on the same fruitless mission, and is going yet for all that I know. We were almost in the shallow water, and shutting my teeth together with a firm resolve to hold steady, I sent a bullet through the neck of the deer, and with a convulsive start he sent flying the spray in every direction, and then lay kicking upon the water.

" Towing the deer to the shore we got him into the boat, and as I took the bow again Bill took up the paddle and we started for camp.

" How fine the old buck looked in the evening light with his white belly up and legs gracefully bent as his head lay between my knees and I stroked his smooth ears and opened the closed eyes and patted his neck.

" As we neared the camp the stars were sending silvery gleams over the ripples in our wake. A glimpse of the back-log burning low showed us where to land, and the smell of the smoke hanging heavily over the water was a reminder of the comforts in store.

" The boat grated on the pebbly bottom, and, jumping out, we rolled out our game and dragged him the short distance to camp. Lichen-covered sticks were soon snapping and roaring on the camp-fire, and the forest around was all aglow as the sparks arose with the smoke and floated off among the branches of the trees overhead. The red embers settled in a ruddy heap; and the last piece of venison from the deer which Bill had killed a few days previously, and half a dozen big trout were pulled from the moss by the spring, where we

IN CAMP ON THE MAGALLOWAY.

had stored them ready for use. As they broiled and browned before the birch logs, the juice trickled out and fell sizzling among the coals, sending fragrant aromas in every direction. Our birch-bark plates were filled as only a millionnaire could afford to fill them in the city. And then, in a condition of supreme contentment, I leaned my back against a giant pine, crossed my feet over the buck's glossy flank, and lit my pipe. Bill stretched himself out at full length upon the moss near by; and as the blue puffs floated around our heads, we told of former exploits with deer and bears until the pipes and the camp-fire burned low."

This ended the conference, and the boys bidding the gentlemen "good-night," retired to rest. In the morning after breakfast the Parson settled the bill, and they went back to their boats. Launching them, they put in their things, and started up the river. Between the forks and the dam at the outlet, they encountered many obstacles, but by hard and steady work they reached the dam about eleven o'clock, and after unloading their boats, carried their things around the dam, and then tackled the boats. The distance being short, four of them handled the boat quite easily, and at noon they had rowed up the outlet, turning to the left, and landed near where the carry road ended, and here they camped. It was a beautiful place, and commanded a fine view the entire distance of the lake. They built their camp, set up their table and bench, had their dinner, and then George and the Parson went down to the dam fishing, while Dick and Ned with the shot-guns sallied out on the carry road in quest of partridges.

FLINT'S CAMP, SUNDAY POND.

The fishermen took five trout during the afternoon, one of which weighed three pounds, and was captured by George. He was proud of his trophy, this being the largest fish they had taken, and George told the Parson they would bake him for breakfast. When they reached camp about half-past four they found Dick and Ned had come in ahead, nearly empty-handed, having shot only three partridges, and Ned declared that they had skirmished lively for those.

"We shall have to make a business of getting a deer after we go to the head of the lake," said Ned. "I don't believe we shall find many partridges up here, we are so far away from any settlement."

"You can shoot one whenever you please, my boy," answered George with a laugh, "I won't blow on you."

A PARTY WE SAW ON THE WAY.

"Now, let's have some supper," cried Dick, "I am getting hungry. Shall I build a fire, George?"

"Yes, go ahead."

"We have reached Parmachenee at last," said the Parson.

"True as preaching," returned Ned, "and now for some fun."

CHAPTER XIV.

UP THE LAKE. — DANFORTH'S CAMP. — THE HEAD OF THE LAKE. — UP THE RIVER. — LITTLE BOY'S FALLS. — A PERMANENT CAMP. — WOOD RAMBLES. — RARE FISHING. — A MOOSE HUNT. — BREAKING CAMP. — THE START FOR HOME. — ALMOST AN ACCIDENT.

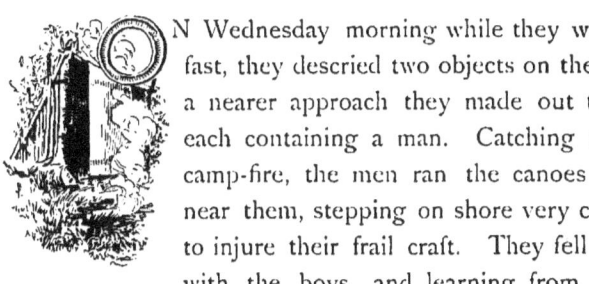

N Wednesday morning while they were eating breakfast, they descried two objects on the lake, which upon a nearer approach they made out to be two canoes, each containing a man. Catching sight of the boys' camp-fire, the men ran the canoes up on the beach near them, stepping on shore very carefully, so as not to injure their frail craft. They fell into conversation with the boys, and learning from George that the water was very low between the outlet and the forks, they concluded to sack their canoes across the carry, although it had been their intention only to carry around the dam, and then run the river. After making up their minds to do the carry, they lost but little time. The canoes were taken out, and each of them turned bottom up, and thrown on the shoulders of the two men with the same ease that one of the boys would have tossed a biscuit into the water, and off they started.

"Did you notice, George, how those fellows handled their canoes? You would not suppose each weighed a hundred pounds or more," and Dick looked after them in astonishment.

"They carry one a little easier than you or I would, Dicky, but I wonder why they use the word 'sack' so much in this country. They never lug or carry anything here, it is always 'sack,' or 'sacked,' or 'sacking.'"

"Like old Falstaff," put in Ned with a grin, "they are fond of 'sack.'"

"I wonder what day of the month it is?" queried the Parson.

"The fourteenth," answered George; "and we ought not to stay up here more than two weeks longer, for it will take us a week to get home."

"Suppose we pack up then, and be off," suggested Dick, "it is nine o'clock now."

"How about that trip over to the Little Magalloway," said Ned. "We have not been there yet."

"Why can't we go to-day, and start off up the lake to-morrow?" proposed Dick.

"Nothing to hinder, if you wish to go," replied George.

SACKING CANOES.

"Then let's make the trip there to-day," said the Parson.

"Little Magalloway it is, then," returned George; "but, as we shall be gone all day, we must take a luncheon with us."

In a few moments a pail had been filled with whatever was cooked, and, taking the luncheon and their guns, they crossed the carry to the landing, then followed the Little Magalloway up to the Stone Dam. They rested here half an hour, then continued up the stream till they reached a pool of dead water, and here they disposed of their refreshments. While enjoying a social chat, Ned proposed they should strike through the woods for the lake. They made the attempt, but got turned around, and after several hours' hard tramping, came out on the carry road, just where it pitches down to the lake. With a cry of joy, they recognized the road, and in a few minutes were at camp, tired and hungry. They all assisted in making supper ready and retired early.

The next morning George was up at six o'clock, and after lighting the fire, called his friends, who were yet asleep, but who arose quickly when they saw he had the fire blazing.

STONE DAM, LITTLE MAGALLOWAY.

Breakfast was quickly prepared and eaten, baggage and stores packed up, and the boats launched.

"Away we go now!" cried Dick.

"All right," returned George, and the two boats were a moment later heading up the lake. A little after ten they reached Danforth's camp; and as George wished to add to their stock of supplies, they concluded to stay there the rest of the day and over night, and board with Danforth. They were much interested in the camp and what they saw there. The buildings, five or six in number, stand on an island at the head of the lake, and contain a dozen or more rooms. Mr. Danforth owns a number of other small camps in the vicinity of the lake, that he uses for shelter when caught out over night, and George obtained permission to use them, if it came in their way to do so.

The next morning, having procured what additional stores they needed, among which was a hind quarter of venison, the Parson settled the bill, and embarking they made their way to the inlet, and soon lost sight of the lake. They reached Little Boy's Falls about ten o'clock, where they stopped, deciding to build a permanent camp at this locality. They moved everything on shore, then carried one of the boats around the falls, as they could use it as far as the First East Branch, sometimes called Otter Creek. Thus, with a boat above and below the falls, they could cruise either up or down the river.

THE POOL, LITTLE MAGALLOWAY.

George selected a high, dry knoll for their camp, and under his instructions they went to work. They set up the poles as they had done in building the other camps, put on the front stick, and ran the rafters back to the ground. Then he cut half a dozen smaller poles, which he ran cross-way of the rafters, making the frame-work more secure.

Then obtaining some cedar splits, he covered the frame with a double course, ran another pole across the top to keep them in place, and rolled a large log against the bottom, holding the splits securely at that end. On the sides he drove down several poles perpendicularly, and cutting shorter splits, wattled them in between the poles, from the ground to the top of the camp, thus making both ends secure against the weather. By setting every other pole on the end a little out of line, the walls were made fast. A few long splits were also cut, and one end of each being sharpened, were driven into the ground on the front of the camp, only leaving an entrance four feet wide.

PARMACHENEE LAKE, FROM CARRY LANDING.

A lot of spruce boughs were then cut, and piled on the roof, and around the ends, making the little shanty both warm and water-tight. A floor was made by cutting fir poles the right length, hewing one side flat, and laying the smooth side uppermost. The floor was plentifully strewn with fragrant cedar boughs, and two of their rubber blankets spread over it. One of the other blankets was reserved for a door, which was hung before the entrance in the front part of the camp, the other as an additional precaution was thrown over their provisions, which they kept in one corner of their camp. It took them the rest of the day, with the exception of the dinner-hour, in completing their building operations; but when they had finished, George declared himself satisfied, and said they had the "boss camp." The only tools used in its construction were axes and jack-knives, and the only articles except what nature had furnished them on the spot, were a few pieces of stout marline, that had been brought around some of their bundles.

They were all well tired out at night, and after supper, soon retired to rest, sleeping heavily until seven o'clock the next morning.

George was the first to awaken, and looking at his watch, was surprised to find it so late.

"Come, fellows, wake up," he called, as he turned out and began to dress. "It is seven o'clock, and to-day is Friday, and to-morrow is Saturday, and the week is all gone and nothing done. For shame, sluggards!"

"Who are you calling a slug, you old angle-worm," retorted Dick, sleepily rubbing his eyes.

"Come, Ned, where are you? It's a lovely morning out," stepping to the front of the camp, and throwing the bottom of the rubber blanket up on the roof, the way they opened the door, "just look out."

"Here goes," replied Ned, springing to his feet and giving the Par-

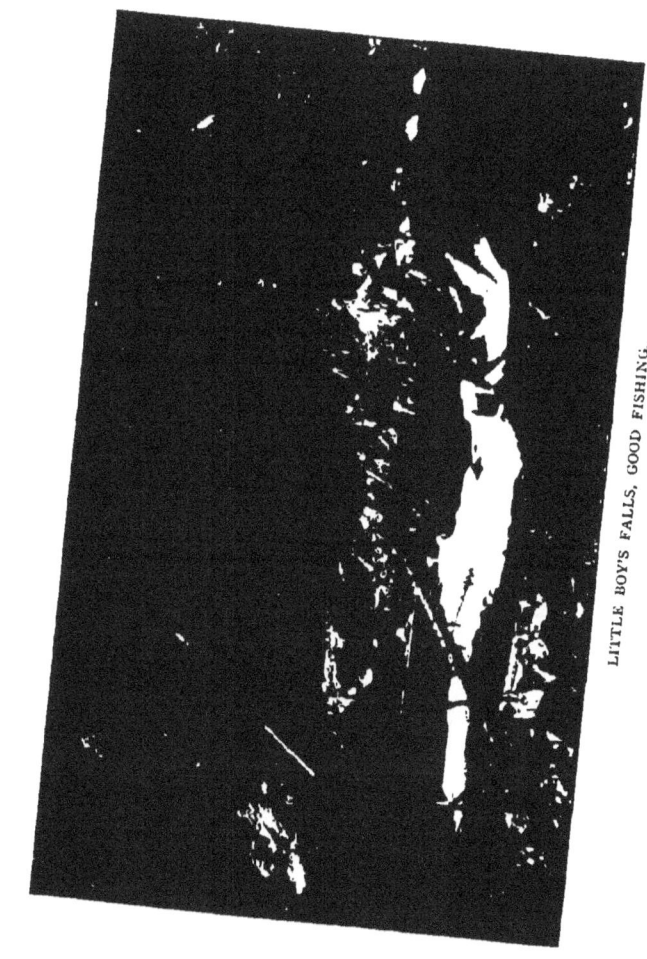

LITTLE BOY'S FALLS, GOOD FISHING.

son who had not yet stirred, a gentle kick, "Roll out, Fred. All hands on deck!" and Ned bawled loud enough to frighten a moose to death if there was one in that locality.

"Friday, is it," said Dick. "Fish-day with the Catholics. It is funny they don't eat meat on Friday. You are going to cook some of that venison this morning, aren't you, George?"

"Yes, that's all our larder contains in the way of solid food, that I can cook quickly. I'll take off a few slices and fry them. Build a fire before you wash, will you, Ned, and I'll go and perform my twilight."

CHASING A CARIBOU.

"Suppose," proposed George at breakfast, "that we go up to Otter Creek to-day. We can go to the mouth of the stream in the boat, and then take a ramble in the woods. We can carry a little luncheon with us, and plan to get back to camp about four o'clock, and have an early supper. What do you say?"

All were agreeable; and after the dishes were washed they launched their boat above the falls, and started up the river. They had only made about a mile from camp when they saw some distance ahead a large animal wade across the river, and disappear in the woods.

"A deer!" cried Dick.

"A moose!" yelled Ned.

"Neither," returned George decidedly, "it was a caribou."

"A caribou?" cried his three friends in concert.

"Yes, gentlemen, a caribou. If you had not been so excited you would have noticed that it was too small for a moose, and too large for a deer. It is claimed by naturalists that it is the same animal as the Northern reindeer of Europe. It is very fleet, and it is a 'cold day' for a hound, every time, when he gets on the trail of a caribou. But hurry up, and let's find where he landed. Perhaps we can stalk him if he does not hear us."

They soon reached the spot where the animal had left the river, and hauling up the boat, divided into two parties, George and the Parson going one way, and Ned and Dick in another direction. This gave each party one rifle and one shot-gun.

"Be careful, now, how you shoot, if you see any game," whispered George as the boys separated, to Ned, "I don't want you to make a target of the Parson and me."

"Excellent advice. Follow it yourself," retorted Ned, as the two parties disappeared from each other's sight.

They spent two hours in hunting the caribou, but it was emphatically a "still hunt," so still, that they never saw a thing to waste a charge on, and they returned to the river bank within a few moments of each other, rather chagrined at their ill-luck.

"Where's your caribou, Ned?" laughed George, as the boys reached the boat.

"*Our* caribou?" queried Ned. "Well, if you haven't cheek. You had better ask yourself the same question."

"The Parson and I left him for you and Dick," returned their leader, as they launched the boat.

"That's where you made a mistake," put in Dick. "You should not have been so generous."

"Well, better luck next time," said George, as they started up river.

A short time after a flock of black duck went over their heads, but too far away for a shot.

"TOO FAR AWAY."

"This is regular Friday's luck," grumbled Dick, as he eyed the birds wistfully.

"Don't be superstitious, Dick. Some of the most important events in the world occurred on Friday," and George laughed at his companion's long face.

It was twelve o'clock when they reached the mouth of the Creek, and hauling the boat out, they sat down awhile and ate their lunch.

After half an hour's debate as to what should be done next, they finally divided as they did when they went after the caribou, and two of them went into the woods on the north side of the stream, and two on the other.

"Be back here by three o'clock," shouted George to his companions, as he and the Parson struck into the forest.

At the hour appointed for the rendezvous, the parties met at the boat, but neither had seen any game. Ned and Dick had "struck it rich" on spruce gum, and their jaws were grinding like crushing-machines. They each had a pocket full, and offered some to their friends. The Parson "took a chaw," but George told them "it was too much like work, and didn't pay for the trouble."

"Did you see any game, George?" inquired Dick, as they rowed down river.

"Not a thing; but we ran across the tracks of some large animal that I think must have been a bear. We followed them a while, but the trail did not pan out well, and we left it. We had better try and get a mess of trout at the falls for breakfast to-morrow morning, and I will roast a piece of that wild meat for supper."

When they reached camp Dick and the Parson offered to go fishing if Ned would help George. He expressed himself as ready to do anything for the common good, and proved it by at once building the fire, while George proceeded with the supper, and Fred and Dick went down below the falls to try their luck with the trout.

"You need not be in a hurry about coming back," remarked George, as the fishermen started away; "with this meat to roast and potatoes to boil, I can't have supper before six o'clock. If you leave off fishing at six you will be here early enough."

"Do you want me to wash the potatoes, George?" asked Ned.

"Yes, if you please. Take about a dozen fair-sized ones and run down to the river; get a pail of water after you wash the spuds, and put two quarts in that kettle, and a tablespoonful of salt. After you get the potatoes on, pick a quart of beans: I must put them in soak to-night."

"All right," said Ned, who made a good assistant.

Supper progressed favorably, and when the fishermen appeared a few moments after six with a fine string of trout, it was all ready.

"I was never so hungry in my life," declared Dick, as he passed the trout over to Ned to be taken care of, and set his rod away. "Oh, crimini! I wonder how that venison will taste roasted: it smells mighty nice. Any water in camp, Ned? No? of course not. I shall have to wash my hands, any how, before I eat, for they smell fishy."

"Give us a rest," replied Ned. "Take the pail and get some water. The river is right before you."

The evenings had grown considerably cooler since the storm, and after supper the boys built a huge fire and sat around it all the evening, enjoying its warmth and light.

"There is one good thing about this country," remarked George, as they lay around their camp-fire. "fuel is plenty here and costs nothing. What a pity it is that the poor people, who in some of the large cities actually freeze for want of fire, could not have some small part of the enormous quantities of wood that annually go to waste in these forests."

"That's a fact," replied Ned: "what a blessing it would be to them if they could only get it."

"George, did I ever tell you about a little incident I read of last winter, about a bear in a lumber-camp?"

"No. What was it, Dick?"

"There were a lot of boys visiting a lumber-camp near some town in New Hampshire, and a bear suddenly appeared. The boys were

LITTLE BOY'S FALLS, LOOKING UP RIVER.

frightened and ran, and so did the bear; and the bear knocked over one of the boys, who straddled him without meaning to, and was carried half a mile on his back. Mustn't that fellow have looked funny?"

"Get out with your nonsense. Do you suppose we swallow such a yarn as that?"

"I don't care whether you swallow it or not. I read it in the *Boston Journal*."

"I wouldn't believe it if you read it in *Zion's Herald*. Let's go to bed," and the boys turned in.

The next morning after breakfast the Parson produced his sketch-book, and calling to Dick, said, "I have illustrated your bear story. Want to see it?"

"Yes," replied Dick, and the boys gathered around the Parson, who showed them a clever sketch of a boy on a bear's back, and they had a good laugh over it.

"That fellow on the bear don't look very happy," suggested Ned.

"No," replied George, laughing, "he looks about as happy as a stockholder in the Pacific Bank."

"What shall we do to-day, George?" queried Dick.

"Anything you please. But I shall have to stick to camp, if we are to have those beans for supper to-night."

"Then you will need some one to assist you."

"I ought to have one of you with me. The other two can go out."

"I will help you," said Ned, and George accepted his services.

"To-morrow is Sunday," remarked Dick: "we shall not go gunning or fishing, and you ought to get up a nobby dinner, give us a regular tuck-out in fact."

"What a little gourmand you are, Dick; you think a great deal of your stomach."

"Why shouldn't I?" urged Dick stoutly. "If it were not for a fellow's stomach, where would a fellow be?"

"Give it up," returned George, laughing. "Let's have a harder one."

"Come on, Dick," said the Parson, "let's be off if we are going. Don't stand here and argue all day about eating."

"Take my compass with you, Dick, it may come handy." And George went into the camp and brought it out. "You had better get back to dinner; and Dick, if you can prevail on the Parson to go down to where Cleveland's camp used to stand, this afternoon, and get a lot of the raspberries we saw growing there, I will promise you something for to-morrow that will tickle your palate."

"All right. I'll go any way. Will you go with me, Fred?"

"Yes, I suppose so. And now let us be off;" and the Parson seized his gun, and Dick his rifle, and crossing the river in their boat below the falls, the boys struck into the woods to the westward.

"Now," said George as his friends disappeared, "I want to make a bean-hole."

"A bean-hole?" repeated Ned curiously.

"Yes. We will have our beans cooked in backwoods style;" and seizing an axe he sharpened a stick at one end, and dug a hole in the ground about as large around as a half-bushel, and somewhat deeper. When he had finished, he told Ned to cut some wood from an old-growth maple that the recent storm had prostrated, and make up a rousing fire over the hole. This his assistant did.

"Keep your fire well supplied with fuel, Ned, and get as large a bed of coals as you can."

"All right; I will."

George then took his beans and rinsed them twice thoroughly in cold water, turned them into an iron pot (they had no earthern one), added a pound of pork, sliced across, half way through, two table-spoonfuls of molasses, and a little salt, the pork being well buried in the beans. He procured a tin plate that would fit inside the kettle, placed it on the beans, and going down to the river obtained a clean flat rock, which he laid on top the plate. The kettle was then set aside until the fire should be right.

"What are you going to get up for dinner, George?"

"I guess I'll take the lower part of that leg of venison and make a stew. Think you would like it?"

"Yes, a stew would be a change from what we have been having."

"All right, then, here goes." And taking the meat from where it was covered up, with the axe he cut off the lower part of the leg, and put the rest away. The piece he had selected he gave a good washing, then placed in a kettle half full of water, and added ten potatoes, which he peeled and sliced, an onion served the same way, and a little rice, and then set it over another fire that he had Ned build.

"I have a regular pyramid of coals here," cried Ned after a while.

George looked at the fire, and said it would do. Then dug out about half the coals from the excavation, set the pot of beans in, heaped coals all around it, and piled them on top until the pot was buried from sight, then covered the top with dirt, exclaiming, "There Ned, if those beans don't make your mouth water when they are are done, then I am a sinner."

"You are, any way, old fellow," replied his friend. "But I have no doubt your beans will be good. How did you catch on to this dodge, though."

"Lowe gave it to me."

"What is there to be done now?"

"Nothing special. I have got to keep an eye on that stew, and I guess we had better cut up a pile of wood. I shall have to make some dumplings by and by."

The boys worked and talked by spells, and about half-past eleven, George took a pint of flour, a heaping teaspoonful of Royal Baking Powder, and some water, and mixing it up, made his dumplings, which he dropped in the kettle, adding at the same time a little pepper and salt. Then he set the table. In the fifteen minutes the dumplings were pronounced done, and the stew was taken off the fire just as the boys made their appearance. Ned had made the coffee under George's directions, and that was sending forth an appetizing smell.

"I smell something good," cried Dick, as he came up to the fire sniffing: "is dinner ready?"

"All ready," answered George, "sit down," and the boys needed no second invitation.

"Where have you been?" inquired Ned.

"I don't know exactly. Over on the other side of the river, rambling about. We ran across two or three small ponds, and saw a lot of ducks. I should think there were hundreds of them, but we never got a shot at one. We saw any amount of deer-tracks and a good many were fresh. This is a good place to hunt deer."

"Yes," put in Ned, laughing, "you can hunt for them a week, and not find one."

"But they are around here all the same," asserted the Parson.

"And so are moose, caribou, bear, fishers, wild-cats, lucivees, and I don't know what else, but we don't find any," retorted Ned triumphantly.

"We'll have a moose before we go home, and don't you forget it," put in George. "We'll go over to Arnold's Bog next week; that is where Danforth shoots them."

"And Danforth knows how to hunt them, and we don't; that's the difference between us," observed Ned dryly.

"George, these dumplings are boss," and Dick who was too much interested in his dinner, helped himself to the third one.

"Look out, boys," cried Ned in mock alarm, "while we are talking, Dick is eating up all the dinner. He is death on dumplings."

"Each man for himself, on an occasion like this," mumbled Dick with his mouth full.

"Each man will have to be for himself where you are," remarked Fred, "or he will get left on the dinner question."

"What have you buried under that pile of coals?" queried Dick as they rose from the table.

"DEATH ON DUMPLINGS."

"Beans," said George. "Are you going to get those berries this afternoon?"

"Yes, if the Parson will go with me. What shall we pick them in?"

"Take those two lard-pails, that Danforth gave us. They will hold about three quarts apiece, and if you fill both, you'll do well."

"We had better take the guns with us," remarked the Parson; "there are likely to be a few partridges around the camps, and up those old logging-roads."

"Correct, my boy," replied Dick. "Will you lend me your gun, Ned?"

"Of course, take it."

"Where are your shells?"

"In my knapsack. Help yourself."

As soon as they were ready, Dick and Fred with the guns and

pails, embarked in the boat below the falls, and pulled down river. They reached the little clearing, and having secured the boat, proceeded at once to fill their pails. The berries were beginning to get scarce, and this caused them to wander about considerably. They had been picking an hour, and were working over toward the woods, when they heard a rustling in the bushes near by, and to their astonishment beheld a full-grown brownish colored bear, who squatting on his haunches, was bending the bushes toward his

THE BEAR AND THE BERRIES

mouth with his fore paws, while with his long tongue he swept the berries into his mouth, and devoured them with charming gusto.

"By Jove! That's a bear!" cried Dick, as he turned toward their guns.

"You're right, it is," yelled the Parson. "You ought to have your rifle here now, Dick."

The bear heard the noise made by the boys, and catching sight of them just as they picked up their guns, gave a frightened snort and fled. The boys gave chase, but the bear could cover two feet of ground to their one, and seeing but little chance to overtake him, they both gave him the contents of their guns. They could hear the shot rattle among the trees, and judged the bear was uninjured.

"Is it any use to chase him, Fred?" asked Dick, as he extracted the empty shells from his gun, and put in loaded ones.

"No, sir, he's a mile away now, and it's lucky he didn't chase us. What could we have done with partridge-shot? I didn't bring any buckshot, did you?"

"No; I guess on the whole that you are right. It's lucky we didn't get to close quarters with him; there might have been trouble *bruin* for us."

"You ought to be fined five dollars for that," laughed the Parson, "and now let's finish picking our berries. I have no fear of the bear returning."

After filling their pails, they carried them to the boat, and then took a turn for a mile or so up a logging-road, where they were lucky enough to flush a covey of partridges, and secured five birds. They followed those that flew, for a short time, in the hopes of getting more, but the frightened birds kept out of the young sportsmen's way, and they were fain to content themselves with what they had bagged, and walked back to the boat, and rowed up river.

They reached camp about half-past five, and found supper about ready.

CHAPTER XV.

BAKED BEANS. — CAMPFIRE MUSIC. — THE GREEN COOK. — A COOK'S TRICK. — ARNOLD'S BOG. — A SUCCESSFUL MOOSE HUNT. — "THROUGH THE WILDS."—ALMOST AN ACCIDENT. — RETURN TO CAMP.

"FIVE partridges and six quarts of raspberries," said Ned inspecting their plunder. "Pretty good for greenies."

"Who are you calling a greenie?" queried Dick. "I want you to understand that we shot a bear."

"Hurt him much?" laughed George.

"I guess not," said the Parson, joining in the laugh, and he told about peppering bruin with partridge shot.

"If George and I had been there," remarked Ned with a provoking smile, "the bear would have been ours."

"He's yours now, if you want him," chuckled Dick; "'I resign my share in him."

"How about those beans?" queried the Parson.

"I guess they are done, and we may as well have supper;" and Ned set the table, while George raked the coals away and uncovered his pot of beans.

The beans were baked to a turn, and sent forth an aroma that brought the hungry boys speedily to the table, and they were not slow in helping themselves to the steaming viands before them.

Between jokes and laughter, their food was sandwiched in, and after supper George invited them all to help him to get up a good pile of wood, enough to last over Sunday.

"You fellows have appetites like Polar bears," remarked George, as they sat around the blazing camp-fire in the evening, "and I don't intend to cook all day to-morrow for you. We will only have two meals Sunday, breakfast say about ten o'clock, and dinner about four, and if any of you want anything to eat before, between, or after those hours you can get it yourselves."

"BAKED BEANS!"

"A good idea, George," acknowledged Ned. "We can all stand it but Dick, and he can fill up on cold beans."

"If I can't go without eating as long as you can," retorted Dick, "you may tie me up in a meal-bag, and pitch me into the river. Just make a note of that, will you?"

"Saturday night, boys, let's have a good old-fashioned sing," and George started off on "Home, Sweet Home," his friends joining in. One song followed another, and then they changed off on Moody and Sankey hymns, and it was ten o'clock before they knew it; then the social circle was broken up, the fire scattered a little, and they retired to rest.

"Well, we have slept it out this morning," said George, as he arose to a sitting posture, and looked at his watch, "half-past eight by all that's lovely. Wake, ye sleepers!" and he gave the boys a shake, that opened all their eyes suddenly.

"What's the row?" inquired Ned, gaping.

"Only half-past eight, that is all. I should think it was about time for us to get up unless we intend to lie all day."

"I should say so, too," echoed the Parson, as he started up and began dressing. In ten minutes the boys were all dressed; and having completed their toilets at the river, which served them for a wash-basin, they were ready, as Ned suggested, to assist the *Chef* in preparing breakfast.

The Parson started a fire, and Dick offered to make the coffee, while Ned went to the river for some water.

"How do you make coffee, George?" queried Dick. "I'll be hanged if I know how," and he stood with the coffee-pot in his hands, looking from that to George.

"Set down that coffee-pot the first thing," and George stopped a moment over the pork he was slicing. "Take one of those pint tin basins, get an egg, break it into the basin, and put the shells in the coffee-pot."

Dick took an egg, seizing it much as he would if he had grasped a hammer to strike a nail. The result was that he crushed it in his hand, it flying all over him, and he threw it away.

THE GREEN COOK.

"Let me show you," said George, laughing; and taking an egg, he gave it a deft rap on the edge of the basin, broke it in two, inverted the half shells, drained them, and tossed them into the coffee-pot. "Now take a fork, Dick, and beat it."

Dick grabbed a fork in one hand, and the basin in the other, and at his first attack on the glutinous substance sent a lot of the yolk into his eye. While he stopped to dig this out, George, with another laugh, took the fork and the basin, tipped the latter up a little, and with that slight-of-hand movement that cooks understand so well, soon had the egg in a froth.

"Now, Dick, see if you can finish it," handing him the basin. "Put four tablespoonfuls of coffee into your basin, and mix it thoroughly with your egg. When you have made a paste of it, scrape it into the coffee-pot, rinse out the basin with cold water, and pour that in, and then fill the coffee-pot with cold water, up to the bottom of the spout, and set it on the fire. It's as easy as falling off a log."

BEATING EGGS.

Dick succeeded in doing this part of the business correctly, then George set him to watching the pork fry out that he had put in the spider. When it was cooked, George laid the pork on a plate which he put near the fire to keep warm, and then filled the spider with potato and fish.

"That looks like minced fish," remarked Dick.

"Smart boy," replied George, "that is what it is."

"But how did you make it: you have no tray or chopping-knife."

"Let the fish soak in water all day yesterday until it became soft, then picked it to pieces with my fingers. Boiled the potatoes, mashed them, mixed the potatoes and fish well together, and here you have it."

"Well, if that isn't one way of making hashed fish! What did you have for fish, some of that dedicated codfish?" The boys roared.

"Desecrated, you mean," said Ned.

"No, I don't," replied Dick, laughing at his blunder, "I mean desiccated. That's the fellow, George."

"Yes, Dick, that was what I used. Desiccated codfish."

While the fish was browning under Ned's supervision, George made some biscuit and put them to bake. Then running a knife under the fish in the frying-pan, he pronounced it well browned; and lifting the pan from the fire, he slipped the knife under the fish in all directions, until it was entirely loose from the bottom of the spider.

"Now, boys," he said, "I am going to show you a cook's trick." And giving the frying-pan a quick upward flip, he sent the fish flying into the air, where it turned over, and as it came down he caught it in the frying-pan, the beautifully browned bottom being now on top; and he placed it back on the fire, to brown the other side.

"That beats Hermann," cried the Parson, his eyes opening like twin stars.

"I'll bet you a dollar you can't do that again, George," remarked Ned.

"I always let well enough alone," replied the *Chef* with a merry twinkle in his eye. "But I would not advise the rest of you to try it, because if you do you will be very likely to find your fish in the fire." And George turned the biscuit.

After breakfast the boys wrote letters home, and taking their boat below the falls went down to Camp Caribou, and left them with Danforth, who told George he should have a chance to send mail out the next day. Returning to camp they spent the time until dinner in reading papers they had procured at Parmachenee.

For dinner they had a piece of roast moose with mashed potatoes, cold biscuit, hot coffee, raspberries sprinkled with sugar, and a raspberry-pie George called it, although Ned said it was something like a short-cake only better.

"How did you manufacture this pie, or cake, or whatever you choose to call it. I was busy reading, and did not notice what you were up to."

"I took one can of that condensed milk, and dissolved it with half a cup of water. Beat up two eggs, one at a time, threw in a cup of sugar, a teaspoonful of Royal Baking Powder, and a piece of butter about as large as an egg. Beat it all together, put it in one of those tin pie-plates and baked it. When it was cold I cut it in two flat-ways, piled in raspberries about two inches deep, sprinkled them with sugar, laid on the other half of the pastry, and it was ready to sample."

"And I'll sample it," added Dick, as he proceeded to do so.

"Is it good, Dick?" asked Ned as he helped himself to a piece.

"Good? That's no name for it. Can't you make another one for breakfast, George? I could eat all of this myself."

"Can't do it, Dick: it is too much trouble."

GREAT FISHING.

The evening was spent in singing and conversation, and nine o'clock found stillness in the camp.

Monday morning after breakfast they took some lunch with them, and carrying their guns and fishing-tackle paid a visit to Rump Pond. On their way back, they stopped at another small pond, and went to fishing at its outlet, and soon found it was alive with trout. They fished until they were fairly tired of the sport, capturing in two hours over three hundred fish.

"Suppose we leave a few for the next fellow," suggested George as he found his companions showed no signs of stopping. "I am going home. It will be dark now before we can get there."

As George started, his friends followed; and although they lost no time on the way it was dark before they reached camp, and they were obliged to cook their fish and eat their supper by the light from their fire and lantern.

Tuesday, leaving their fishing-rods at camp, but taking their guns and rifles with plenty of ammunition, also all the lunch they could carry, for they expected to be away from camp one or two nights, they started for Arnold's Bog about ten miles distant. They went in their boat as far as the First East Branch, and pulling it out there hid it in the bushes. Then taking their guns, axes, and provisions, they struck into the woods, following Danforth's trail. A good deal of the way was hilly, and they

YOUTHFUL HABIT STRONG IN AGE.

crossed several large brooks whose names they did not know. They arrived at the bog about one o'clock, and took possession of a small camp at the lower end that Danforth had built. After dinner they procured a supply of firewood, and then took a walk around the pond. Moose tracks were plenty, but the animals did not show up. The crow's-nest built by Danforth from which to call moose excited their curiosity, but as the boys did not know how to imitate a "moose-call" it was of no use to them.

George thought their chances would be best in the night; and after supper they scouted around, and built a fire on the shore some distance from their camp, but they saw no moose. And at ten o'clock, cold and sleepy, they returned to camp and went to bed. The night passed without alarm; and the next day they tramped about the country for many miles, but reached camp at night completely tired out, without having seen a single animal larger than a squirrel.

Wednesday night they retired early, but along in the middle of the night were awakened by a series of noises that George declared were made by moose. And flushed and excited they dressed, and taking their arms and extra ammunition, went silently out in the dark.

At George's suggestion they kept quiet a few moments until they heard the noise again.

"Whatever it is, it is coming this way," said George. "I will throw a few sticks on the fire and liven it up. It is said to attract wild animals at times, and we will keep back in the shadow."

This they did; and shortly their patience was rewarded, by seeing a large moose, shambling slowly along, and stopping occasionally, and lifting his head, send forth the queer noises they had heard.

The moose gradually approached them until he was within about one hundred yards, and George told Dick to fire when he gave the word, and asked Ned and the Parson to reserve their fire.

"Aim behind his fore shoulder, Dick: now let him have it."

The two rifles spoke almost as one, and both bullets hit the animal, who came down on his knees, but soon rallied and stood upon his feet. When the moose fell, all the boys rushed out to him, thinking he was dead; but as he regained his feet, Dick and George stopped and put fresh cartridges in their rifles.

"Give it to him, boys," cried George, as the moose, having caught sight of his enemies, charged upon the group, and Ned and the Parson emptied four charges of buck-shot into him from short range.

SHOOTING A MOOSE.

This was more than the old fellow could carry. He stopped in his onset, gave a muffled bellow, staggered a few times, and went over on his side, his legs bending under him. He never kicked again.

"He is our meat," shouted Ned. "Three cheers," and they were given with a will.

"Now what shall we do with him?" queried Dick.

"Leave him where he is till morning." Looking at his watch, "It's three o'clock now. I'll risk him till daylight, and we'll have his tongue for breakfast. Now let's go back and get what sleep we can."

This advice was followed; but they could not sleep very well after the excitement of the night, and at six o'clock they were all up. A fire was started; then they went over to the moose, and after two hours hard work succeeded in skinning him, and getting his head off, and cutting him up. Then they had breakfast. After breakfast they packed up a little of the meat, and took the skin, and the head which had fine horns, and started over the trail on their way back.

Their load was heavy, and they stopped frequently to rest. When they were within about four miles of their boat they stopped for a lunch; and while they were eating, a party of six came along who had left Danforth's in the morning, and who were on their way to the bog. They were piloted by John Eastman, their guide, and George told him of their good luck, and told him to help himself to the moose-meat the boys had left behind at the bog, which John was very willing to do.

After a short conversation, the two parties separated; and the boys after a tiresome march reached their boat, launched it, and went down the river to camp, where they found everything secure. They were sleepy and hungry, as well as tired, and George cooked a good supper, to which they all paid their compliments; they retired early, their bed never having felt better than it did that night.

Friday, after breakfast, they carried the moose head and skin to the lower boat, rowed down to Danforth's, and made arrangements with him to preserve the head and skin, and send them to Boston as soon as he could. George told him they should start for home the next Monday, and informed him that Mr. Lowe wished them to leave the boats in his charge, and Danforth agreed to take care of them. They ate dinner and supper at Camp Caribou, and returned to their camp in the evening.

The whole day Saturday was passed in climbing a mountain off to the eastward of them, from which they obtained a good view of the surrounding country, tramping through the woods to it by compass; they returned to camp about five o'clock weary and footsore, and hungry as usual.

A LUNCH BY THE RIVER.

Sunday they did not rise very early, and George announced two meals as the programme for the day. Breakfast was served about ten, and dinner at four; and as it was the last day they would spend in their present camp, George made a plum-pudding in its honor. All hands assisted in getting dinner; and as Dick was very anxious to help make the pudding, George set him to picking and stoning raisins, and buttering crackers, while he attended to the rest of it.

When the pudding was in the baker, Dick told George that he knew how to make the pudding now, and much to his friend's amusement he tried to tell him how it was done.

"I am afraid you will never make much of a cook, Dick, for all you love the goodies so well. But I will tell you again how the pudding is made, and you can write it down."

When the pudding was baked they had dinner, and after clearing up the dishes, read and sang until they retired for the night.

Monday morning they were all astir at six o'clock, and after breakfast, lugged the upper boat around the falls, loaded them both, and rowed down river. They called at Danforth's, and left some things they had borrowed from Mr. Lowe, and everything else that they could dispense with, for they were going to have a hard tramp "Through the Wilds," and told John where he would find the boats, and shaking hands with him started off. They pulled to the east side of the lake, a short distance above the outlet, where they left their boats, and entering the woods travelled by map and compass, for about five hours, when they reached Cupsuptic River, coming out at a huge chasm, or flume, nearly a mile long, and varying in height from five to eighty feet. Here they came near meeting with a bad accident.

A NARROW ESCAPE.

They had followed down the bank of the river, from where they first reached it, until they could cross the stream without difficulty, and then leaving their packs on the east bank, proceeded to explore the rocky flume, they had so unexpectedly discovered. When opposite the deepest part, they found an old pine lying across the chasm, that had probably lain there for years. George crossed on it all right; but Dick, who came behind him, slipped, and came very near going to the bottom, where it is almost needless to say he would have been instantly killed. But the youngster's muscles were good, and hanging on to the tree, he succeeded in lifting himself up, straddling it, and getting back on the side from which he had started, when he dropped down on the rock weak and faint.

With unusual care, George recrossed the log, and in a moment was beside Dick, where Ned and Fred were already.

"Are you hurt, my boy?" asked George anxiously, taking one of Dick's hands in his.

"No, but I am awfully frightened. It was seventy-five feet to the bottom of that hole if it was an inch," and Dick shuddered.

A SYMPATHETIC FRIEND.

"Thank God, you did not go down," cried Ned fervently, and the others said "Amen!"

"It was a narrow squeak," remarked Dick faintly. "The log was slippery, and I thought one spell I should go sure, but I didn't want to die," looking up with a queer little smile, "and I dug my nails right into the wood. But — I — tell — you — George — it — was — a — hard — chance," and he burst out crying.

This made his friends feel badly, and they looked sympathetically from one to the other.

"It's the reaction," said George. "It's better for him to cry. His nerves have had a fearful shaking up. I don't believe he can go any farther to-day."

"Yes — I — can," replied Dick through his sobs, "I — shall — be — all — right — in — a — few — minutes."

"Well, cry away, old fellow, all you wish to, it will do you good;" and George sat beside him, and laid Dick's head on his shoulder as tenderly as a woman could have done, and taking off his hat, stroked his hair soothingly.

In about fifteen minutes Dick ceased crying and stood up on his feet. Looking around him, while the color came into his face, he said, " I hope you won't think I'm a coward, but I couldn't help crying."

" Of course, you couldn't," remarked Ned, seizing his hand and shaking it heartily. " If it had been me, I should have bawled like a spanked baby."

The boys laughed at this sally, and then made their way back to where they had left their packs.

" It is two o'clock," observed George, "and we have eaten no dinner. I'll make you a cup of hot coffee, Dick, that will set you on your feet again."

" It will be three o'clock," said Ned, "before we are through dinner," and he began starting a fire. " I don't know how the rest of you feel, but I am confounded tired. Suppose we camp here to-night, and get an early start in the morning."

This proposition met with favor, and the boys accepted it, and during their talk around the camp fire that evening concluded to go to Seven Ponds instead of directly to Kennebago Lake, as they thought of doing at first. George said it would only take them a few days longer, and he thought they would have no difficulty in going there by compass; and when they turned in that night it was fully decided. Before going to sleep, George thanked their heavenly Father for the almost miraculous preservation of their young friend's life, and solicited the kind continuance of his care.

CHAPTER XVI.

THROUGH THE WILDS. — TRAVELLING BY COMPASS. — SEVEN PONDS. — HEAD OF KENNEBAGO LAKE. — FOOT OF KENNEBAGO LAKE. — JOHN'S POND. — DOWN THE KENNEBAGO RIVER. — INDIAN ROCK AGAIN. — DOWN THROUGH THE LAKES. — CAMBRIDGE. — STAGE-RIDE THROUGH GRAFTON NOTCH. — MOOSE CAVE. — THE JAIL. — SCREW AUGER FALLS. — BETHEL. — HOMEWARD BOUND BY RAIL. — FAREWELL.

SEVEN o'clock the next morning found them on the march, heading north-east. George had studied the map attentively before starting, and had set their distance from the Seven Ponds to be about eight miles, by the course which they would travel. Allowing for variations from a beeline, which they were likely to make, and the fatigue of travelling through an unbroken wilderness, over mountain and valley, through close growth and swamps, he calculated that they ought to reach the lower pond sometime during that day, and he knew if he once struck the Kennebago stream, all he would have to do would be to follow it north-west to the pond.

They travelled slowly, George thinking it best not to get tired out too early in the day; and when they pulled up at noon for dinner, he calculated that they had made about five miles. They stopped to lunch beside a little mountain brook, whose waters were as clear as crystal, and as cold as ice. They spent an hour in resting and conversing, and then resumed their march. At three o'clock they reached a stream which George declared must be Kennebago. Crossing it, they found a trail on the east side, and following this up, in less than half an hour they came in sight of the lower or L pond. They followed the southern shore of this pond to its head, reaching a stream that made an outlet to the waters of the other ponds, and continuing along the south side of the brook, at six o'clock they discovered the outlet of Big Island Pond, having travelled over fifteen miles through an almost primeval forest.

Here they found a camp, of which they took possession and made themselves at home. It was too dark to try to do anything that night, although there was a young moon; they made their supper from moose-meat and hard-tack, and turned into their blankets at nine o'clock, well fagged out after their long day's tramp.

On going out Wednesday morning, they were surprised to find there had been a snow-squall in the night, leaving about an inch of snow on the ground, while the trees were covered with the same feathery coating, giving them a beautiful appearance. The sun was just coming up over the forest, and striking upon the snowflakes on the trees, made them sparkle and scintillate like diamonds.

"This looks winterish," said Ned. "If we are going to have snow we had better make tracks for home. If we should get snowed in up here we should not get out all winter."

"I guess it will be safe to risk two or three days," answered George, laughing: "winter don't usually begin the latter part of September, even as far north as this."

"How beautifully these trees look with the snow on them," remarked the Parson; "while you are getting breakfast I will make a sketch, for I suppose it will be all melted by noon."

"It will if the day is pleasant. Dick, can't you go down to the pond

THE FOREST TRAIL.

and catch a few trout, while Ned and I cut up a little wood, and make preparations for breakfast?"

"All right, George. How many do you want?"

"Anywhere from six to a dozen, according to their size."

In half an hour Dick made his appearance with ten trout weighing about half a pound each, and they were quickly cooked. After breakfast, George proposed that they should try still-hunting for deer. He thought the snow would last on the ground until two or three o'clock, and that if they could find fresh deer-track they might follow one easily in the light snow, and if they had good luck run him down.

The Parson declined the invitation on the ground that he had not finished his sketches, and Dick said he didn't feel equal to much of a tramp that day. Ned, however, offered to go with George, if Dick would lend his rifle. Dick told him to take it; and about eight o'clock, George and Ned, with a little luncheon, for they did not know how long they might be away, started out to try their luck at still-hunting.

"I hope you will get a deer," said Dick as they moved away: "you have taken the last of the moose-meat, and Fred and I will have to catch trout for our dinner."

"We shall do our level best," returned George; "and I wish you and the Parson would cut up a good lot of firewood to-day, will you?"

"Yes," replied Dick; and the Parson promised to make the chips fly as soon as he had finished his sketching.

George and Ned sauntered slowly along the border of the pond, examining the shore narrowly for signs of the game they were in quest of.

Two or three times they were fooled by holes made in the snow from some of the snow on the trees overhead falling to the ground in little patches. The wind came out from the north-west and blew a moderate breeze; and although the sun was shining brightly, the air was crisp and cool, and made their hands and faces tingle. The snow on their boots, also, felt uncomfortable, and they had to stop every little while, and stamp their feet vigorously. Occasionally the wind would send a lot of snow whirling down on them, and some of it would find its way on their necks and down their backs, much to their discomfiture.

They followed the shore of the pond around until they reached the stream connecting with the pond north of them, and as it was then noon, sat down on an old windfall to eat their lunch.

"I don't think there is much fun in this, George, do you," and Ned brushed the snow off the log where he was sitting.

"It is rather a disagreeable day to be out, I acknowledge, this confounded snow coming down on one so, but we may strike game yet before we get back to camp."

"The sooner the better, then."

"How long shall we stay here, George?"

"Leave Friday morning, I guess. I thought I should like to take to-morrow if the rest of you are willing, and cross the outlet of this pond near the camp, and go up and take a look at the others. They are not more than a mile and a half or two miles in a straight line from

LOOKING FOR GAME.

where we are camped. And now we are up here we may as well see all there is to be seen."

"I will go with you for one. But suppose we start back now. We may pick up our deer on the way home."

"I hope we shall, Ned. I hate to go back skunked."

Turning to the east again, they followed the shore of the pond back, going over their own tracks in returning. No sign of deer rewarded their efforts; and they were within two miles, they judged, of the camp when George, looking up from the snow, which was now nearly melted, for a few moments cast his eyes out over the pond and saw something that brought him to a dead halt. It was a deer swimming across the pond, and making for the shore where they stood, — a slight cove, that set back from the main body of the pond perhaps an eighth of a mile.

A DEER IN SIGHT.

"Ned, if my eyes were not dazzled so by the snow I should call that a deer heading straight for this spot where we are," and George pointed to the object in the water.

"Where? Oh, I see, now. By gracious! it is a deer. Let's draw back a little, and give him a chance to come on shore; the wind is in our favor anyway, and he won't scent us."

A LUCKY SHOT.

The boys concealed themselves a short distance from the shore in some bushes, and waited fifteen minutes impatiently before the deer reached the shore. As he walked out, George nudged Ned and whispered, " Give it to him, and I'll reserve my fire in case you miss."

Ned took deliberate aim, the deer being only about four rods away, and pulled trigger. The bullet struck the deer fair in the breast, and the buck gave one leap high in the air and came down as dead as Julius Cæsar. Poor fellow! His troubles and trials, if he ever had any, were ended.

" That was a good shot, Ned, and you deserve his head; but you never can lug it out from here in the world."

" I suppose not. But I'll have his skin, anyway. I can carry that on my back. Would you carry him to camp whole, or dress him here ? "

" Dress him here, and take the skin, and all the meat we can lug, and I'll send Dick and Fred back for the rest. He'll weigh a hundred and thirty pounds, and is bulky for us to carry."

The next day, Thursday, they spent in exploring about the ponds, and Friday morning they packed up, and after a hard tramp, during which they were twice nearly lost, they reached the head of Kennebago Lake, and spent the night at the hotel camp.

The next morning the Parson went over to a point near and made a very pretty sketch of the head of the lake.

About nine o'clock, having hired a couple of boats and two men from the camp, they were rowed down to the foot of the lake ; and as the scenery was very fine, the Parson asked the boys to wait while he obtained a sketch as a companion to the one he had made at the other end of the lake. Accordingly the boats were hauled up on the south shore near an old camp, but a short distance from the outlet, and for an hour the Parson busied himself with his book and pencil, while his

SADDLEBACK MOUNTAIN, GRAFTON NOTCH.

friends talked to the guides. The sketch being finished, they embarked again, and the men pulled down the river as far as they could go, and the Parson paying them for their services, the boys landed on the west side of the river, and followed the path that led to the falls. Here the Parson's sketch-book came into requisition again, and after doing the falls they continued on down the river. At the outlet of John's Pond, they crossed the river, and took a look at the westerly end of this sheet of water. But it did not pay them for their trouble; and re-crossing the Kennebago again, they tramped on down the right-hand bank, and about one o'clock reached a small log camp, where they stopped and took lunch.

After dinner they continued their way, and reached Indian Rock about half-past five, just in time to take passage on the steamer Oquossoc, which was about starting for the Upper Dam. They reached the Scow Landing in Trout Cove about half-past seven, passing a sail-boat that lay at anchor, containing two men, and went up to the house, where they obtained some supper, and stopped over night. They expected to have to stop there over Sunday; but about half-past nine they heard the whistle of the Welokennebacook, and paying their bill, carried their things over to the landing where they found the steamer.

The captain told them they could not get down to Cambridge that day, but that they could stop at the Middle Dam or the Arm until Monday.

After conferring among themselves for a few moments they concluded to visit the Arm, as there was a very pretty, well-kept house there; and the steamer sailing at half-past ten, they reached South Arm at twelve, ate dinner, and spent the afternoon in writing letters home.

Monday morning they strolled around the house, the Parson making several fine sketches in the vicinity, and after dinner embarked on the

ALONG THE CAMBRIDGE RIVER, GRAFTON, MAINE.

steamer for Middle Dam, then rode on the buckboard to Sunday Cove, where they found the steamer Parmachenee, and their old friend, Captain Farwell, awaiting them.

THE LANDLADY AT SOUTH ARM.

A few moments sufficed to transfer their luggage from buckboard to steamer, and they were soon speeding down the lake, their tongues flying like millwheels, as they related their adventures to the captain and engineer. At six o'clock they reached Cambridge, and going up to "The Lakeside," found their baggage all right, and they busied themselves during the evening in packing up, and thereby avoiding having to hurry in the morning. Tuesday morning they left the hotel in a private team, so they could take their own time and see all there was to be seen. Fred wanted to make sketches on the way, but the stage could not wait for that sort of business.

They left "The Lakeside" at eight o'clock, after bidding good-by to their friends, and drove slowly away. It was a lovely October morning, just cool enough to be pleasant, and the ride proved to be all that could be desired.

READY TO START.

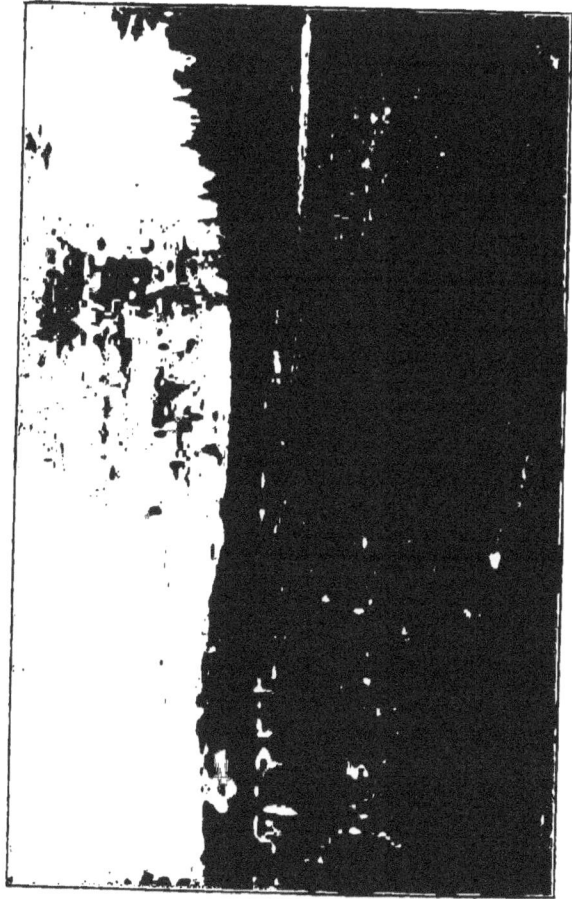

UMBAGOG LAKE FROM RAPID RIVER.

They followed the valley of the Cambridge and Bear Rivers, and admired the huge mountains that formed the sides of the notch, paid a visit to Moose Cave, the Jail, and Screw Auger Falls (here the Parson made a sketch), and reached a wayside hotel about one o'clock, where they stopped an hour and a half to dinner.

In the afternoon they continued their way down the rugged

LOOKING EAST FROM LAKESIDE HOTEL.

valley of Bear River to Newry Corner, and then up the picturesque and romantic valley of the Androscoggin, one of the most charming localities in Maine. Through their entire drive they were never out of sight of mountains, peaks of greater or less height surrounding them on every hand. Between Newry Corner and Bethel they came up with a lady and gentleman who was travelling in a private carriage: the lady was seated by the roadside painting a view, which took in a lovely bend in the river, with high mountains in the background.

The Parson thought the view very pretty; and asking the driver to wait, he jumped from the carriage, and so to speak, "doubled" on the fair artist, for climbing over the fence into a field on the right-hand side of the road, he mounted a large rock, and made the same picture the lady was painting, and put her, her attendant, and carriage

SPECKLED MOUNTAIN, GRAFTON NOTCH, MAINE.

in the foreground of his own sketch. He was much pleased with this effort, and showed it to his friends, who acknowledged it was very pretty.

About six o'clock they reached Bethel Hill, as the principal village was called, and were driven to the hotel where they stopped over night. They found Bethel a very pretty place, and its hotel a good one. As they had once more reached the pale of civilization, after being shown to their rooms, they discarded the clothing they had been wearing in the woods, and which from constant use was pretty well worn out, and put on their home clothes, and they appeared at supper looking a little different from what they did when entering the hotel.

SCREW AUGER FALLS.

After supper they inquired the way to a barber's, for their hair had grown very long in the woods, and needed cutting badly; and after "going through a course of sprouts," as Ned expressed it, at the hands of the barber, they came out feeling like new men. While having their hair cut, they were much amused by listening to the stories of the barber, who was a very loquacious individual.

According to his version he had camped all through the wilderness about the lakes, and had shot more deer, moose, and caribou than one man often sees in a lifetime.

"What did you think of the barber, George?" asked the Parson, as the boys left the shop, still laughing at some of the barber's "twisters."

"I think he would make a capital mate for the pilot of that steamer on which we made the trip in Portland harbor."

"You are just right," put in Ned, and all the boys roared as they thought of the fog story.

VIEW ON BEAR RIVER.

They found letters awaiting them at the hotel, both from their friends at home, and from the young ladies whose acquaintance they had formed so pleasantly that summer, and were delighted to learn that all their relatives and friends were well.

In the evening they fell into conversation with the landlord, and told him of their trip and its adventures. He was surprised that they should go into the northern wilderness without a guide, and wondered that they had not been lost. George told him "it was easy enough when a fellow knew how," and that he intended to do it again some time.

The next morning they took the cars for Portland, and continued through to Boston by rail, reaching home as brown as Indians and as hearty as woodsmen, after an absence of nearly three months.

And now, after having taken my readers nearly through the wilderness of north-western Maine, I close up my desk, throw away my pen (which is all worn out), and say "Farewell!" not without a vague hope, however, that we may meet again. Till then adieu, and may happiness attend you!

www.ingramcontent.com/pod-product-compliance
Lightning Source LLC
Chambersburg PA
CBHW020739020526
44115CB00030B/632